After the Campfires:

The Simpson Family In Oregon & Beyond, 1846-1945

THIS PUBLICATION
WAS PRODUCED BY:

PUBLISHING
415 388-7779
DH@HEALY1.COM

After the Campfires:

The Simpson Family In Oregon & Beyond 1846-1945

By Kirke Wilson

June 13, 1938 ~ June 25, 2026

HEALY

David Healy's notes about the production of this publication:

Back in 2024, Diane Eubanks discovered that a distant relative, Kirke Wilson, had written five books about their shared Simpson ancestors. She found these on my brother, Don Healy's website: ***https://bdhhfamily.com/***.

She initiated the effort to compile these volumes into a single book. Don scanned the volumes, and I compiled them into a 400+ page work titled ***The Simpson Family in America, 1688–1880***, available here: ***https://www.simpsonhistory.org/Simpson1688-1880.pdf.***

In April 2025, I met with Kirke, who lent me the manuscript for another unpublished work, ***After the Campfires: The Simpson Family in Oregon & Beyond, 1846–1945***. I was captivated by the accounts of the achievements and escapades of my great-great-great grandfather, Ben Simpson and his sons, Samuel and Sylvester, and decided to produce this book.

This work led me to further discoveries about Sylvester's sons—Lynn, Kirke, and Ernest—as well as Ernest's wife, Anna Pratt, whose story and accomplishments I was able to expand upon.

 This icon on a photo or illustration indicates that it has been enhanced or generated with the assistance of AI.

Questions and comments are welcome at: info@simpsonhistory.org

Go to **simpsonhistory.org** for additional information and links related to this branch of the Simpson family, or search Facebook for "**Simpson History 1846–1945**."

 Published by **HEALY Publishing**
Book Design & Production: **HEALY Publishing** | Clackamas, OR 97015 | ***healy1.com***
ISBN: **979-8-234-06195-9**
Library of Congress Control Number: **2026911509**
Printed in the United States of America
Second Edition 7/1/2026

Contents

About the Author

Kirke Wilson grew up hearing the stories his Simpson grandmother and her sisters had heard from their grandfather of restless ancestors crossing the plains in covered wagons and raising families on the frontier of settlement. The stories exaggerated some events, Grandfather Simpson, for example, was unlikely to have known General Washington, and neglected others, like the assumption that vacant Indian lands were available for settlement. There were accounts of ordinary people, dissatisfied with their prospects, moving westward over several generations to unclaimed lands and better opportunities. The adventures were exciting for young ears but they were incomplete. They were vague about why these folks kept moving and what, if any, guidance their stories offered their descendants.

The exploration of family history consumed more than half a century of intermittent travel and research following the Simpson family from the shores of Maryland's Chesapeake Bay, to North Carolina, Tennessee and Missouri where they converged in Platte County, Missouri with the Cooper family who had followed a similar path from Virginia to Kentucky and Missouri. The exploration included visits to places where the two families had lived and the libraries, historical societies, cemeteries and battlefields where their lives and those of people like them are remembered. The research was backwards, from west to east, from well-documented to more speculative. It was guided by the precision of local genealogists, contextualized by historians and enriched by contributions from remote relatives, some of whom were descendants of the family members who chose to remain in North Carolina, Tennessee or Missouri rather than complete the transcontinental journey to the Pacific Ocean.

Kirke Wilson retired in 2005 after 31 years as director and president of the Rosenberg Foundation in San Francisco. He had previously been the West

Coast Vice President of a public policy consulting company, a Staff Assistant in the office of the Governor of California and an organizer of migrant and seasonal farm workers in the San Joaquin Valley. He graduated from Yale where he majored in philosophy.

In addition to several iterations of family history, Kirke Wilson has published articles, reviews and opinion pieces covering a wide range of subjects. His articles have appeared in Boonslick Heritage, Foundation News, The Nation, Overland Journal and other publications.

1 Westward the Course of Empire

At the beginning of 1845, the map of the United States was still a work in progress. Texas was an independent republic, California was part of Mexico and Oregon was an immense territory which the United States shared with Great Britain. The United States was emerging from an economic depression and in a mood to flex its muscles and grow. Emigrants from the United States were increasing their numbers in the contested regions, shifting the political balance and creating work for the mapmakers. In his 1845 inaugural address, President James K. Polk paid tribute to the emigrants, "The world beholds the peaceful triumphs of the industry of our emigrants".[1] The "triumphs" the President celebrated were the relentless territorial expansion of the United States across the continent to the Pacific Ocean and south to the Rio Grande. The expansion was by no means entirely peaceful, but it seemed inevitable as families loaded their wagons and moved west. Polk was, as he had promised, a one-term president. Within his term, the United States would become a continental nation adding what would become part or all of twelve western states. The map would be nearly complete. Texas, California, Oregon and other western territories would become part of the United States. The industry of the emigrant families would create a nation unified from the Atlantic to the Pacific.

Territorial ambitions were not new to the United States, and they were not confined to land-hungry settlers on the frontiers. In 1811, at a time when the United States was only beginning to advance westward from the Atlantic states, future president John Quincy Adams predicted that the country would eventually expand to fill the continent:

> *The whole continent of North America appears to be destined by Divine Providence to be peopled by one nation, speaking one language, professing one general system of religious belief and political principles, and accustomed to one general tenor of social usages and customs.*[2]

Adams, like other proponents of national expansion, attributed the growth to "Divine Providence". Expansion was inevitable because it was part of God's plan. Because it was part of God's plan, it was also something to be desired.

At the same time President Polk was talking about the "peaceful triumphs" of the emigrants, a political journalist in New York was writing about "the irresistible army of Anglo-Saxon emigration" that was bearing down on California. John L. O'Sullivan's "irresistible army" would overcome those forces,

> *... thwarting our policy, hampering our power, limiting our greatness and checking the fulfillment of our manifest destiny*[3]

The opposing forces, he predicted, would be overwhelmed by the "still accumulating momentum of our progress". Later that year, O'Sullivan wrote of Oregon,

> *... that claim is by the right of our manifest destiny to overspread and to possess the whole of the continent which Providence has given us for the development of the great experiment of liberty and federated self-government entrusted to us*[4]

The concept was not new but a writer in New York had coined the phrase that would come to characterize the western expansion. Manifest destiny was the justification for the nation's territorial ambitions. Spreading liberty and self-government from coast to coast was a sacred obligation.

The "industrious emigrants" had been moving west and overspreading the continent for generations. For some of them, habit and destiny had become interchangeable. They had moved over the mountains into the frontier areas of Kentucky and Tennessee and across the Mississippi River into the frontier areas of Missouri. Some had simply outgrown the land they owned while others moved to escape debts or misdeeds. But for most, the primary objective was to acquire land and begin anew. In some places, like the Platte Purchase of western Missouri in 1838, the process was relatively orderly. The federal government acquired the land through purchase from the Indians, surveyed the land and sold it to settlers. In other areas, like the Boonslick region of central Missouri in 1810 or Oregon in 1846, the process was not as tidy. The land was Indian territory and there was, at the time, no legal way for settlers to acquire title.

Perhaps they assumed it was destiny, but the technicalities of land ownership did not deter the settlers. They knew from experience that the Indians would eventually give up their claims and that those settlers living on the land, often with official disapproval, would eventually be rewarded for their persistence. The assumption among the pioneers was that those Indian lands not being used for farming were not needed by the Indians. Such surplus lands should be acquired from the Indians and opened for settlement. In situations where the land remained in Indian ownership, the experience had been that circumstances would change. The Indians, either voluntarily or as a result of coercion, would pull back leaving the land available for settlement. The assumptions were deeply tainted by the settler's sense of racial superiority and entitlement, but they accurately described the pattern that would repeat itself across the country.

The overland emigrants traveling to Oregon during the 1840 to 1860 period were primarily family groups rather than the single men and adventurers attracted by the gold in California. The Oregon emigrants were pioneers, but they were far more likely to be farmers than frontiersmen. They were individualists but they traveled in groups of relatives, friends and strangers to protect themselves against the Indians they feared and to have assistance crossing streams, repairing broken equipment or replacing depleted food supplies. They were proudly patriotic, stopping on the trail July 4th for speeches and celebrations, and knew they were part of a larger movement. They would have been sympathetic with the notion of manifest destiny if they had known about it. They considered the United States exceptional in its liberties, but few were motivated by a compelling desire to displace the British in the northwest. They did not think much about who currently owned the land but assumed that land would be available for them. These emigrants were not visionaries trying to build a perfect society like the Mormons in Utah and they were not motivated by duty like the missionaries in Oregon. They were common but restless people who made uncommon decisions like moving 1900 miles with their families across prairies, deserts and mountains to Oregon.

The emigrants of the mid-19th century in their iconic covered wagons were familiar with the frontier pattern of settlement, migration and resettlement. The settlers fended off the Indians who claimed the land, cleared the land, built cabins and planted crops. For them, there was relatively little change in how they lived over several generations. As these families moved west, they splintered with some members remaining behind building permanent communities with churches, schools and commerce while others moved on to a new frontier. The families who moved west left little record of why they kept moving. By the 1840s, they had experienced a lengthy and devastating economic crisis that had depressed the price of agricultural products and the value of farmland, and many had found the valleys of the Missouri River and Ohio River unhealthy. In the broadest sense, they were dissatisfied where they were and were seeking opportunity elsewhere. At a minimum, they were seeking land.

The distance and duration of the transcontinental journey involved expense and risk. Families needed sufficient capital to acquire the wagons and supplies to sustain them during the trip and the first few months in Oregon. They would be traveling in the spring and summer and have to be able to survive without income for a year. Emigrants were aware of the increased risk of the longer trip and prepared for it by consulting guidebooks, quizzing returning emigrants and accumulating the necessary supplies and equipment. They organized themselves into traveling companies, with written rules and elected leaders, and sometimes engaged experienced mountain men as trail guides. Within days, the wagon trains would stop to depose elected leaders and reorganize. As they moved west, families left one wagon train to join another or whole trains divided into smaller and more compatible units. The emigrants were simultaneously dependent on their traveling companions for their safety and independent in their judgment and behavior. They prepared for several months of wagon travel through unforgiving terrain, potentially hostile Indians and severe weather. Many families, anticipating what they were likely to need in Oregon, carried construction tools, seeds and farming implements. Others transported supplies to start a business, like nursery stock, dry goods, parts for a mill or medical books.

Before reaching Oregon's Willamette Valley, the overland emigrants of the mid- 19th century traversed a wide band of land that they considered uninhabitable except by Indians. Few of the emigrants had thought much about how they wanted to be governed. In general, they wanted a government that would protect them and their property and otherwise leave them alone. In most of the places they had previously lived, they had not been required to make decisions about shape or purpose of government. Such decisions had been made by others long before and could be taken for granted. Many of the Oregon emigrants were corning from Missouri which, for example, had been a state since 1820 and an organized territory of the United States since 1805. In Missouri, the choices were to accept the existing system of governance or move on.

Moving to Oregon was different than the move from one county to another in Missouri. The distance, duration and risk of the overland trip were different, but the largest difference was that Oregon in the mid-1840s was not part of the United States. Its residents were Canadians, British and a growing number of newcomers from the United States but the place had no actual government until 1843 when the weak provisional government was formed. These residents were divided by nationality as well as religion and they had different ideas about what they wanted from a government. Not surprisingly they were also suspicious about each others' motives.

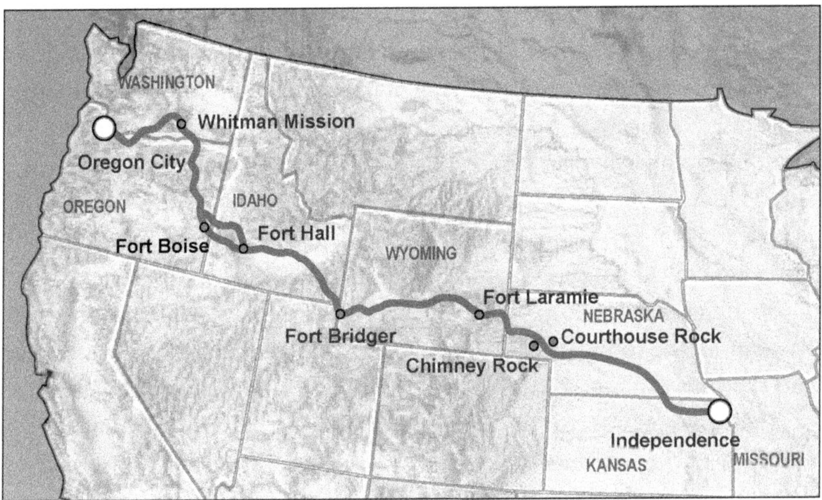

The Oregon Trail

In the past, if the settlers became dissatisfied, they could move to another place. In Oregon, these restless people could still load their children and goods in a wagon and move but it would become increasingly difficult to find a place where there was good land and no other people. They continued to move, often from farm to town and town to city but it was increasingly difficult to reinvent themselves on a new frontier by moving west. The alternative to movement was to put down roots and build where they were. Building for permanence involved patience and different skills than simply building a cabin and planting a crop. The settlers would need a vision of commonwealth that extended beyond the individualism of subsistence agriculture. They had demonstrated that they could work together when necessary while crossing the plains, but they had also demonstrated distrust of leaders, impatience and impulsive decision-making. In general, their experience in previous settlements had been that decisions about the structure and finance of government were made elsewhere in territorial capitals or Washington, D.C. Unless they were lawyers or aspiring politicians, they did not have to concern themselves with the details of statecraft.

Oregon experienced change in nearly every aspect of life between 1846 and 1900. Some of the changes were simply part of the process of settlement including the distribution of public lands among the pioneers the building of towns and the creation of schools, churches, newspapers, political parties and other instruments of civil society. Some of the changes were the result of external events like the Gold Rush in California, the Civil War or the national economic depressions of 1857, 1873 and 1893. Other changes were the product of individual and group initiative like the growth of trade and transportation and the flourishing of private educational institutions. In some cases, change was the product of government action like the removal of Indians to reservations, the use of land subsidies to promote development and the expansion of public education. Some of the changes, like school reform and women's rights, seem modern while others like the temperance movement or the advances in transportation, seem dated.

The pioneers of 1846 experienced change as they traveled. When they left Missouri in the spring of 1846, Oregon was a region shared by Great Britain and the United States. By the time they arrived in the Willamette Valley that fall, Oregon was part of the United States with a flimsy provisional government the residents had created. Within three years, the provisional government would give way to a territorial government and a decade later, in 1859, a state government. Some of the pioneers ignored the changes occurring around them and lived agrarian lives very much like those their parents had lived on another frontier a generation earlier. Others contributed to the change by building the enterprises, institutions, cultural artifacts and governmental structures of the new society.

The focus on external change obscures the role of the individual in initiating and shaping change. The pioneers of the territorial and early statehood period expected to work hard building homes and farms, but they were slow to recognize that they also would be called upon to create a new society. The models they had were not particularly useful. California had been a colony of Spain and Mexico before it was catapulted by the Gold Rush into statehood. It was too dynamic to be a useful model for Oregon. The border states, like Missouri and Iowa in which many of the emigrants had lived, were too static. The pioneers brought with them prejudices from other places like racial attitudes and a reluctance to pay taxes as well as positive ideas about popular democracy and individual liberty. In contrast to the homogeneity of many of the places they had previously lived, Oregon had attracted a healthy diversity of educational backgrounds, religious denominations and political affiliations. There seems to have been a disproportionate number of educated people among the early settlers of Oregon including preachers and lawyers as well as people who had held responsible positions in other places before coming to Oregon. The pioneers set about creating a state. With the exception of the divisions regarding slavery, they seem to have shared a broad consensus about what sort of state they wanted and the proper role of government in protecting citizens, building roads, educating children and encouraging commerce.

During the last half of the 19th century, the pioneers of 1846 became old timers. The memories of the Overland Trail faded but the pioneers and their children were building what they sometimes called empire. The three generations of Simpsons, all of them pioneers, reacted in different ways to the Oregon they encountered. The oldest ignored much of the change around him and lived as he had on the frontier in Tennessee and Missouri. The second generation embraced change and exploited every opportunity that emerged and several that did not. The youngest generation had advantages that were not available to previous generations and chose career paths that did not exist for their parents or grandparents.

Overland in 1846

The Simpson and Cooper families had been moving west since the 18th century. Over 150 years, the Simpson and Cooper families had followed parallel paths from the mid-Atlantic colonies across the mountains into the frontier areas of Tennessee and Kentucky before moving to Missouri. In 1843, the two migration routes converged in Platte County, Missouri, when Benjamin Simpson married Nancy Cooper. Each of them was of the sixth generation of their family in North America and each of them was part of a large clan.

Benjamin Simpson was descended from Richard Simpson (c.1663-1711) who settled on the Maryland shores of Chesapeake Bay in the 1680s where his son Thomas Simpson (1691-n.d.) and grandson Richard Simpson (1714-1795) lived until the 1750s when they moved with their families to Guilford County and later Rockingham County, North Carolina. In the fourth generation, another Thomas Simpson (1739-1833) moved his family to Warren County, Tennessee about 1804. With his son William (1793-1858) and grandson Benjamin (1818-1910), Thomas Simpson's family moved to Howard County, Missouri in the early 1820s and Johnson County, Missouri in the 1830s. When the Platte Purchase of western Missouri was opened for settlement in 1838, William Simpson of the fifth generation, his son Benjamin and several relatives and in-laws moved to Platte County.

Nancy Cooper was descended from a distinguished frontier family. James Cooper (1661-1732) had come from Great Britain to Philadelphia where his son, the first Benjamin Cooper (1697-1776), was born. Francis Cooper

(1726-after 1802) of the third Cooper generation settled in Culpepper County, Virginia sometime before 1750 where he acquired land and served in the Culpepper militia during the French and Indian War (1756-1757) and Lord Dunmore's War (1774). His son, another Benjamin Cooper (1756-1841) served six years in the Revolutionary War in Virginia and Kentucky. He participated in the defense of the Kentucky settlements, military campaigns into Ohio in 1779 and 1780 and the Battle of the Blue Licks in 1782. Benjamin Cooper moved to the Missouri frontier in 1806 where he led the defense of the Boonslick settlements during the War of 1812. His son William Cooper (1796-1848), Nancy Cooper's father, participated in the War of 1812 in Missouri and the Black Hawk War. In Illinois in 1832. William Cooper died crossing the plains to Oregon in 1848.

Benjamin Simpson, his father William and his infant sons Sylvester and Samuel were among the industrious emigrants who crossed the Oregon Trail together in 1846. They traveled from Platte County in western Missouri to the Willamette Valley of Oregon. Platte County had been Indian land until 1838 when, after purchase from the Indians, it was opened to settlement. Within a year, ten families related to William Simpson and ten families related to William Cooper had acquired land in Platte County. By 1846, members of the Simpson and Cooper families owned 2600 acres in Platte County. Some members of these families remained in Platte County while others sold land and prepared to move west[5] The Simpsons were members of a larger group including relatives of Dr. James McBride and others who traveled together most of the way from St. Joseph, Missouri to Oregon City on the Willamette River. (Appendix I) The Simpson and McBride groups began as part of a larger wagon train but soon reorganized electing the young Ben Simpson captain. The wagon train had no particular name at the time but, for convenience, is here referred to as the Simpson-McBride wagon train.

The Simpson family group traveling together consisted of 47 people in twelve households including three generations of Simpsons and Kimseys as well as their Anderson, Jones, McLinn, Price, Smith, Wilson and Wisdom in-laws. William Simpson was a farmer and preacher and, at 53, the oldest member of the family group. His son, Benjamin Simpson, was 28 and the captain of the wagon train. Sylvester was two years old, and his little brother Sam was less than a year old. They were among the thirteen members of the Simpson family who were less than ten years old while crossing the plains.[6] Over the next half century, each of the four Simpson pioneers would leave his mark on Oregon. William Simpson organized Baptist churches in

Yamhill and Marion Counties. Benjamin Simpson was active in business and politics at several locations in Oregon. A generation later, the two younger Simpsons would graduate from Willamette University and become lawyers and journalists. Sylvester Simpson would become known as a versatile public administrator and popular lecturer in Oregon while his younger brother would be remembered as an Oregon poet.

Like the Simpson family, members of the McBride family would also distinguish themselves in public service in 19th century Oregon. James McBride (1805-1885) was a physician and preacher who served four terms in the territorial and state legislatures. He also served as Surveyor General of Oregon and as Resident Minister for the United States in Hawaii. His son John (1832-1904) was the author of a reminiscent narrative of the 1846 trip on the Oregon Trail and a delegate to the Oregon Constitutional Convention in 1857. He was elected to the Oregon Legislature and the U.S. House of Representatives and was appointed Chief Justice of the Territory of Idaho. Another son George McBride (1859-1911) was the Secretary of State of Oregon and served one term in the U.S. Senate. A third son, Thomas McBride (1847-1930) served as Chief Justice of the Oregon Supreme Court.

The Simpson-McBride wagon train arrived in the Willamette Valley in late September 1846 after five grueling months on the overland trail. The families that had traveled overland together paused briefly in Oregon City to celebrate what they had accomplished. They shared the relief that they had completed the trip and the sadness that they would be scattering to their final destinations. William and Mary Simpson and their younger children continued to Yamhill County where they spent the winter of 1846-1847 in a cabin on the North Yamhill River near the present-day town of Carlton. William Simpson and another 1846 emigrant established the first Old School Baptist Church in Oregon. In 1847, William and Mary Simpson moved to the Waldo Hills of Marion County where they claimed 640 acres of land, built a small log house and established a second Old School Baptist Church.

William Simpson's son Benjamin was a restless and enterprising pioneer. Raised on the Missouri frontier where formal education was sporadic, Ben Simpson owned stores, sawmills, a warehouse, a steamboat, a newspaper and two ocean-going schooners at various times during a 40-year career in Oregon. He secured government contracts to build a sawmill at Fort Yamhill, a wagon road across central Oregon and a lighthouse at Yaquina Bay. He was elected to the legislature seven times from four different counties, and he was appointed to positions as an Indian Agent, Surveyor General, Postal Inspector and Indian treaty negotiator. T.T. Geer, who served as governor of Oregon, described Ben Simpson as "One of the prominent men in Oregon for many years in its formative period."[7] He used his political influence to obtain government jobs and to benefit his private interests. He failed as often as be succeeded and was no stranger to political intrigue, public controversy or ethical ambiguity.[8]

Sylvester Simpson and Samuel Simpson had obtained in Oregon the formal education that had not been available to their father being a generation earlier on the Missouri frontier. The two brothers and three of their sisters attended Willamette University in Salem. Sylvester Simpson earned a master's degree from Willamette in 1864, and Samuel earned a bachelor's degree the following year.[9] The two brothers briefly edited a newspaper before becoming lawyers. Sylvester Simpson served in a series of senior appointive positions in Oregon government. He was chief clerk of the Oregon State Senate, State Librarian, State Superintendent of Public Instruction and Private Secretary to the Governor of Oregon. He was also an inspiring and informative public speaker on a variety of topics. He and his family moved to San Francisco in 1879 where he devoted the rest of his career to legal editing and research. Samuel Simpson worked briefly as a lawyer before following a career as a writer. He was the editor of four newspapers, the author of textbooks for 4th and 5th grade students and the editor of Bancroft's History of the Northwest. Sam Simpson was also a prominent Oregon poet. His poem Beautiful Willamette was recited by generations of Oregon school children.

NOTE For accounts by Barnet Simpson and Mrs. Mary Elizabeth Munkers Estes that were on the same wagon train see page 191.

2 The Pioneer Preacher

William B. Simpson (1793-1858) and Mary "Polly" Kimsey Simpson (1797- 1858) had been moving all their lives. He was born in North Carolina and she in Virginia. They had married in Warren County, Tennessee in 1813 and moved west to Howard County, Missouri in 1820, Johnson County, Missouri in 1831 and Platte County, Missouri in 1839. In each place they settled, William Simpson had farmed during the week and preached the rigid, Calvinist gospel of the Old School Baptists on Sunday. William and Mary Simpson were the senior members of the three-generation wagon train that left St. Joseph, Missouri in April 1846. Five months and nearly 1900 miles later, the wagon train reached the Willamette Valley in late September and split up. William and Mary Simpson, along with their three unmarried children, Martha, James and William Barnet, their grandson John as well as their son David and his wife crossed the Willamette River and continued to Yamhill County where they settled near present day Carlton.[10] Before leaving Oregon City, William Simpson visited the Hudson Bay Company outpost to claim the equivalent in bacon, flour and cornmeal of the supplies he had left at Fort Hall two months earlier.[11]

They wasted no time recovering from their five-month ordeal on the Overland Trail or celebrating their accomplishment. It was early fall and winter was coming. The day after arriving on the North Yamhill River, 18-year-old David Simpson found a job splitting rails. He was paid two and a half bushels of potatoes for splitting one thousand rails.[12] William Simpson, who had a reputation for being handy with tools, erected a sixteen-foot square log house, said to have been built without nails, where he and his family spent a cold, crowded and wet winter. John Simpson, living with his grandparents in Yamhill County, remembered 1846-1847 as:

> *an extremely hard winter, on emigrants, both man and beast. Grandfather [Simpson] lost all his stock that winter but one cow and one horse; and for quite a time we lived on pea coffee and bran bread.*[13]

The younger Simpson boys were enrolled that winter in a subscription school. Barnet Simpson remembered that the teacher was a disabled cooper who made tubs and barrels during school hours rather than providing instruction to the students. John Simpson remembered the resourcefulness of one of his teachers:

> *... we had very few [books] not near enough to go round. The teacher cut the alphabet out of the books and pasted them on paddles; and these were passed around, from one another. I learned the alphabet that way.*[14]

As soon as he completed the log house for his family, William Simpson and Joseph Turnidge (1819-1857), a fellow preacher and 1846 emigrant, began the construction of a building nearby to serve as a schoolhouse during the week and as an Old School Baptist church on weekends.

In the spring of 1847, William Simpson leased nearby land where he grew a wheat crop.[15] He had no farming equipment but was immensely resourceful. He fashioned a plow out of scrap wood and metal. He used oxen to draw the plow through the field and "turkey-wing cradles" assembled by a Wisdom in-law, to harvest the grain. The cut grain was piled in a corral where livestock walked over the piles to separate the wheat from the chaff. The grain was thrown in the air to clean out the chaff. The ancient methods were crude but effective. According to John Simpson, "they raised the finest grain I ever saw."[16]

The Old School Baptists

William Simpson had grown up in North Carolina during a period of religious ferment. His parents had been devout Methodists who had entertained circuit riding preachers in their home and provided the land for what became Simpson's (Methodist) Chapel in Rockingham County. At the same time, traveling evangelists had attracted thousands to camp meetings which went on for days and featured multiple preachers and emotion-laden religious conversions. During this period of heightened religious awareness, some Protestant denominations were struggling with internal disputes. The Baptists were torn between two factions. The dominant group, called at various times "Regular" or "Missionary" Baptists, was challenged by Baptists calling themselves "Particular", "Anti-Missionary", "Old School" or "Primitive".[17]

The Old School Baptists believed in a strict interpretation of the Bible and rejected most forms of religious structure and authority. They were opposed to theological seminaries, Bible Societies, Sunday schools, Bible tracts, temperance organizations, missionary associations and camp meeting revivals calling them "the inventions of men and not warranted by the word of God". Attending a theological seminary, for example, was an admission that the word of man was as important as the word of God. In their view, seminaries were unnecessary as "... any man who was truly called of God, would also be equipped by God".[18] The Old School Baptists combined a literal interpretation of the Bible with frontier independence and distrust of elites and concentrated power. The Old School Baptists were not opposed to missionary activity; in fact they saw themselves as missionaries. What they opposed were the missionary societies and other religious institutions which, in their view, collected money, had leaders with "great swelling titles" and lost sight of their purpose. For the Old School Baptists, these powerful and remote religious institutions were without biblical basis and were a threat to religious liberty.

William Simpson, the son of Methodists, first encountered Old School Baptists as a child in Rockingham County, North Carolina. He became an Old School Baptist minister at the age of 23 in Tennessee and preached the gospel as he moved west. In 1833, he established High Point Baptist Church in Johnson County, Missouri. On February 27, 1847, the building that Elder Simpson and Elder Turnidge had constructed on the North Yamhill River became the Hillsborough Baptist Church. It was the first Old School Baptist Church established west of the Rocky Mountains. The new church had a congregation of ten including the families of the two builders.

The Old School Baptists in Oregon

Within eighteen months, the number of Old School Baptist Churches in Oregon had grown to three with a total of 44 members. In October 1849, representatives of the three churches convened at the Hillsborough Church to form an association of Old School Baptist churches in Oregon. Elder Simpson presented the introductory message explaining why an association was needed and was elected Moderator (chair) of the new association. He was also a member of the committee which drafted the founding documents for the association including a constitution, articles of faith and rules of decorum.. The "Constitution" contained twelve concise provisions including one reaffirmation of the independence of each church and another, somewhat longer, rejecting church-related institutions:

> *... we deny fellowship with [the Baptist Board of Foreign Missions) together with Sunday schools and temperance societies.*[19]

The "Articles of Faith" were eight short statements affirming belief in the Trinity, the scriptures, the doctrine of "election by grace" and baptism by immersion. The eighteen "Rules of Decorum" included a limitation on the number of times a particular speaker could address a single issue (three) and the preferred form of address for another member of the association ("brother").[20]

Named the Siloam Association, the group of Old School Baptist churches met annually and expanded gradually as new churches were formed. By the time of the 1851 annual meeting, the association had five churches with a total of 86 members. A participant in the 1851 meeting reported that

> *The preaching was all of the right kind, and all of a piece, and according to the ancient way marks... all the various institutions and inventions of man were exposed...* [21]

Elder William Simpson was one of the preachers "of the right kind" at the 1851 meeting. He also attended the 4th annual conference of the association with his son Ben in 1853.[22] Ben Simpson was a member of the church ("brother") and sometimes appears as an "elder" (preacher) although there is no record of him preaching.

The Simpsons attended their last conference of the Siloam Association. Sometime in 1853, William Simpson objected to what Elder John Stripp and Elder John Mansfield were preaching about "limited atonement". Limited atonement, the doctrine that Christ died only for the elect, was the defining belief of the Old School Baptists and one of eight Articles of Faith of the Siloam Association. The objection resulted in charges that William Simpson and his son Ben

> *... have repeatedly of late been preaching and contending for a system contrary to the faith of this church particularly on the subject of atonement, denying that it has alone for its object the Church or body of Christ (or in other words his chosen and elect people) contending that none are redeemed until regenerated...*[23]

The tiny congregation of the Hillsborough church voted seven to one to approve the resolution that "Elder Wm. Simpson and Br. Benjamin Simpson are no more of us". William Simpson and his son were expelled from the church William Simpson had built seven years earlier.[24]

With the two Simpson men excluded from the church, the congregation considered the objection William Simpson had raised about the two preachers. The Hillsborough members voted 15 to 4 to reject the objection. Within months, the Hillsborough Church purged itself of "disorderly" members by expelling six additional persons including the four members of the Simpson family.[25] William Simpson had been an Old School preacher for forty years when he provoked the confrontation at Hillsborough Church in

1853. He had been one of the founders of the denomination in Oregon and the first leader of the Siloam Association. He knew the singular importance of limited atonement within the beliefs of the Old School Baptists and the severity with which the denomination treated deviation. It is unclear exactly what he was challenging but he surely must have known the outcome of a vote in his little congregation. By the time the dispute within the Hillsborough Church reached its unpleasant conclusion, Elder Simpson had already built a second Baptist Church in the Waldo Hills of Marion County where be assembled a small congregation and continued unimpeded.

The Hillsboro Church remained unyielding, and William Simpson was now portrayed by his former church as some sort of enemy:

> *Some with whom we once took sweet counsel together, have separated from us; and have been and are now siding against us, proclaiming another Gospel, and have led off some into Babylon.*[26]

Elder Simpson ignored his critics and preached what he believed in the little Waldo Hills Church the rest of his life. The Waldo Hills Church made no effort to join the Siloam Association. The Association grew slowly, split into two bickering factions and fell into decline.

The Oregon Donation Land Act

Settlers had been occupying Oregon land since the late 1830s, and growing numbers of emigrants were arriving each year expecting land to be available. The settlers formed a provisional government in 1843 which adopted land laws but did not approve any land claims. The 1848 law making Oregon a territory of the United States established the Territorial government but made no provision for title distribution of public land to settlers. Samuel Thurston, the Territorial Delegate from Oregon advocated vigorously for the land law the U.S. Congress enacted in 1850. The Donation Land Claim Act provided for a survey of public lands in Oregon and authorized land grants for settlers who had arrived in Oregon prior to December 1, 1850, and those who arrived between 1850 and 1853. White male adults who had occupied and cultivated the land for four years or more were eligible for a half section (320 acres) of free land. If the settler was married, the family could claim a second half section in the name of the wife. This was the first time that women held title to federal lands in their own right. Settlers who arrived in Oregon between 1850 and 1853 were eligible for up to 160 acres with all the same requirements. The 1850 law applied only to white settlers and biracial

Native Americans. The law excluded African Americans, Native Americans, Asians and Hawaiians from obtaining free land.[27] (Appendix III)

The Donation Land Act was generous toward the settlers and retroactively legitimated their squatting on Indian land. The 1850 law created the position of Surveyor General for Oregon and authorized a General Land Office in Oregon City where land claims could be filed. The surveyor began work in May 1851. The 1850 Land Act was somewhat premature since there was no land to distribute. Indian tribes, many of them severely depleted by disease, held title to the land the government proposed to give away. In 1850, the U.S. Congress appropriated $29,500 to acquire title to Indian lands in Oregon. Three Treaty Commissioners were appointed to negotiate with the tribes. During 1851, the Commissioners successfully negotiated eighteen treaties in which Oregon tribes relinquished land in exchange for cash and goods. In several of the Treaties, the tribes ceded large parts of their traditional lands but retained small parcels rather than accept relocation. At the same time the treaties were being negotiated in Oregon, the U.S. Congress, nearly 3000 miles away in Washington, D.C., abolished the Treaty Commission. The U.S. Senate refused to ratify any of the eighteen treaties.[28]

In 1853-1854, Indian Agents undertook a second round of negotiations to acquire Indian land in Oregon and Washington. The negotiations resulted in fifteen treaties in Oregon and Washington. The Indians of the Willamette Valley and surrounding areas ceded their land to the federal government in exchange for cash, manufactured goods and food to be paid over several years. The Indians agreed to relocate to reservations and the government agreed to provide schools, houses, hospitals, livestock and mills as well as teachers, farm managers and physicians. In the January 1855 Treaty of Dayton, Oregon, 46 Indians representing Clackamas, Kalapuya, Molalla and other tribes traded their rights to the Willamette Valley for $135,000 worth of goods to be delivered over twenty years. Five years after the enactment of the Donation Land Act, the federal government could open the General Land Office in Oregon City to begin to process land claims. By the time all the donation land claims had been reviewed, early Oregon settlers had obtained 7437 patents for 2.6 million acres of land.[29]

To the Waldo Hills:

In the fall of 1847, William Simpson harvested his wheat crop and moved from Yamhill County to Marion County. In November 1847, William and Mary Simpson settled land adjacent to property their oldest daughter Eleanor

Anderson and her husband James had claimed in April 1847. Their son David Simpson and his wife Julia followed in December.[30] The Simpson land was in the Waldo Hills about ten miles southeast of Salem and north of the communities of Aumsville and Sublimity. William Simpson built a one-room, sixteen foot square log house.[31] As settlers who had arrived in Oregon prior to 1850 and who had occupied and improved their land for four years or more, William and Mary Simpson together qualified for a full section (when surveyed the land turned out to be 641 acres) under the Donation Land Act. Their property was surrounded by land claimed by their children and their families. Their son-in-law Napoleon B. (Dick) Wisdom was immediately to their north and their son-in-law James Anderson was to their east. Son-in-law Larkin Price was east of the Anderson property and son-in-law Ninevah Ford was south of the Anderson land. Their son David Simpson and his wife claimed land adjacent to the Price property. In all, William Simpson, his son, four sons in-law and one Kimsey relative received patents for 404 acres of Donation land in Township 8 South, Range 1 East. (Appendix II and III)

Benjamin and Nancy Simpson claimed 600 acres about ten miles away in Township 9 South, Range 3 West, while Kimsey relatives claimed 1921 acres in Polk County and 644 acres in Yamhill County.[32] The Simpson-Kinsey clan which had left 2600 acres in Missouri (much of it owned by relatives who remained in Missouri) was rewarded with more than 6700 acres of land in Oregon.[33]

Many years later, an adoring grandson remembered William and Mary Simpson and their old armchair:

> *There sat the venerable Grandfather as the words of kindness & admonition dropped from his lips. There he sat as he read the old family Bible & explained & enforced its precepts. There too, sometimes sat our beloved Grand Mother, whose countenance beamed with kindness & sympathy. From it she would watch our childish sports & direct our amusements. And when the stormy passions would arise, like a queen on her throne, she would decide all our disputes & settle all our difficulties.*[34]

William and Mary Simpson had moved for the last time. They lived together in the Waldo Hills house they had built surrounded by their children and grandchildren. Mary K. Simpson died in February 1858 and William Simpson died the following November. They are buried, with more than 30 other Simpson relatives, in the Lone Fir/ Rocky Point Cemetery on Anderson Road three miles northwest of Sublimity in the Waldo Hills.

3 The Empire Builder

The contrast between father and son was striking. Where William Simpson was content to plant the seeds and collect the harvest of his small farm and congregation, Ben Simpson (1818-1910) was a man of action who saw opportunity everywhere he looked, and he looked everywhere. The local newspaper called him a "pioneer of prominence".[35] He was energetic, ambitious and endlessly optimistic. Rather than accompany his father to Yamhill County, Ben Simpson, his wife Nancy Cooper Simpson (1820-1883) and their two young children spent the winter of 1846-1847 in Oregon City where he, like other recent arrivals, earned money splitting rails. They redeemed the food credits they had obtained at Fort Hall and Simpson built a sawmill, the first on the Clackamas River above Oregon City.[36]

Oregon City, with a population of about 600, was the largest settlement north of San Francisco and the only city in Oregon.[37] Located immediately below the Falls of the Willamette, Oregon City was the transfer point for cargo between the upper and lower parts of the Willamette River. The town had been laid out in 1842 by John McLaughlin of Hudson's Bay Company who had since retired and was seeking United States citizenship. By 1846, Oregon City was the center of economic, cultural and political activity in the region with stores, taverns, water-powered mills, lawyers, doctors, skilled craftsmen and a hotel. Oregon City had a school building, the only subscription library in the territory and an active literary society called the Falls Association.[38]

Rachel Fisher, an overland emigrant from Iowa, saw Oregon City for the first time in 1847. She was favorably impressed by the character-building institutions she found in the little frontier town:

> *Oregon City appears to be quite A flourishing little town "... there is a temperance meeting a licium (sic), two common day schools, two different religious meeting[s] ... "*[89]

Oregon City had been the nominal capital of the region since 1844 when the legislative assembly of the provisional government began meeting. For a recently-arrived emigrant with political and business ambitions like Ben Simpson, Oregon City was the place to start. In the spring of 1847,

Simpson and his family moved to the French Prairie section of Marion County where he planned to claim land.[40]

The Provisional Government

Before 1846, Oregon was the entire northwest region extending north into what is now western Canada and east to the Rocky Mountains including all of what is now Idaho, Oregon and Washington as well as those parts of Montana and Wyoming west of the crest of the Rocky Mountains. The United States and Great Britain had competing claims to the area which they had been unable to resolve in treaty negotiations dating back to 1818.[41] As an interim measure, the two countries agreed to a joint occupancy arrangement in which the nationals of both countries were free to use the area for commercial purposes or settlement. The joint occupancy agreement was flexible enough to enable the British to operate a fur trading monopoly throughout the region while increasing numbers of United States citizens were settling in the Willamette Valley.[42] For all practical purposes, Dr. McLoughlin (1784-1857), Chief Factor of the Hudson's Bay Company, had been the governor of Oregon from 1823 until the formation of the provisional government in 1843.

By the early 1840s, missionaries and settlers in the Willamette Valley were agitating for self-government and eventual affiliation with the United States. The French Canadians living in the area, many of them retired fur trappers married to Native American wives, were uneasy about the proposed new government and the relationship to the United States. In an open letter, they objected strenuously to taxes ("we don't want them") and to the creation of a militia ("useless at present... danger of bad suspicion to the Indians").[43] In 1843, the settlers formed a provisional government "for mutual protection" and adopted an interim constitution to operate" until such time as the United States of America extends their jurisdiction over us". The elected officials of the provisional government included a three-person executive committee, a nine-person legislative body and, among others, a judge, sheriff and three constables. The Constitution of 1843, sometimes called the First Organic Laws of Oregon included high-minded statements of intent that education would be "forever encouraged" and that Indian lands would never be taken "without their consent" and authorized the governor to "call out the military force of the territory, to repel invasion or suppress insurrection... " The 1843 constitution was adopted at a public meeting by a vote of 52-50. Recognizing that a proper government needed laws, the participants in the

1843 meeting had adopted more than 500 pages of the 1839 laws of the Territory of Iowa as the laws of the provisional government of Oregon.[44]

The stated purpose of the provisional government was "mutual protection", but, to placate the French Canadians, there was no provision in the 1843 constitution for a militia and there was no revenue to support a militia if an invasion or insurrection should occur.[45] The framers of the 1843 constitution agreed to compromises, like the three person executive and the silence about taxes and militia, to maintain unity among those seeking self-government for the Oregon region. The unproven assumption was that Oregon residents would voluntarily pay "subscriptions" to government.[46] The following year, Oregon settlers approved a second provisional constitution. The 1844 constitution eliminated some of the unworkable features of the 1843 version and added provisions that had been neglected the previous year. The second constitution replaced the unwieldy three-person executive with a single governor and explicitly authorized the legislature to impose taxes and to mobilize the militia when necessary. In 1844, a group of American settlers obtained the approval of the legislative assembly to form a militia unit called the Oregon Rangers. The Rangers drilled briefly and disbanded without ever seeing active service.[47]

The settlers were impatient about their right to land. With a few exceptions, like the Hudson's Bay forts, all the land in Oregon remained Indian land. Confident that the land would eventually become available to them, the settlers built cabins and planted crops on land where the tribes had hunted for game, grazed livestock and harvested roots. They also began to pass laws in anticipation of the availability of land. The provisional government had no land but approved a land law in 1843 specifying when and where land claims should be recorded and limiting individual claims to 640 acres (one square mile) with an exception for religious missions which could claim up to 36 square miles (23,040 acres). The 1843 constitution had pledged that no Indian land would be taken without consent of the Indians. The pledge survived one year before the Legislative Committee of the provisional government narrowed the definition of which Indian lands were protected. The protected lands, it turned out, were only those lands the Indians actually used or occupied. The provisional legislature noted the declining Indian population and the difficulty in negotiating with the tribes before redefining Indian lands:

> *The Indians inhabiting this country are rapidly diminishing, being now mere remnants of once powerful tribes now disorganized, without government, and so situated that no treaty can be regularly be made*

with them... The Indians are not engaged in agriculture and have no use for or right to any tracts, portions or parcels of land, not actually occupied or used by them.[48]

The 1844 Land Law maintained the 640-acre limit, required that claims be square if possible and reduced the period required for improvements from six months to two. The 1844 law also repealed the special provision allowing religious missions to claim 36 sections, the recording requirements and race, gender and age restrictions on land ownership. The land law was a convenient fiction. The provisional government had no authority to determine Indian land rights, but the land law was useful to demonstrate to prospective emigrants that land would be likely to be available in Oregon in the future.

The residents of Oregon began their exercise in self-government during the time that Oregon remained subject to the joint occupancy agreement between the United States and Great Britain. In his 1845 inaugural address, President Polk had warned the British awkwardly but unequivocally that the United States intended to settle and claim Oregon.

...title to the country of Oregon is "clear and unquestionable" and already are our people preparing to prefect that title by occupying with their wives and children.[49]

In 1846, after nearly forty years of diplomatic negotiations, the long-standing dispute between the United States and Great Britain was resolved and the boundary between the United States and Canada was defined forever at the 49th parallel.[50] The United States conceded its claims north of the boundary and acquired uncontested jurisdiction over an immense region stretching from the Rocky Mountains to the Pacific Ocean.

Apart from the settlement in the Willamette Valley and a few isolated trading posts, forts and missions, the Oregon Country was populated entirely by Indians. Several tribes, particularly those in the Columbia River region, were uneasy about the growing number of wagons crossing their lands each fall and the proliferation of settlements on Indian lands. The Indians of the Northwest who had contact with settlers were dying from diseases for which they had no immunity. Among the Cayuse and nearby tribes, in the late 1840s, the contagious disease was measles and the results were devastating.

Children and adults were dying in large numbers and some Indians wondered whether the epidemics were part of a plan to exterminate the Indians and make land available for settlement.

The Cayuse War

From: https://nativeamericannetroots.net/diary/839

The peaceful settlement of the Willamette Valley was suddenly threatened in late 1847 when a group of Cayuse Indians attacked residents at the Whitman Mission, called Waiilatpu, where they killed Marcus Whitman, his wife Narcissa and eleven others and took three men, eight women and 39 children captive. The news of the November 29-30 killings at the mission reached Oregon City, about 225 miles away, December 7. Settlers were outraged about the killings but apprehensive that this was the beginning of a wider Indian uprising to drive the settlers out of the Willamette Valley. The short-lived Oregon Rangers had disbanded and the provisional government, now in its fifth year, had no organized military force to use to repel invasion or suppress insurrection. Fortunately the provisional legislature was in session when the news about the Whitman killings arrived in Oregon City. The legislative assembly and Governor George Abernathy immediately called for volunteers for a military campaign to free the captives, capture the killers, punish the Cayuse and protect the Willamette Valley.[51] Oregon leaders believed that the Indians would only respect a show of force and that it was essential to engage the Indians on their own lands rather than waiting for them to invade the settlements.

The provisional government of Oregon had no weapons, ammunition or other supplies and no money or credit to purchase the supplies a military campaign would require. As the war started, the Oregon treasury had a cash balance of $43.72 and owed $4079.[52] Volunteers were expected, as best they could, to supply their own saddle horses, rifles, ammunition and blankets.

Within two days, a company of 46 young men from Washington County had volunteered and departed to protect the mission at The Dalles. The company was under the command of Capt. Henry A.G. Lee and included Ben Simpson's former brother-in-law Alvis Kimsey and Ben's cousin Thomas Kimsey.[53] Within weeks, several additional units mobilized including three companies from Marion County, the most populous county in Oregon.[54] Company D, sometimes called the 6th company, was under the command of Capt. Thomas McKay, a respected retired fur trader and step-son of John McLaughlin of Hudson's Bay Company. McKay's company had 36 men and was primarily composed of French-Canadian fur trappers who had retired to farming on the French Prairie of Marion County.

Ben Simpson and his family had been living in Marion County since the spring of 1847. On January 28, 1848, Ben Simpson and his brother-in-law Ninevah Ford enlisted for three months as privates in a second company of volunteers organized in Marion County.[55] The second company, designated Company E, had 44 men under the command of Capt. Leven N. English. Captain English (1792-1875) was an experienced frontier fighter. He had served in the War of 1812 and was a Captain in Black Hawk's War.[56] The mobilization stripped the Willamette Valley of its supply of fighting men and left families feeling vulnerable. In a scene repeated throughout the settlements, John Simpson remembered his step-mother hugging his father,

John T. Simpson - *Son of Ben and his first wife, Eliza Jane Wisdom*

> *...crying, begging him to stay with his family, that they would all be killed; but father told her to be of good cheer that they wouldn't be molested by the Indians*
>
> *...while I believe her to have been one of the bravest women [who] ever lived, at this time she was scared. And it is the only time I ever saw her to show any fear whatsoever...* [57]

Ben Simpson reassured his wife, as best he could, and departed for Cayuse Country with Captain English's company leaving Nancy Simpson and four little boys, the oldest seven, with her worries in their Marion County cabin.

Capt. William J. Martin, who had been the original captain of the 1846 wagon train the Simpson family joined, organized a third company of Marion County volunteers. The three Marion County companies, along with the companies raised in other counties comprised the First Regiment Oregon Mounted Rifles. The regiment was under the overall command of Colonel Cornelius Gilliam (1798-1848), a veteran of Black Hawk's War in Illinois in 1832, the Seminole Indian War in Florida in 1835 and the 1838 campaign to expel Mormons from Missouri. In all, about 700 officers and men enlisted in the First Regiment at various times but, with desertions and expiring enlistments, the effective force rarely exceeded 200.[58]

While the volunteer regiment was forming, Peter Skene Ogden of Hudson's Bay Company took the initiative to rescue the Whitman Mission captives.[59] The Company represented British interests in the Northwest and was in competition with the settlers for control of Oregon. It was also a business and aware that an Indian war, whether it was initiated by the Indians or the by the settlers, would be disruptive to business and would create lasting animosities in Oregon. Acting independently of the provisional government, Ogden met with Cayuse Chiefs in December 1847 and used the influence of Hudson's Bay Company to persuade the Indians to release the captives. Ogden paid a ransom of 50 blankets, 50 cotton shirts, ten guns, ten fathoms (60 feet) of (rope) tobacco, ten handkerchiefs and one hundred loads of ammunition to the Cayuse.[60] The ransom was paid by Hudson's Bay Company and was never reimbursed by the provisional government or by the United States.[61] The 47 Whitman captives, along with nine missionaries and children evacuated from another mission arrived in Portland January 8. The generosity of the Hudson's Bay Company leadership secured the captives but also averted what would have been a full-scale war with several Indian tribes had the provisional government attempted to recover the captives by force.

Oregon was desperate for assistance. The provisional legislature had no army and was unable to supply its own troops with horses, weapons, and food. The provisional government had to rely on a British company to ransom the captives and suffer the humiliation of being denied a loan for war expenses from the same company. The legislature sent Jesse Applegate to California and Joseph Meek to Washington, D.C. for help. Applegate encountered severe snowstorms in the Siskiyou Mountains and was forced to turn back. Meek, paying his own expenses, delayed his departure until spring and crossed overland to Missouri in a remarkable 66 days. He reached St. Joseph, Missouri May 11. By May 28, he was in Washington, D.C. where he was influential in persuading the Congress, in August 1848, to make Oregon a territory of the United States. The military assistance Oregon needed in January 1848 arrived in October 1849.

The Whitman captives had been rescued but the Whitman killers remained free, and the settlers continued to believe that the tribes of the Columbia River region were a threat to invade the Willamette Valley settlements. The Cayuse War of 1848 was a series of brief skirmishes between units of the Oregon regiment and shifting combinations of Columbia River tribes. The skirmishes involved intermittent attacks by one side or the other, followed by withdrawal to defensive positions and resumed attacks. In three instances, the skirmishes extended beyond one day and across ten or twenty miles. The battles were themselves inconclusive. No land was permanently lost or gained, and casualties were not great enough to reduce the capacity of either side to fight. In each of the three major battles of the Cayuse War, the Oregon volunteers prevailed when the Indians withdrew from the battle ground. In two of the three battles, tribes allied with the Cayuse agreed to a separate peace.

The campaign against the Cayuse began in January 1848 when advance units of the Oregon Mounted Rifles secured the mission at The Dalles. Beginning February 16, a detachment of about 130 volunteers, what one historian characterized as "all that could be mounted and equipped"[62] engaged Indians from three tribes in a series of skirmishes twenty miles up the Deschutes River. The Indians retreated into the nearby mountains after several days of intermittent fighting. The Oregon volunteers, despite their lack of supplies, chased the Indians from the battlefield, recovered about forty stolen horses and achieved a peace agreement with the Deschutes tribe.[63]

From the Deschutes River, Colonel Gilliam's army continued eastward along the Oregon Trail. Morale was poor throughout the regiment. The troops were impatient with the delays caused by a peace delegation meeting with tribal representatives. They were also frustrated by the way the inadequate supplies of food and ammunition were being distributed and complained about endless minor irritants like their order in the column. Some volunteers simply left their units. One company went so far as voting on whether to turn around and return home (they stayed). During this period, two Marion County companies, those of Captain McKay and Captain English, joined the regiment. The Marion County companies had been slowed by a nine-pound cannon they were transporting. The cannon was the only one in Oregon and something of a nuisance. It had been part of the armament of a ship that had stopped in Oregon and was presented to Oregon City in 1846. The municipal cannon was unwieldy to transport and thoroughly unsuited for the hit and run warfare of the Columbia River Indians. The Marion County companies fashioned a makeshift vehicle to carry the cannon using the rear half of an abandoned emigrant wagon. The cannon was fired twice during the Cayuse campaign with little effect. It was loud enough to attract attention but useless on the battlefield.[64]

Gilliam's Oregon Regiment comprising five companies with a total of about 150 men followed the emigrant road eastward toward the Umatilla River crossing. On February 24 the regiment encountered a large number of Cayuse at a place called Sand Hollow about ten miles west of present-day Hermiston. Estimates were that 400 Indians were blocking the trail of whom three-quarters were prepared to fight and the rest were women and observers from other tribes. The Indians had selected the dry sandy battleground and had the advantage in numbers and terrain. Colonel Gilliam arranged his regiment along the emigrant road with two companies on each flank and one in the middle protecting wagons and supplies. Gilliam placed his most experienced troops, McKay's French Prairie company, on the right flank and English's Marion County company immediately adjacent. The Indians circled the regiment on horseback taunting the volunteers and threatening to attack. The battle began on the right flank when the Indians shot a dog accompanying the regiment. The experienced mountain men and crack shots of the French Prairie company responded killing one Cayuse Chief and severely wounding another. The battle continued into a second day and moved east toward the Umatilla River before the Indians withdrew leaving the Oregon volunteers victorious in the decisive battle of the 1848 campaign against the Cayuse.[65] Ben Simpson and the other volunteers from Marion County fought in the battle of Sand Hollow.

The regiment proceeded north into what is now southeastern Washington and arrived near the Whitman Mission March 2. Colonel Gilliam elected two companies, including Captain English's company from Marion County to accompany him the site of the Whitman Mission at Waiilatpu. The troops found a gristly scene. The Mission building, furnishings and possessions had been vandalized and burned. The troops also discovered that the shallow grave that survivors had hurriedly dug had been disturbed by animals. Bodies of victims had been uncovered and were scattered about. The soldiers reburied the bodies of those killed the previous November and used the ruins of the mission to build fortifications while the peace commissioners engaged in negotiations with the Indians. Growing impatient with the delay, Colonel Gilliam divided his force. He sent 158 men northward toward the Snake River following the retreating Cayuse and kept 42 men under Captain English at the Waiilatpu fort.[66]

The larger force fought a thirty-hour, running battle against the Cayuse and their allies the Palouse. The battle began near the Touchet River moved toward the Tucannon River and eventually returned to where it had started. Ben Simpson remembered Colonel Gilliam receiving a message in the middle of the night from the troops chasing the Indian. They reported that they had exhausted their supplies of food and ammunition and were camped eight or ten miles away from Wailatpu where they were surrounded by Indians. According to Simpson, Colonel Gilliam immediately:

> *... ordered two wagons to go to their camp with provisions and ammunition and he asked for volunteers to go to guard the wagons and I volunteered and went as one of the guards.*[67]

By the time the relief wagon arrived, the Indians had withdrawn. The Oregon regiment had won the battle but the Whitman killers they were pursuing escaped eastward.

Enlistments were beginning to expire and spring crops needed planting. The Oregon Regiment began to return to the Willamette Valley. On March 20, Colonel Gilliam left Waiilatpu to travel to Oregon City where he planned to confer with Governor Abernathy. He was accompanied by Captain English and his Marion County company. On March 24, Colonel Gilliam was accidentally shot and killed.[68] A halter rope he was pulling off a wagon snagged on the trigger of a loaded rifle and killed him instantly.[69] Ben Simpson wrote about the death of his commanding officer:

> *... my commanding officer was with Col. Gilliam when he was killed at Wells Springs with his own gun. His death left Cap'n Maxen in Command [of the troops returning to Oregon City] being the oldest Cap'n. He ordered me to take Gilliam after he was shot, and to wash, shave and dress him and prepare for conveyance to The Dalles... I did dress him and put him in the wagon, and we traveled all night never stopped any more till we got to The Dalles.*[70]

Captain English and his company continued to Salem where Benjamin Simpson was discharged April 17, 1848. Simpson remained in Marion County through the growing season but returned to Clackamas City in the fall of 1848 where he resumed work at his sawmill.

Gilliam's campaign against the Cayuse had achieved most of its objectives. Despite persistent problems of morale and supply, the Oregon regiment had defeated the Cayuse in each of the three battles they fought. The regiment held the ground and the Indians eventually withdrew. The volunteers had displayed bravery and discipline which surprised the Indians who were accustomed to the more conciliatory responses they had encountered among the families in the wagon trains. While it is unlikely that the Columbia River Indians ever planned an invasion of the Willamette Valley, Gilliam's campaign had impressed the Indians and convinced many of the tribes to reconsider their alliances with the Cayuse. The War had left the Cayuse isolated among the Indians and punished by the settlers. Ben Simpson and his Marion County company missed the first battle of the war but fought in the crucial Battle of Sand Hollow and escorted the relief wagons to resupply the troops who had fought in the final battle of the war. The Marion County Company also reburied the bodies of those killed at the Whitman mission and constructed a fort at the site.

The Whitman killers had eluded the Oregon regiment during the military expedition of 1848. They had fled to remote places and remained fugitives until 1850 when the Cayuse tribe surrendered five men to Territorial authorities. According to the Cayuse leaders, the five were the only living members of the group who had murdered the Whitmans and others in 1847. The five were brought to trial in Oregon City for the killings. Surviving eyewitnesses testified in a jury trial where the five defendants were represented by experienced defense lawyers. The five were found guilty and hanged in Oregon City June 3, 1850.[71]

The 1848 Cayuse War was over, but the financial problems of the Oregon government continued. The provisional government had promised to pay the members of the regiment $1.50 a day for their service, horse, equipment, supplies and weapons, a total of $109,000. In 1853-1854 the United States Congress approved payments of $148,000 to the Territory of Oregon for expenses of the Cayuse War of 1848. The Congressional appropriation included the payment to the volunteers but did not include any reimbursement of Hudson's Bay Company expenses in ransoming the Whitman Mission captives.[72]

The people of Oregon were justly proud of their young men and the victory they had achieved in the Cayuse War. The volunteers had responded promptly to the call for troops. With no training and limited resources, the Oregon volunteers dispersed the Indians in every battle they fought and successfully prevented an Indian invasion of the Willamette

Valley. The victory celebration overlooked how unprepared the provisional government had been and how dependent it was on the generosity of others. The settlers were ecstatic about the release of the Whitman captives but overlooked the fact that the Hudson's Bay Company had used its relationships with the Indians to locate the captives and its supplies to pay the ransom. The provisional government sought help from the Federal government but was unable to pay the expenses of Joseph Meek's heroic overland journey to Washington.

In its celebration, Oregon failed to recognize that its isolation entailed greater self-reliance. It could not depend on the federal government 2500 miles away for protection nor expect a British company, with which it had ambivalent relationships, to pay its bills. Despite its success, the campaign against the Cayuse exposed how poorly organized the settlers' government was. The Indians were impressed that the Oregon volunteers would dig in and fight in the face of vastly superior numbers, as they did at the Battle of Sand Hollow. The unlearned lesson of the Cayuse War was that Oregon needed to find a way, other than brute force, to deal with its Indian neighbors. The settlers believed that they were entitled to land in Oregon because of the privations of the overland trail and that the United States government would eventually provide that land. The settlers were primarily farmers and, from their perspective, the land they wanted was vacant and unused. The Indians used the land differently but, like tribes before them, would be unable to protect their lands against the land-hungry settlers. For the next forty years, Oregon policy makers, including Ben Simpson, would struggle with Indian land issues. The outcome of the struggle would always be the same. The Indians would give up part of their land in exchange for assurances that their remaining land would be protected.

The California Gold Rush

The volunteers of the Oregon Regiment returned home from the Cayuse War during the spring and summer of 1848. They soon learned that gold had been discovered in California and that fortunes were waiting to be made. Within a few months, a large proportion of the young men in Oregon had departed for California. John R. McBride, whose family had accompanied the Simpson family on the Overland Trail in 1846, estimated that two-thirds of the men in Oregon left for the gold fields of California between July and November of 1848.[73] Ben Simpson was attracted by the opportunities in California. Rather than trying to strike it rich as a miner, he decided to take advantage of gold rush prices and shortages by shipping lumber from his mill on the Clackamas River to California. In 1850, he began cutting lumber for prefabricated wooden houses, that were called "knock-down houses" which he transported to California by ship and sold for $1000 each before returning to Oregon in July 1850.[74] The transaction may have been very profitable. Another Oregon businessman claimed to have made $40,000 from a single shipload of lumber he sold in California.[75]

The Territorial Government, 1850

After five years of provisional self-government, Oregon became a territory of the United States in August 1848. As a territory, Oregon was essentially a colony of the United States with appointed officials in the executive and judicial branches of government and limited local control. The territory was administered by a governor appointed by the president of the United States. [76]The first territorial governor, Joseph Lane, was a popular choice in Oregon. He was a southerner and pro-slavery. He had been a general in the Mexican War and a state legislator in Indiana. The new governor arrived in Oregon City in March of 1849 and immediately began organizing a government. He appointed territorial officials, directed the ubiquitous Joe Meek to conduct a census (which found 8795 citizens in the territory, 298 "foreigners" and did not count Native Americans) and called for the election of members of the territorial legislature and a non-voting delegate to represent the territory in the United States Congress.

The first territorial election was held in June 1849 and voters elected eighteen representatives from eight counties to the Legislative Assembly which convened at Oregon City the following month. The first assembly organized itself into two bodies, the House and the Council, and voted to make Salem the seat of the territorial government. The territorial election of June 1849 also elected Samuel R. Thurston (1816-1851) to be Oregon's non-voting delegate to the Congress. Thurston was a Democrat and lawyer who had come overland to Oregon in 1847 from Iowa. Thurston received 470 of the 943 votes cast and acknowledged Ben Simpson's role in his success:

> *... to Simpson, I owe my election. I do not mean he elected me, but I so trace influences, that had it not been for him, I should never have been a candidate.*[77]

Ben Simpson was, like Thurston, a Democrat. He did not run for a seat in the first territorial legislature but, as Thurston reported, played something of a behind the scenes role in assuring that his preferred candidate prevailed. Many years later, Simpson explained:

> *In 1849, I took an active part in bringing out Samuel R. Thurston for Congress. I wanted to beat Jim Nesmith... Thurston was the best timber we had to do it with. I thought.*[78]

In 1850, voters elected representatives to the second session of the territorial legislature. Benjamin Simpson was elected to represent Clackamas County in the House.[79] At a time when political parties were only beginning to emerge in Oregon, Simpson attributed his election to the bipartisan support he had received. He explained to Thurston,

> *I received the highest vote polled in the county for a seat in the house of representatives... I did not get to be a candidate without the strongest solicitations from both whigs and democrats".*[80]

Simpson was a confidential advisor to Thurston. He kept the Territorial Delegate informed about recent developments in Oregon but also sought to take personal advantage of his relationship.

In late 1849, Ben Simpson and Isom Cranfill opened a general merchandise store on Water Street in Oregon City. The store sold cloth (blue drilling; hickory; shirting), manufactured products (China ware; tin ware axes; harnesses; shoes; rope), imported spices (pepper; ginger; allspice; cayenne), soap and "segars". Cranfill (1807-1877) was an 1847 emigrant to Oregon and pastor of the Old School Baptist Church in Molalla. Simpson & Cranfill were competing with several Oregon City merchants offering equally improbable combinations of goods like J.D. & W.C. Holman (clothing and "resurrection pills"), William Kilborn (dry goods and groceries), S.M. Holderness (ready-made clothing; crockery; lamps, lanterns and candlesticks) and Abernathy & Clark (medicine; rice: rubber cloth; tobacco). Oregon City merchants were dependent on goods imported from San Francisco and Hawaii. Simpson & Cranfill claimed a competitive advantage because "one of the firm is now at San Francisco purchasing... goods suited to the Oregon market." [81] Ben Simpson, who was transporting lumber to San Francisco, could now make efficient use of the same ships returning to Oregon.

Soon after the Simpson & Cranfill store opened in Oregon City, Ben Simpson's lumber mill on the Clackamas was damaged by flooding. Simpson described the December 1849 flooding in a letter to Thurston:

> *The country has been considerably flooded with water which has damaged many persons very much. I lost myself at the Clackamas*

> *mills about four thousand dollars... Still our mill is running and doing tolerable well...* [82]

Simpson discussed commodity prices (lumber in California, low; flour, beef and pork, high) before abruptly shifting from public issues to the private realm. He asked the Territorial Delegate to buy three or four thousand dollars" worth of merchandise for his store:

> *... goods that would suit this market. Such as fine clothing for gents and articles for ladies, dresses of the finest quality of goods sell best since the gold has become so [plentiful]...* [83]

Simpson offered to pay the Territorial Delegate a commission for his efforts and to pay Thurston's wife for the merchandise when it arrived in Oregon.

The interplay along the boundary of public service and private benefit was a recurring theme in Simpson's career in Oregon. Simpson's letter reveals his view about the intertwined relationship of public service and private interest. He conflates issues in the public sphere, like flood damage and commodity prices with private issues like the astonishing request that the delegate purchase goods for Simpson's store.

The second session of the Territorial legislature met in Oregon City from December 2, 1850 to February 8, 1851, and established much of the framework for governing the territory. In the second session, the legislature determined the boundary line between Oregon and Washington, established a public school system, incorporated the cities of Portland and Oregon City, created three counties, located county seats in six others, changed the names of three counties and established the boundary line between Linn County and Benton County. The second territorial legislature also organized judicial districts and defined crimes and misdemeanors, approved seven roads, incorporated a bridge company and granted a charter for an insurance company. The legislature appropriated funds to pay officers who had served in the Cayuse War and petitioned the US Congress to make payments to Cayuse War widows. [84]

Ben Simpson was elected to represent Clackamas City in the second territorial legislature. He served on committees on education, claims, commerce and counties and vigorously represented the interests of his Clackamas County constituents. He sponsored successful legislation incorporating the Young Ladies Academy of Oregon City and the First Congregational Society of Oregon City and was active in shaping controversial legislation confirming title to lots in Oregon City[85] and regulating the fees charged by grist mills. Simpson introduced a resolution to build a territorial road from the Willamette Valley to the coast at Astoria and to authorize a company to supply water to residents of Oregon City. The legislature did not approve the water charter, but the territorial road became one of the major issues of the session and was adopted with amendments. On December 20, Simpson presided as the house considered a bill "allowing grants of land to widows who have become such on the road to Oregon, and those who have become such since coming to Oregon..". The following day, Simpson proposed a resolution requesting that Territorial Delegate Samuel R. Thurston call the attention of the Congress to the issue of land donations to widows and orphans in Oregon.[86]

Oregon residents were ambivalent about their status as a territory. They were dissatisfied with their lack of control over executive and judicial appointments, but they were apprehensive that statehood would result in tax increases. Ben Simpson was one of five members of the Second Territorial Legislature appointed to a committee to consider convening a constitutional convention in preparation for statehood. The committee evaded the statehood question by sending a resolution to the Congress asking that Oregon be delegated the power to appoint its own governor, judges and other officials. In other words, Oregon wanted the authority of statehood without its responsibilities. The Territorial Legislature agreed that Oregon should have a statewide vote on the propose constitutional convention if the U.S. Congress rejected the Oregon proposal for territorial self-government.[87]

In 1851, the restless Ben Simpson sold his Clackamas River sawmill and Oregon City store and moved his family to Marion County where he promptly became a candidate for the Third Territorial Legislature. A rival candidate, a recently-arrived judge from Ohio, objected to Simpson because he was a preacher. With restraint and the proper use of the English subjunctive, Simpson responded:

> *I regard this style of argument as unworthy of a reply, but if I were disposed to stoop to its level, I might warn you against the danger of electing lawyers to make your laws so that no one but themselves can understand them. But I forbear. The fact is that our professions ought not to be an objection to either of us, for while I think I am not minister enough to be dangerous, I know that Judge W— is not lawyer enough to hurt.*[88]

The voters of Marion County agreed that Simpson's ministerial work was not disqualifying and elected him to the House in the Third Territorial Legislature.

Simpson was elected to a special session of the legislature in 1852 where he served on committees on education and printing.[89] The voters of Marion

County reelected him to the regular session of the House in 1852. The legislature returned to the question of statehood. A member introduced legislation scheduling an election in 1853 to determine whether or not to convene a constitutional convention. Ben Simpson recognized that his fellow citizens remained opposed to statehood and proposed that the election be postponed until 1854. Simpson's amendment was adopted in the House, but the measure died when it failed to pass in the Council (upper house of the legislature).[90]

In 1853, Simpson was elected to represent Marion County in the Council in the Fifth Territorial Legislature. Among other matters, the fifth legislative assembly devoted a great deal of time to resolving disputes about the names of places and erasing Indian names from the map. Chemeketa became Salem and Marysville became Corvallis. The Council, although it only had nine members, had a spirited and extended debate about the name for Salem. Like realtors naming the streets in a subdivision, Council members proposed alternatives. When Chemawa, the first choice of the Council, was rejected, Ben Simpson proposed the name Valena. Another member of the Council amended Simpson's resolution with the name Pike and a third substituted Chemawah. Simpson tried again, this time with the name Victoria, before the legislature adjourned leaving the name of Salem unchanged.[91] After four terms in the House of the territorial legislature representing two counties and one term in the Council, Benjamin Simpson did not serve in the legislature again until after 1859 when Oregon became a state. (Appendix V)

The Willamette Valley

Most of the pioneers who arrived in Oregon in the 1840s settled in the valley of the Willamette River and its tributaries. The area had open prairies, gentle, rolling hills, a long growing season and ample water but limited access to markets for farm products. Existing roads were primitive, poorly maintained and often muddy or flooded. River transportation was an attractive alternative but was limited by the falls in the Willamette River at Oregon City. Most of the agricultural production was above the falls while the growing market in Portland and transportation to San Francisco and Hawaii were below the falls. By 1849, ocean-going schooners and steamships were common on the Columbia River and lower Willamette. Taking advantage of the demand created by the California Gold Rush, sailing ships were transporting lumber, agricultural products and passengers from Oregon to San Francisco.

River travel was slow to develop above the falls of the Willamette. The flatboats used on the river could only carry small loads and were slow moving upstream against the current. Each fall loads of perishable freight, much of it locally-grown wheat, began to pile up at the river landings. During 1851, steamboats began transporting freight and passengers on the Upper Willamette. Ben Simpson was operating a store at Parkersville in Marion County where he sold general merchandise and groceries and accepted payment in wheat. The Parkersville store was located on the Pudding River about twelve miles east of Fairfield Landing. In 1852, Ben Simpson and a group of French Prairie farmers built their own steamboat at Fairfield. Late that year, Simpson wrote his friend and colleague from the 1850 legislature Matthew Deady:

> *I am still doing all in my power to get my boat running, I got the boilers up to there [sic] place today. I think though I will be able to give you a trip to Marysville in Christmas holiday if not sooner.*[92]

The steamboat Simpson and others built was 120 feet long with a 22-foot beam and 5-foot draft. Christened ***The Oregon***, it was designed to carry freight and passengers on the Upper Willamette between Chenemah and Corvallis.

The Oregon side-wheeler *Source: The Oregon Historical Society ohs.org*

During the same period he was operating the Parkersville store and the steamboat on the Willamette, Ben Simpson exchanged property he owned for a sawmill on the Santiam River in Marion County. He expanded his Marion County enterprises in the spring of 1853 when he built a warehouse at Fairfield Landing. The warehouse enabled Simpson to store grain for himself and the French Prairie farmers while they waited for a boat to arrive. Fairfield Landing was convenient to the French Prairie and its wheat growers and about 16 miles downstream from Salem. That summer, J.C. Waldo and Company built a two-story warehouse at Fairfield increasing business for the steamboat but also increasing the competition for Simpson's warehouse.

Simpson and his partners operated their steamboat for two years before concluding that it was too small to be profitable. In 1854, ***The Oregon*** was badly damaged when he hit a snag in the river four miles below Salem. Ben Simpson and the other owners, were losing money and only too happy to abandon their steamboat.[93] According to John Simpson, his father "..always believed the boat was wrecked purposely… the men who had gone in with father could not get along together".[94]

During this period, Ben Simpson purchased the Peter Poley farm in Marion County. He operated the farm for a short period before trading it for the Neal sawmill on the Santiam River. About 1855, Ben Simpson was severely injured when he fell at his Santiam River sawmill. John Simpson was working with his father at the sawmill,

> *...while he was trying to roll a log onto the carriage with his cant hook he lifted so hard that he broke through the floor and fell into the tail race, 10 or 12 feet below. He struck his head on a timber, which disabled him so that he had to sell the sawmill. For more than a year his head hurt him most of the time, and during most of that time he walked with a reeling gait and at times it affected his memory.*[95]

Simpson was unconscious for an extended period and unable to work for several months while he recovered. With the loss of the steamboat and the injury at the sawmill, Ben Simpson began to explore other opportunities.

Grand Ronde Reservation

The settlement of the Willamette Valley and the Columbia River Valley resulted in conflict between the Native Americans who lived in the area and the settlers who demanded that the Indians be moved away from the settlements. Between 1853 and 1855, Joel Palmer, Superintendent of Indian Affairs for Oregon, negotiated a series of treaties with Oregon tribes involving relocation to temporary and permanent reservations. In 1855, a large permanent reservation, later called Siletz, was established along the Oregon Coast and a smaller reservation was created in the Grand Ronde

Valley on the South Yamhill River. The Grand Ronde Reservation included about 69,000 acres of land in Yamhill and Polk Counties and was adjacent to the larger Coastal Reservation. Members of about twenty tribes and bands, most of them from the Willamette Valley were relocated to the Grand Ronde Reservation where Fort Yamhill was constructed in March 1856.[96].

In 1856, Ben Simpson secured a government contract to build a dam and sawmill on the Reservation at Grand Ronde. He also purchased and operated the sutler's store at Fort Yamhill. Sutlers were civilian storekeepers selling a wide variety of merchandise to Indians, reservation employees and the local military garrison. Sutlers were subject to government regulation regarding the goods they stocked and the prices they charged. The regulation of goods and prices was often ineffective. Sutler stores were located in remote places and some inflated prices and sold substandard merchandise. Other sutlers were honest businessmen who built long relationships with their customers.

In the ten years since he had arrived in Oregon., Simpson had become an experienced businessman and well-connected politician. By 1856, he had owned and operated two stores, a warehouse, two lumber mills and a steamboat. He had also served five terms in the territorial legislature. Simpson would have known Absalom F. Hedges, the territorial Superintendent of Indian Affairs, who had represented Clackamas County in the provisional legislature.[97] As sutler, Ben Simpson, his wife Nancy and their eight children lived in a house on the grounds of the fort. The older Simpson children, including particularly Sylvester and Sam who were twelve and eleven when they arrived at the fort, became friends of the young soldiers garrisoned there including Lieutenant Philip H. Sheridan (1831-1888). According to family legend, Sheridan encouraged Sam Simpson's interest in poetry by giving him a book of Byron's poems.[98]

Philip Henry Sheridan (1831 – 1888)

Lieutenant Sheridan, later a Civil War General, was stationed at Fort Yamhill intermittently from July 1856 to September 1861.[99] Sheridan had a mediocre record at West Point where he ranked 34th in a class of 52 cadets and had been suspended for fighting.

As a consequence, he spent the years after his graduation in backwater posts like Fort Yamhill where there was little to do and few opportunities for advancement. Sheridan was stationed at Fort Yamhill from April to July 1856, from June 1857 to February 1860 and from March 1860 to September 1861. He served as Commanding Officer at the tiny post in June and July 1857 and June to September 1861.[100]

The sword that Sheridan gave to Ben Simpson

The Slavery Question in Oregon

Slavery and racial exclusion had been among the issues which divided Oregonians from the earliest days of self-government. Oregon was far from the populated parts of the United States but was not sufficiently remote to escape the bitter disputes over slavery and states' rights that were tearing the country apart. Many of the pioneers who had come to Oregon on the Overland Trail were from Missouri and other slave states. A small number of emigrants brought slaves with them to Oregon. Others were strongly opposed to slavery in Oregon. The provisional government of Oregon had outlawed slavery in 1843 and again in 1845. In 1849, the Territorial legislature prohibited black persons from settling in Oregon.[101] The Donation Land Act of 1850 provided land grants to white settlers but explicitly excluded African-Americans, Asians. Hawaiians and Native Americans. As Oregon approached statehood, the issues of slavery and free blacks remained contentious.

The first significant legal challenge to slavery in Oregon occurred in April 1852 when Robin Holmes, a former slave, sued Nathaniel Ford of Polk County for custody of Holmes' three minor children.[102] Ford, a former legislator and sheriff in Missouri, had, brought the Holmes family with him to Oregon in 1844 as slaves. Ford had freed Robin Holmes and his wife Polly but kept three children in bondage. The case dragged on unresolved until July 1853 when Chief Justice George H. Williams of the Territorial Supreme Court, newly arrived in Oregon, assumed responsibility for the case. Williams ruled that there was no statutory authority for slavery in Oregon and immediately set the Holmes children free and returned them to their parents.[103]

The United States Supreme Court complicated the matter in 1857 by ruling in the ***Dred Scott*** case that territories did not have the authority to prohibit slavery because that power rested exclusively with the individual states.[104] For Oregon to have control over slavery within its boundaries, it would have to become a state. Oregon political leaders had previously considered seeking statehood, but the voters rejected statehood proposals, sometimes narrowly, in 1854, 1855 and 1856. Public opinion was shifting as Oregonians grew dissatisfied with territorial status. They resented the political appointees sent to govern them and the meager influence they had in Washington where they were represented by a non-voting Congressional delegate. The Oregonians were particularly concerned about collecting federal reimbursement of expenses the territory had incurred in Indian Wars. In June 1857. Oregon voters overwhelmingly approved a statewide a referendum to convene a Constitutional Convention.

The debate over slavery in Oregon intensified as the Constitutional Convention approached. Public figures saw to it that their ideas were known. The arguments, whether they favored slavery or opposed it, were strangely devoid of ethical or moral content. They were not critical of the institution of slavery or defending the rights of slaves. They were narrowly legalistic or based on speculation about the impact of slaves on the labor market in Oregon. Ben Simpson was not a delegate to the Constitutional Convention but be wanted his views known. In June 1857, he wrote his friend Matthew Deady a long and somewhat rambling letter setting out his opinions about slavery in Oregon. Simpson knew that Deady was sympathetic to his views and that Deady would be likely to play an influential role in the Constitutional Convention.

Simpson was a typical Oregonian with southern sympathies. He was born in Tennessee, grew up in Missouri and married to a woman whose family was from Kentucky. The Simpson family had never owned slaves, but slavery appears to have been an open question for Ben Simpson in 1857. He seems not to have had moral objections to slavery or even to have considered the possibility that slavery had a moral dimension. In his letter to Deady, Simpson acknowledged that his opinion about slavery had changed somewhat, without explaining how or why, and argued that slavery was an issue of southern loyalty, national unity and social control. He justified slavery in Oregon as a method of reducing labor costs in Oregon which had been inflated by mining wages in California. He wrote Deady:

> *As the time will soon arrive when we will be called upon to vote for or against slavery in the Territory of Oregon or I would say the state of Oregon, it's highly necessary that the advocates of slavery were up and doing as the opposition are... Now Sir, I must confess to you that I have somewhat changed my opinion in regard to the propriety of slavery in Oregon "... I now think that l shall vote for it for various*

> *reasons... In the first place, when we become a state, we must take our place in the Union of States either with the North or South. Then, in that case, we wish to be identified with the Southern Libralists [sic] and not with the Northern Fanatics and again I am of the opinion that the perpetuity of our glorious Union greatly depends on the position we take in Oregon upon that question as the South has not and never will interfere with the institutions of the north while the North would crush the South if they had the power. Then let us come up and do battle on the side of Justice. And again, as in all probability, under a free constitution we cannot prevent free Negroes coming to Oregon let us have them as slaves and we can control them... I am of the opinion that a reasonable number [of slaves] would pay a fair per cent as it would enable the farmers to work on a much securer basis. He would be able to raise wheat for fifty cents per bushel while he cannot now afford to raise it for one dollar. This is owing to our being as it were almost surrounded by an extensive mining country and instead of Farm Labor being regulated as it should be by the price of produce, it is controlled by the price of labor in the mines...*"[105]

Simpson went on to complain about the high cost and limited availability of household help in Oregon which he attributed to a pattern of early marriage. Simpson was writing from the isolation of the Indian Reservation at Grand Ronde but his opinions were similar to those of many of his fellow Oregonians.

The opposition to slavery came in several forms. David Newsome (1805-1882) was a successful Marion County fruit grower, temperance advocate and astute social critic. He strongly opposed slavery but was apprehensive that the voters, if given the chance, might approve slavery in Oregon. He observed sadly that

> "*... a majority of the voters are from the Slave States, and are as completely under the control of a set of political mountebanks, as ever men can be... I hope the curse of slavery will not be permanently fastened on this beautiful "Italy of America".*[106]

Newsome was a lonely voice in opposition to the Democratic Party, its Salem Clique and the willingness of the voters to act as directed by the politicians. He attributed the situation in Oregon to what he called "Locofocoism" and its "kindred institutions... brandy, slavery and ignorance in general".[107]

In contrast to the Republican views of David Newsome, George Williams, was a Democrat who opposed slavery. He was the author of the 1853 decision that freed slave children in Oregon. In 1857, he was still Chief Justice of the Territorial Supreme Court and an elected delegate to the Oregon Constitutional Convention. A few weeks before the Convention, Justice Williams published a long letter in the ***Oregon Statesman*** explaining his opposition to slavery. Like Ben Simpson's letter, Williams avoided any moral reflection. The letter did not condemn slavery but merely concluded that it would be impractical in Oregon. In what has come to be known as the "Free State Letter", Williams argued that slavery would be a burden and not a blessing in Oregon". His analysis was that slaves were only economically practical in certain high value crops like cotton, rice and sugar which could not be grown in Oregon. He compared population growth in pairs of adjacent states and found that growth was uniformly greater in the free states. Williams acknowledged the shortage of household help in Oregon but argued that slavery would not solve the problem. He also observed that the interests of Oregon would best be served if the state were allied with the North. Justice Williams was critical of slaves but not of slavery.

On the day Justice Williams published his open letter, his colleague on the Territorial Supreme Court Mathew Deady responded to Ben Simpson's June letter. Deady confirmed his support for slavery in Oregon. He ignored Simpson's arguments regarding wages and Southern loyalty but passionately defended slavery as a fundamental property right. His family never owned slaves but, for him, the issue was very clear. Private property was sacred. Slaves were property like any other property. They could be bought, held and sold without government interference. He wrote:

> *... There are some millions of Africans owned as property in the United States, and whatever shallow-brains or Smatter-much may say about "property in man". they are just as much property as horses, cattle or land because the law which creates all property makes them such. Governments like ours were instituted not to teach or compel me to own this or that kind of property, but to protect me in the possession and enjoyment of any kind of property which it may be my good or bad fortune to lawfully acquire.*[108]

The slavery question loomed over the proceedings as sixty white male delegates, thirty of them farmers and nineteen lawyers, convened in Salem in August and September 1857 to draft a constitution for Oregon. The first order of business was to elect Justice Deady to preside over the Convention. Delegates voted down a proposal by slavery opponents to prohibit discussion of the slavery issue, but they deliberated about state boundaries, the location of the capital, public education, liquor laws and a variety of other issues without directly confronting the question of what to do about slavery. The Democrats had dominated Oregon politics during the territorial period and had a strong majority among the convention delegates. Like the national Democratic Party, Democrats in Oregon were deeply divided over slavery. One faction was sympathetic to the South and slavery while the other, "Unionist", faction was opposed to secession. Both factions were represented in the Constitutional Convention along with representatives of an ascendant Republican Party which was against slavery and in favor of statehood only if Oregon was admitted as a free state

After 31 days of debate and deliberation, the Convention delegates approved a draft constitution for ratification by the voters. The constitution enumerated 33 fundamental rights (freedom of speech, religion, assembly, right to bear arms) but left the questions of whether or not to allow slavery and whether or not to exclude free Negroes to the voters to decide. The delegates approved language for each of the possible outcomes.

> *The voters were asked to respond yes or no to three questions:*
>
> *Should Oregon adopt the Constitution drafted at the Convention?*
> *Should there be slavery in Oregon?*
>
> *Should free Negroes be allowed in Oregon?*

On November 9, 1857, Oregon residents approved the proposed State Constitution by a vote of 7195 to 3195. They voted against slavery in Oregon 7727 to 2645. Article 34 was added to the enumerated rights in the constitution:

> *There shall be neither slavery nor involuntary servitude in the state, otherwise than as a punishment for crime, whereof the party shall have been duly convicted.*

The clause prohibiting slavery had been prepared by John McBride, a Republican delegate from Yamhill County. McBride had been a teenage member of the 1846 wagon train of which Ben Simpson had been the captain.[109]

At the same time the voters prohibited slavery in Oregon, they also voted 8640 to 1081 to exclude free Negroes from Oregon.[110] The exclusion clause, which specified the absence of rights, was, incongruously added as Article 35 among the list of rights in the constitution. Article 35 prohibited any "free negro or mulatto" in Oregon from owing land, making a contract or bringing a lawsuit. In Benjamin Simpson's home precinct the vote was 18 to 1 to adopt the Constitution, 13 to 12 against slavery and 23 to none to exclude free Negroes. Ben Simpson voted in favor of the Constitution and, as he had predicted the previous June, he voted in favor of slavery in

Oregon.[111] The statewide vote reflected the changing attitudes of the people of Oregon. They voted 74 percent to prohibit slavery while also voting 89 percent to exclude Negroes from Oregon. They opposed slavery, perhaps because they believed it would be impractical in Oregon, but they remained even more opposed to having African Americans in their state.

In February 1859, Oregon was admitted to statehood. Oregon is the only free state admitted to the union with a prohibition on free Negroes in its constitution. The exclusion was never enforced but it remained part of the state constitution for nearly seventy years. Oregonians voted against the repeal in 1900 before finally voting to repeal the exclusion in 1926.[112]

4 Statehood

As the framers intended, statehood brought few obvious changes to Oregon. The state congressional delegation increased threefold from one non-voting delegate to two Senators and one voting member of the House but the names and faces were familiar. Of the two Senators, one had served two terms as territorial governor and the other had served three terms in the territorial legislature. Statehood resulted in some reorganization of the judicial branch with George Williams moving to the Senate and Matthew Deady moving to the federal District Court. Reuben Boise and Riley Stratton became Associate Justices of the Oregon Supreme Court. Williams, Deady, Boise and Stratton had been delegates to the 1857 convention drafting the constitution. To assure continuity, the delegates had incorporated all existing Oregon law into the State Constitution.

The Civil War in Oregon

The outbreak of the Civil War in 1861 brought changes to Fort Yamhill. The veteran troops who had been stationed at the fort were reassigned to the war zone in the East. Philip Sheridan, after seven uneventful years as a Lieutenant, was promoted to Captain in May 1861 and transferred to the battlefields of the Civil War where he distinguished himself as a ruthless and effective officer. Within eighteen months of his promotion to Captain, Sheridan was a Major General in the Union Army and, by 1864, commanding officer of the Army of the Shenandoah. Meanwhile, the regular army troops at the fort were replaced by volunteers from California. Company D of the 4th California Infantry was garrisoned at Fort Yamhill from March 1862 to October 1864.

Before the war, Ben Simpson had made no secret of the fact that his sympathies, in the struggle between the northern states and the southern, lay with the South. Once the war began and the Union was threatened, he changed his mind. He explained his abrupt but enduring change in a letter to his friend Matthew Deady:

> *So far as my own course is concerned, that was fixed with the commencement of the war, and I assure you that under no circumstances shall I act with any person or party that have not as*

> *their object the unconditional support of the administration to put down the present wicked and unjustifiable rebellion.*[113]

As sutler at Fort Yamhill, Benjamin Simpson was a federal contractor and was subject to General Orders #29 of October 20, 1861, which required that he swear an oath of allegiance to the United States. The oath was administered at Fort Yamhill by Captain Lyman S. Scott, commanding officer of Company D, 4th California Volunteer infantry.[114]

Ben Simpson continued as the sutler at Fort Yamhill through much of the Civil War. In 1862, he added the duties of postmaster.[115] The sutler's store was an attractive target for Indians who were hungry, angry or simply bored with inactivity. In late 1862, three Indians were caught stealing from Simpson's store at Fort Yamhill. The three were tried and convicted by a military court which attempted to make the punishment fit the crime and deter future misbehavior. The three Indians were required to give three horses to the sutler as restitution for the goods stolen and each received 20 lashes in punishment before being released.[116]

After several years as sutler at Fort Yamhill, Benjamin Simpson began to grow restless and look for new opportunities. He had hired Gilbert C. Litchfield (1832-1924) in 1861 to work as a clerk in the store. With a full-time employee, Simpson could devote time and attention to political and business opportunities off the reservation. For the first time since Oregon statehood in 1859, Benjamin Simpson sought public office. He was elected to represent Polk County in the lower house of the Oregon legislature in 1862.

He wrote his friend Senator James Nesmith, "we are now exulting over our victory".[117]

The 1862 Legislature

The legislature Ben Simpson joined in 1862 was the first to convene in Oregon after the beginning of the Civil War and the second after Oregon had achieved statehood. Oregon had elected the unionist Addison C. Gibbs governor replacing John Whiteaker, the first governor after Oregon became a state. Whiteaker was a Democrat and supporter of slavery. He had the dubious distinction, along with the governor of Kentucky, of having declined to provide troops to the Union Army when requested by President Lincoln. Governor Gibbs had been elected with an astonishing 67 percent of the vote as a fusion candidate representing Republicans and pro-union Democrats. In his inaugural address Gibbs had reminded the legislature that "a wicked rebellion is raging". The 1862 legislature was no longer debating slavery or the right of states to secede but was struggling with issues like whether loyalty to the union required that federal notes be accepted at face value. Federal notes were commonly traded at a discount, sometimes as much as 30 percent, but the legislature concluded that they should be considered legal tender in the payment of taxes and debts.

The 1862 legislature also considered administrative issues which the previous legislature had left unresolved. These included the location and operation of the state penitentiary and insane asylum, the creation of two new counties and a new judicial district and the adoption of the collected codes of the new state that Judge Deady had compiled. Governor Gibbs emphasized the importance of education in Oregon and proposed changes in teacher certification and increased accountability of county school Superintendents. The most pressing education issue in Oregon involved public lands granted to the state for the support of education. The federal government had granted the state 90,000 acres to support a college for "agriculture and the mechanical arts" and another 700,000 acres to support common schools. The land grants required that each state identify specific property and manage it until it could be sold with the proceeds used to establish a permanent endowment for the schools. Oregon had delayed compliance as long as possible and was risking the loss of the land grants. The 1862 legislature passed laws to begin the selection of public lands to be reserved for the support of education.

The land grants were crucial for the common schools of Oregon but were delayed by several obstacles including the fact that most of the public land in Oregon had not been surveyed. As late as 1869, only 8.4 million acres of the 61 million acres in the state had been surveyed.[118]

The Coast Reservation

In June 1862, Ben Simpson, wrote Senator Nesmith urging him to intervene if there should be an effort made at Washington to remove [the Indian Agent at Grand Ronde]" where Simpson was the sutler.[119] James B. Condon, the Indian Agent, had fired some employees who retaliated with a campaign to get Condon replaced. Condon resigned in 1863, and Simpson was appointed to serve as temporary Indian Agent at Grand Ronde until July 1864 when a permanent replacement for Condon was named.

In March 1863, President Abraham Lincoln appointed Ben Simpson to be Indian Agent at the Siletz Reservation replacing another agent who had been removed.[120] An anonymous writer in the ***Daily Statesman*** published a long letter describing Simpson's character and defending Simpson's qualifications for the position:

> *Simpson is an "old settler" in these parts and by dint of indomitable energy, tact and ready adaptation to passing events, has written his scotch name along the pages of our provincial chronicles... Simpson is a big-hearted, impulsive, generous fellow-loves his friends and does not altogether hate his enemies; but he is a born partisan, a ready-made people's man, and is always willing to give or take blows in their cause be it fair or foul. When heading a party raid against some unpopular one, who has dared to dispute the divine right of the majority, he can become as fierce and relentless as a border chief of old on a Clan-avenging foray in the Scotch Marches (sic).*
>
> *Simpson was originally a Baptist preacher of what particular shell, l know not; but soon after coming to Oregon he engaged in trade and politics principally. [IIe] was thc principal backer of Ben Harding for the U.S. Senate and the leading man on the floor [of the legislature)... Simpson has plenty of mother wit, which has often done him good service in the rough polemics of the stump where his vocation often calls him...* [121]

Simpson sold the sutler's store at Fort Yamhill to his employee Gilbert Litchfield and his young friend Rockey Preston Earhart and moved to the Siletz Reservation. Earhart (1837-1889) had come to Oregon in 1855 from Ohio. He worked as a civilian clerk for the Army at Fort Yamhill where he was a Ben Simpson protege. Simpson had attempted unsuccessfully to obtain a commission for Earhart as a Lieutenant in the Army.[122] Earhart later served as an Indian Agent, state legislator, assistant to Benjamin Simpson in the office of the Oregon Surveyor Genera] and eventually was elected to two terms as Oregon Secretary of State. Litchfield continued to operate the store at Fort Yamhill for 30 years.

Benjamin Simpson assumed his duties as the fourth resident Indian Agent at the Siletz Reservation in the spring of 1863. The Agency was located on the Siletz River about ten miles from the coast near the boundary between Benton County and Tillamook County. Siletz, or the Coast Reservation as it was originally called, had been created in 1855 through a presidential executive order which set aside nearly 1.4 million acres of land along the Oregon Coast for the exclusive use of Indians in Oregon. The reservation extended along I05 miles of rugged Oregon coastline from Cape Lookout in the North to the Siltcoos River in the South and inland 20 miles to the crest of the Coast Range. Unlike reservations established by treaty or act of Congress, a reservation established by executive order could be modified unilaterally and without any compensation to the Indians through a subsequent executive order.[123]

Indians from 30 tribes and bands representing ten distinct language groups and numerous villages had been forcibly relocated from their traditional home areas to the Siletz reservation at the end of the bloody and bitter Rogue River Wars of 1855 and 1856 in Southwestern Oregon. In 1864, 4164 Indians were living on the Coast Reservation including 1322 at Grand Ronde, 2312 at Siletz and 530 at Alsea in the South. In contrast to the Willamette Valley Indians at Grand Ronde, the Indians at Siletz, were far from home and unhappy to be there. An 1870 report described the Indians at Siletz as "restless and quarrelsome"[124], while an 1872 report from the Superintendent of Indian Affairs for Oregon observed.

> *These Siletz Indians have always been regarded as the most belligerent and refractory of any in this state. Notwithstanding which, however, they are far removed from savage life.*[125]

Siletz, like other reservations, was a place where Indians could be held, protected from settlers and trained to be self-sufficient. Unless authorized to leave by the Indian Agent, Indians were required to remain on the reservation. The Indian Agent was assisted by troops stationed on the reservation at Fort Hoskins to protect Indians living on the reservation and recapturing those who had escaped. In July 1864, Ben Simpson joined Lieutenant James S. Rathbum and a detachment of fifteen soldiers from Siletz in a lengthy sweep of southern Oregon pursuing Indians who had left the reservation and returned to their traditional villages in the Rogue River region. The Indian Agent and troops traveled over 1200 miles in 54 days and apprehended about I00 Indians who they escorted back to the reservation.[126]

By 1865, Simpson could report substantial progress in all aspects of the reservation. Agency farmers had 230 acres under cultivation and had raised 600 bushels of wheat, 2175 bushels of oats, 39 tons of hay and 25,000 bushels of potatoes. In addition, Indians had produced cabbage, carrots, beans and other vegetables in their own gardens. Simpson also reported the construction of fifteen houses during the previous year as well barns and fences. Simpson reported that twelve students were enrolled in the "manual labor school" on the reservation and that all twelve had learned to read and write. Simpson requested additional farming equipment, medical supplies and military assistance to prevent oyster pirates from trespassing in Yaquina Bay.[127]

Oyster Poaching at Yaquina Bay

Early in his tenure as Indian Agent on the Siletz Reservation, Benjamin Simpson became entangled in a public controversy when he tried to enforce tribal control of the oyster beds at Yaquina Bay. At the time, the bay was entirely within the Coast Reservation and part of the Siletz Agency. Indians had traditionally gathered oysters along the shores of the bay and its tributaries. Oyster companies from as far away as San Francisco learned about the oysters in Yaquina Bay and sent boats. In December 1863, Ben Simpson sold rights to Winant & Company of San Francisco to harvest oysters in Yaquina Bay for which the company paid the agency $1000.[128] In February 1864, Simpson learned that a competing firm was gathering oysters in Yaquina Bay without authorization and without paying a fee. Simpson confronted Richard Hillyer, master of the schooner Cornelia Terry, and demanded that he cease poaching oysters on Indian property. Captain Hillyer, who was employed by Anthony Ludlow & Co. of San Francisco, refused to comply. He claimed that, as a United States citizen, he had a right to collect oysters anywhere in American waters.

Hillyer and his crew defied Simpson and continued to harvest oysters in Yaquina Bay. His patience exhausted, Simpson ordered troops from Fort Hoskins to arrest Hillyer. On February 24, 1864, a detachment from Company D, 4th California Infantry boarded the Cornelia Terry where they found 42 baskets of recently-gathered oysters and arrested the captain. Hillyer was released after a few hours and promptly contacted Brigadier General George Wright, the military commander for the Department of the Pacific. General Wright was commander of the troops at the fort, but he had no authority over Simpson. That did not prevent the general from ordering Simpson to stop interfering with Hillyer's "legitimate business". In March 1864, the Ludlow Company sued Ben Simpson and his colleagues in the Benton County Circuit Court claiming $15,000 in damages. The Court ordered Simpson to stop bothering Hillyer. As Ben Simpson reported to his Indian Affairs superiors:

> *Hillyer... procured a writ of injunction from the court restraining me from any further interference. He still continues to trespass upon the reservation while I am prevented by the writ from attempting to check him.*[129]

A. Ludlow & Co. v. Benjamin Simpson, et. al. was still pending in September 1864 when Captain Hillyer and his schooner returned to Yaquina

Bay. Protected by 15 thugs he had hired in San Francisco, Hillyer resumed the oystering in Indian waters for which he had been arrested in February.[130]

In November 1864, Justice Riley E. Stratton of the Oregon Supreme Court, dismissed the lawsuit for lack of state jurisdiction. He found that the federal government was acting within its authority to protect the reservation and exclude trespassers. Captain Hillyer appealed the decision to the Oregon Supreme Court which upheld Judge Stratton's decision and ordered the plaintiffs to pay the court costs incurred by the defendants. Benjamin Simpson and the protection of Indian resources had been vindicated.

The local newspaper made no effort to defend the oyster poachers and agreed, in a somewhat condescending tone, that Simpson was doing his duty protecting Indian property. The newspaper observed however that the poaching problem should be solved by removing Yaquina Bay from the reservation and opening it to settlement by non-Indians.

> *We believe that the fewest number of the people in Benton County have any fault to find with Indian Agent Simpson for any of his official acts. The reserve belongs to the Indians, and it is the duty of Mr. Simpson to see that they are protected in all their rights as long as that remains a Reserve... so far, we accord to him honest motives and good intentions. This county wants the land along the Yaquina thrown open to settlement. The people wish to convert those lands to useful purposes and to accomplish this Mr. Simpson is lending his influence and using his utmost endeavors, because he believes, as all sensible people do, that it would be of no use to the Indians, and as all are working for the same thing, there is no reason why they should not do so harmoniously.*[131]

The newspaper had reported that Simpson was sympathetic to the idea that Yaquina Bay be opened for settlement but implied that "his honest motives and good intentions" required monitoring.

Simpson was a realist about the issue. The settlers wanted the land and conveniently believed the myth that the Indians did not use the land. Simpson could have tried to explain to the white community that Indians used the area for the identical reason the Whites wanted it. But he was a realist. He knew how land disputes between Indians and whites were usually resolved. Simpson did not need the newspaper to encourage him about the Yaquina Bay issue. On October 1865, wrote his Indian Affairs superiors urging that the southern boundary of the reservation be adjusted slightly so that Yaquina Bay would be outside the reservation. He argued that the change would not be "at all deleterious to the interests of the Indians"[132] Within a year of his principled defense of Indian oyster rights, he had conceded to public opinion and accepted the specious argument that the Indians did not use the bay.

On December 21, 1865, President Andrew Johnson signed an executive order removing about 200,000 acres from the Siletz Reservation and opening the area for settlement. Rather than merely adjusting the boundary as Ben Simpson had recommended, the President had removed the entire middle section of the reservation. A decade after it was established, the reservation had been reduced in size by nearly one- fifth, the northern and southern portions of the reservation had been separated, and the Indians had lost the revenue from the oyster beds in Yaquina Bay. The tribes at Siletz received no compensation for the lost lands. The pattern was the same in Oregon as it had been across the West: if reservation land became attractive to settlers, the land was removed from protection and opened for what the Corvallis newspaper had called "useful purposes"

Ellendale Woolen Mill

During the eight years Ben Simpson was Indian Agent at Siletz, he remained receptive to investment opportunities. In December 1864, he was one of the initial investors, along with Reuben Boise, James Nesmith and others, in the Ellendale Woolen Mills Company. Ellendale erected a three-story building near Dallas, Oregon and ordered looms from a manufacturer in Worcester, Massachusetts. The Massachusetts looms were lost at sea and the Ellendale management ordered replacements from a manufacturer in Pennsylvania. The Pennsylvania looms arrived in Oregon in September 1866 and were transported by boat up the Willamette and by wagon overland 17 miles to the factory where they were installed. Ellendale was the fourth woolen mill in Oregon and operated from late 1866 to May 1871, when the mill was destroyed by fire.[133]

The Oregon Central Military Road

Oregon was far from the military action of the Civil War but military strategists in Washington, planning for every contingency, identified what they considered strategic vulnerabilities. One of these was the constricted access to the Willamette Valley of Oregon. The planners were concerned that the Willamette Valley was dependent for resupply or troop movements on roads at the north and south which would be difficult to defend and could be easily severed by relatively small enemy units. The Congress concurred with the military analysis that an additional road was needed in Oregon, but all federal money and manpower were fully committed to the war. The solution was to make land grants which the state could allocate to private contractors for road construction. In July 1864, the Congress authorized the construction of a wagon road from Eugene in the Willamette Valley across the Cascade Range to the Owyhee region of eastern Oregon and the Idaho border. The Oregon Central Military Road was intended to improve the movement of troops and supplies between Oregon and the Snake River Valley of Idaho and increase settlement in central and eastern Oregon. The expense of road construction would be paid through the sale of public lands the federal government had allocated to the state. Oregon would receive three sections of land (1 920 acres) along the road for every mile of road constructed.[134]

The Oregon Central Military Road Company was formed to build the road. Ben Simpson, the Indian Agent at Siletz, was the only contractor to bid on the road construction project. Simpson wrote the directors of the Road Company in 1865:

> *I propose to open clear and grade and erect all necessary bridges on the line of the above-named road from the 20 mile stake to what is known as point look out*
>
> *... For the sum of twenty-six thousand five hundred dollars in gold coin or its equivalent in currency.* [135]

Ben Simpson had previously notified Judge Stratton of the Road Company that he intended to use Indian labor on the road construction. Simpson assured the company that he would provide the Indians the necessary permission to work off the reservation as well as a foreman:

> *... to take charge of the Indians whenever called upon. I shall select the best Indians we have and pay them a fair price in cash. I can raise from fifty to seventy-five [workers] as soon as we can get our spring crop planted which will be by the first of May.*[136]

Once work began on the road-building contract, relationships quickly became strained. The Road Company complained that the Indians were demanding wages of $1.50 a day and Ben Simpson complained about not getting paid. He wrote the Road Company board of directors in May 1866 offering to buy out the remainder of the contract:

> *I will give the company three thousand and five hundred dollars to complete my contract, and they can have my waggon (sic) and two yoke*

> *oxen and all of my tools for working the road. That would leave three thousand three hundred and fifty dollars due me of balance unpaid on contract... The company can have the benefit of having as many Indians as they may desire and I will give them permission to work.*[137]

Ben Simpson's buyout offer was accepted by the Road Company but he continued to have a financial interest in the company. In 1868, he asked "are we going to get anything out of that road or not?[138] As late as 1870, Simpson was still "anxious to get some money out of it."[139]

The road was completed to the Cascade Mountains by the fall of 1867, and to Silver City, Idaho by 1872. The road wandered 456 miles through the wilds of eastern Oregon and claimed 875,000 acres of public land, every odd numbered section of land within three miles of the wagon road.[140] A Congressional investigation of the road in 1888 concluded that it was poorly constructed, little used and primarily a massive land fraud. The headline in the New York Times was "How Big Chunks of the Public Domain Have Been Stolen By Wagon Road Companies in Oregon".[141]

The Shipwreck of the Brother Jonathan

Every generation has its memorable tragedies. Like the Donner Party of 1846, the Johnstown Flood of 1889, the San Francisco earthquake and fire of 1906 and the sinking of the Titanic in 1912, the shipwreck of the Brother Jonathan in 1865 captured the imagination of the West Coast public. The Brother Jonathan was a 220 foot, three masted, wooden hull side-wheel steamer on its regular run from San Francisco to Portland with 190 passengers and a crew of 54 on July 30, 1865, when it encountered a violent storm off the California coast. The captain attempted to return to the harbor at Crescent City but struck a rock four miles offshore where the steamer sank killing all but nineteen of the passengers and crew.

The dead included the ship's captain, General George Wright, the commanding officer of the United States Army in the West, the Surveyor General of Washington, and a prominent San Francisco madam with seven of her employees. The ship also carried two camels and a large shipment of gold coins for treaty payments to Northwest tribes as well as the looms manufactured in Massachusetts for the Ellendale Woolen Mills in Oregon.[142] The shipwreck of the Brother Jonathan was particularly painful for the Simpson family. Nancy Cooper Simpson's younger brother Philomen Cooper (1834-1865), his wife Elizabeth Cartwright Cooper and an infant daughter were among the passengers who died in the summer storm off the California Coast.[143]

Ben Simpson's son Sam wrote a poem in commemoration of the tragedy:

And so, as the sea tides rise and fall
On the rocks at Crescent City,
let the good ship sleep in her gleaming pall And the shrine of our grief and pity.[144]

The wreckage of the Brother Jonathan was located by treasure hunters in the early 1990s. Among other things, the treasure hunters found 1207 gold coins which was sold at auction for more than $4 million.[145]

The Senatorial Election of 1866 and the Oregon Statesman

The Democratic Party controlled politics in Oregon throughout the Territorial period but had become deeply divided during the early years of statehood. Like the national Democratic Party, the division was between those Democrats who supported the union and those who were sympathetic to secession and slavery. The Unionist Democrats had joined with Republicans in the legislative assembly to elect Unionist Democrats to represent Oregon in the United States Senate.[146] By 1866, although Oregon had only been a state seven years, the legislature had elected five Democrats and three Republicans to the U.S. Senate. The six-year term of Senator James Nesmith, a Polk County Democrat, was expiring. Nesmith was a pioneer of 1843 who had been Superintendent of Indian Affairs for Oregon and Washington during the territorial period. Ben Simpson had supported a candidate opposing Nesmith in the1849 race for Territorial Delegate but had subsequently worked with him in the Unionist wing of the Democratic Party and had invested with him in the Ellendale Woolen Mill.

Ben Simpson reviewed the likely candidates for the 1867 Senate seat and concluded that his moderate political views and long record of public service qualified him as a candidate. He had served the people of Oregon in elective and appointive office most of his adult life. He had been elected to the territorial legislature on five occasions and to the state legislature once. Like Senator Nesmith, Simpson had been appointed to a position in Indian Affairs. In 1866, Simpson was not a member of the legislature. He was still the Indian Agent at Siletz and had recently been involved in the Military Road project. He had been part owner of ***The Oregon Statesman***, a weekly newspaper in Salem. Simpson, his boss J.W. P. Huntington, the Superintendent of Indian Affairs for Oregon, Judge George H. Williams and three others had purchased ***The Statesman*** from Asahel Bush and Senator Nesmith in 1863.[147]

Asahel Bush (1824-1913) had been the most powerful figure in the Oregon Democratic Party since territorial days. He had started ***The Statesman*** in Oregon City in 1851 as the voice of the Democratic Party in Oregon. When the territorial capital moved to Salem, Bush had moved the newspaper which reflected the opinions of what was known as "the Salem Clique". The Salem Clique was the informal but actual leadership of the Oregon Democratic Party during the 1850s. The so-called Clique was composed of anti-slavery Democrats like Bush, Harding, and Nesmith as well as pro-slavery Democrats like Joseph Lane and Delazon Smith. When slavery became one of the central issues in Oregon politics, the Salem Clique became divided and lost its influence.

In 1864, the legislative assembly of Oregon elected George H. Williams, a Republican and part owner of ***The Statesman***, to the United States Senate. Judge Williams was a former Democrat and the judge who had freed slaves in Oregon during the territorial period. The decision about the successor to Senator Nesmith would rest with the 47 members of the Oregon House and 22 members of the state Senate of the 1866 legislature. Republicans held a 24-23 majority in the House, a 14-8 majority in the Senate. In the joint ballot of the Legislative Assembly where the United States Senator would be elected, Republicans held a comfortable 38-31 majority. In addition to the Republican majority, many of the members elected to the 1866 legislature were new. Of the 49 members of the legislature who had served with Simpson four years earlier in the 1862 legislature, only one, Sen. D. W. Ballard of Linn County, was a member of the legislature in 1866.[148]

As the 1866 Senatorial election approached, Ben Simpson acquired ***The Oregon Statesman***. In the August 20, 1866, issue, the paper notified readers that controlling interest in ***The Oregon Statesman***... has been sold to other parties, under whose auspices the paper will hereafter be conducted". Although the identity of the "other parties" was not revealed, it was known that Ben Simpson was the new owner and that he had installed his inexperienced but able sons Sylvester and Samuel as editors.[149] Sylvester and Samuel were recent graduates of Willamette University who had no newspaper or political experience. Sylvester was 23 years old and had been teaching Latin and Greek at Willamette since his graduation in 1864 and was building a law practice in Salem. Sam was barely 21. He had graduated from Willamette in 1865 and was reading law with a local judge. Apart from promoting their father's Senatorial candidacy in the city where the

Legislative Assembly would be meeting, the decision to buy the paper served little purpose. Ben Simpson remained an Indian agent and had little time to spend away from the reservation while the two sons were fully occupied. Whatever their motivation, the young editors expressed high hopes for the ***Statesman***. It would be "the great source of the enlightenment and morality of the people" and its writers would be "guide and instructor of the masses".[150]

In an editorial entitled "Salutatoria", the new owners explained that the political philosophy of the ***Statesman***, like its owner, would be moderate, steering between the radical reformers of Reconstruction and those who remained secessionists. Under its new editors, The ***Statesman*** would be:

> *Opposed to the utopian ideas of fanatical reformers, yet having no sympathy with treason, we shall calmly yet earnestly discuss every measure for the restoration of the States and the general wealth of our common country. Boldly criticizing both President and Congress, we shall support truth and loyalty wherever found attacking error and wrong..,*[151]

The editorial announced plans for investigative reporting of Salem doctors ("the knights of the pill bags") but neglected to mention Ben Simpson or his plans to run the "thorny path" for a seat in the U.S. Senate.

The Oregon Statesman was published in Salem each Monday and was available to subscribers for $3 a year (in coin). Much of the front page was devoted to advertising of products and services available in the Salem area. These included: The Capital Hotel (new and splendid); Weitman's Patent Horse Shoes; Parmenter Furniture; Oregon Steam Navigation; Shanahan & Dufrene (pianos for sale or rent); G. W. Hobart (saddles and harnesses); Florence Sewing Machines (gold medal winner at the California State Fair). ***The Statesman*** reported, nearly verbatim, the deliberations of the Oregon legislature and reprinted short articles and curiosities from other newspapers. Political opinions were surprisingly moderate and often conveyed with humor or hyperbole. Simpson's paper was critical of government spending and the reconstruction policies of President Andrew Johnson and supportive of public investment in railroad construction. The editors predicted financial disaster for California and urged that Oregon "not imitate the reckless extravagance of our lavish and dashing neighbor." A severe windstorm in Salem provided the occasion for a gratuitous poke at Reconstruction when it was attributed to "the disastrous results of Andrew Johnson's policy"[152]. ***The Statesman*** seems not to have been used as a propaganda organ for Ben Simpson's 1866 candidacy for the United States Senate. Ben Simpson's name does not appear in the surviving issues of ***The Statesman*** from the fall of 1866. The editorial posture of ***the Statesman*** reflected Simpson's views of current issues like Reconstruction and railroad construction.

At best, Ben Simpson's Senate campaign was a long shot. Republicans held a majority of the votes in the legislative assembly and Simpson's political cronies from earlier years were no longer in the legislature. Ben Simpson's lack of political support did not deter his political opponents who attacked him viciously in the press. When a Salem newspaper published an anonymous letter accusing Simpson of voter intimidation and fraud in a recent election at Yaquina Bay, David Newsome, the Republican essayist and fruit grower, wrote a letter to ***The Statesman*** defending Simpson against the charges which he said, "did great injustice to Mr. Simpson". Newsome explained that he had not voted for one of Simpson's candidates and, contrary to the anonymous letter, Simpson "did not intimidate me nor threaten me about my vote". Newsome also denied that there had been any voter fraud: "I do not believe that there was one illegal vote given by any Union man that day at the election in Yaquina precinct."[153]

Other Oregon newspapers were less even-handed regarding Simpson's Senate candidacy. The ***Portland Morning Oregonian*** published a lengthy and nasty editorial criticizing Ben Simpson for having served as an Indian Agent, the "deficiencies of my early education" and his associations. In a confusing metaphor, the editorial called Simpson and Senator Nesmith "the Chang and Eng of conservatism in Oregon"[154]and sarcastically concluded:

> *We therefore instantly dismiss the idea that Ben is not a suitable man for a United States Senator. Away with the thought which some narrow-minded people seem to harbor that the next position in the line of promotion after an Indian Agency is not a seat in the Senate of the United States...* [155]

The editorial turned serious accusing Simpson of supporting the administration of President Andrew Johnson and being "a traitor from the Union party." The editorial predicted that Simpson "cannot be elected by Democratic votes" and charged that "He is the central figure in all the disreputable dirty schemes that have had their birth at the Capital for the last fortnight or more".

The one true statement in the ***Oregonian*** editorial was that Simpson could not be elected by Democratic votes alone. Republicans held a majority in the Legislative Assembly in 1866 as the legislators prepared to elect a successor to Senator Nesmith. Nesmith sought reelection but was rejected by a coalition of Republicans and Unionists who objected to Nesmith's support of President

Andrew Johnson and Johnson's unwillingness to proceed aggressively with the radical Reconstruction of the South. The Democrats nominated Joseph S. Smith, a former Methodist preacher who had become a lawyer and businessman. The leading Republican candidates were Addison C. Gibbs, a Portland lawyer who had just completed four years as governor, and John H. Mitchell, a Portland lawyer and state senator.

The Republican caucus selected Governor Gibbs by a single vote over John Mitchell but was unable to elect Gibbs on the joint ballot when four of Mitchell's supporters refused to vote for Gibbs. On September 26, the Oregon House and Senate convened in a joint session to elect a U.S. Senator. With 35 votes needed, the vote on the first ballot was Gibbs 33, Smith 21, Nesmith 9, Simpson 3 with three other candidates receiving one vote each. Mitchell received no votes. The balloting continued with a small group of Republicans withholding the votes that would have given Gibbs the majority he needed. The contest dragged on for fifteen ballots before the Republicans substituted Henry W. Corbett, a Portland businessman, for Gibbs. On the 16th ballot, Corbett, the Republican compromise candidate, was elected to the Senate with 38 votes followed by Smith with 14 and Nesmith with 4. Benjamin Simpson received no votes on the final ballot.[156]

Benjamin Simpson never had much of a chance in 1866 and owning a newspaper in Salem, whatever his intentions, was not particularly helpful. He did not use the newspaper to promote his own candidacy or to attack the opposition. Simpson was nominated by Representative J. Stouffer of Polk County but received only the vote of his nominator in the House and no votes at all in the Senate.[157] The multiple ballots in the joint session created opportunities for compromise candidates but the times were changing and the Republicans had the votes. Benjamin Simpson had miscalculated his Senatorial prospects in 1866. The Civil War was over. The Union had prevailed, at an enormous cost in lives on both sides and many of the victors, even in far off Oregon, were not immediately inclined to reconciliation. The Oregon legislature was dominated by Republicans who were seeking to punish the South for breaking away and starting the war. There was little support in the legislature for moderates like Senator Nesmith or Ben Simpson who had been supporters of the Union but who urged restraint in the treatment of the South. The political trends that would result in the impeachment of President Andrew Johnson in 1868 were at work in the Oregon legislature.

In addition to the national issues, Oregon was experiencing a generational shift as the Overland pioneers and veterans of the Territorial legislature, like Nesmith and Simpson, were being replaced by Republican lawyers and businessmen from Portland.

Ben Simpson had missed his chance of serving in the United States Senate. The rural Democrats of the pioneer period were being succeeded by a new generation of leaders. The political winds were beginning to shift. At the end of 1866, Ben Simpson sold the newspaper in Salem and returned to the Siletz Reservation and Yaquina Bay where he began several new projects including building two sailing ships and a lighthouse as well as investing in the construction of a railroad to the coast. His sons, still in their early 20s, left journalism and returned to the law careers for which they had been preparing.

Race and Politics in Oregon

The 1857 plebiscite settled the question of slavery in Oregon but race issues persisted as they had since the days of the provisional government in the 1840s. Oregon never had large numbers of African American, Chinese or other minorities but, few as there were, they were targets of discriminatory legislation nonetheless. When Oregon became a state in 1859, it was the first state admitted to the union with a constitutional provision excluding a particular race from the boundaries of the state. The statutory exclusion of African Americans had persisted from the days of the provisional government and had been approved by 89 percent of Oregon voters in 1857. The exclusionary attitudes continued after the Civil War when the Congress proposed amendments to the federal constitution abolishing slavery (13th Amendment), guaranteeing citizenship lights (14th Amendment) and assuring voting rights (15th Amendment). Two of the three proposed amendments were unpopular in Oregon. Each of the proposed amendments required ratification by three-quarters of the states. The Congress approved the 13th Amendment in January 1865, and it was ratified by three quarters of the states by the end of 1865. Oregon, with its constitutional prohibition against slavery, voted to ratify the 13th Amendment in December 1865.

The 14th Amendment was controversial in Oregon. Its equal protection provisions were in direct conflict with the exclusion clause in the Oregon Constitution. Congress approved the 14th amendment in 1866. Oregon promptly ratified the amendment (the fifth state to do so) but changed its mind and rescinded its ratification in 1868. The 14th Amendment nullified the exclusion provision in the Oregon constitution. Oregon eventually ratified the 14th Amendment more than a century later in 1973. The 1857 Oregon constitution prohibited voting by nonwhites and was in direct conflict with the 15th Amendment right to vote without regard to race. The 15th Amendment was ratified by a sufficient number of states to take effect in 1870. The legislative assembly in Oregon voted against ratification in 1870. Despite the supremacy of the federal constitution, the voters of Oregon rejected referenda repealing the nonwhite voting restrictions in 1883, 1895 and 1916. In 1926, Oregon repealed the exclusion law and in 1927, the voters amended the Constitution to allow nonwhites to vote. The Oregon legislature ratified the 15th amendment in 1959.

Yaquina Bay

Benjamin Simpson was serving as Indian Agent at Siletz in December 1865 when a presidential order reduced the size of the reservation by about 200,000 acres. Yaquina Bay and the surrounding areas were, as the local newspaper had advocated, "thrown open to settlement". Benjamin Simpson would no longer have to protect the oyster beds against poachers because the Bay was located outside the boundary of the shrunken reservation. With Yaquina Bay open to settlement, local boosters envisioned a harbor that would compete with Portland. They estimated that the trip from Yaquina Bay to San Francisco would be 40 hours shorter than that from Portland and would avoid the treacherous reef at the mouth of the Columbia River. In Ben Simpson's always optimistic view, "Yaquina Bay was destined to become one of the greatest seaports on the Pacific Coast."[158]

As soon as Yaquina Bay was opened for settlement, David Newsome toured the area. He immediately became an enthusiastic promoter of Yaquina Bay and its prospects. Newsome had big plans for the area. He envisioned 1000 ships anchored safely in the Bay and a city much like San Francisco overlooking the Bay. Newsome imagined Yaquina Bay becoming the transfer point between shipping from San Francisco and railroads to the interior. With the completion of a railroad 42 miles to Corvallis, Yaquina Bay could serve the Willamette Valley and, using the Central Military Road, could connect to the transcontinental railroad in Idaho. Newsome urged the federal government to authorize land grants to build the railroad and to open of the remainder of the Siletz and Alsea Indian reservations to settlement.

Ben Simpson's maritime experience was limited to the brief and unsuccessful operation of a steamboat on the Willamette River, but, like Newsome, he saw opportunity. Simpson had two ocean-going schooners built. The first of these, the ***Louisa Simpson***, was built by Hillyer and Monroe at Yaquina Bay in 1868 and launched January 17, 1869. The boat was named for Louisa Ann Simpson (1849-1888), the oldest daughter of Benjamin and Nancy Cooper Simpson. The ***Louisa Simpson*** made its maiden voyage to San Francisco in February 1869 carrying 100,000 feet of lumber, freight and passengers. In 1870, Simpson built a second boat at Yaquina Bay. The ***Elinora*** was a 200 ton, three-masted schooner named for his second daughter, Elinora Thurston Simpson (1852-1925). From Yaquina Bay, the schooners could be in San Francisco in four days.[159]

Sample of a 3-Masted Schooner, circa 1870

During the time he was building sailing ships at Yaquina Bay and completing his term as Indian Agent at the Siletz reservation, Ben Simpson was also reconsidering his political future. He had been a life-long Democrat with a deep affinity for the South where he had been born and raised. He had been elected to the legislature as a Democrat six times in 22 years but may have felt disappointed by the tepid support his Senate candidacy had received from his fellow Democrats in 1866. He was also changing. He was becoming more interested in business. He had been a passive investor in a newspaper, a woolen mill and two railroads and the entrepreneur or manager in several ventures. His growing interest in business may have led him to join the Republican Party. The Republican Party had been gaining popularity in Oregon since before the Civil War. In 1868, Ben Holladay (1819-1887), a stagecoach tycoon, arrived in Oregon with his own investment capital and plans to build railroads and control the transportation industry. Holladay immediately became active in the Oregon Republican Party. He hired Medorem Crawford (1819-1893), an Oregon pioneer and Republican loyalist, as an assistant and formed an alliance with Portland lawyer John H. Mitchell, the leader of a Republican Party faction and future U.S. Senator.

Ben Simpson knew Crawford from their days in Oregon City during the territorial period. Crawford had operated a transportation company and served in the provisional legislature. Crawford's loyalty to the Republican Party had been rewarded with military and civil appointments including five years as the collector of federal taxes for Oregon. By 1870, Simpson had become a Republican and was being courted by Crawford on behalf of Holladay. Crawford wrote Simpson soliciting advice regarding Republican candidates who could defeat Lafayette Grover, the likely Democratic gubernatorial candidate in the up-coming election.[160] Republicans had held the Oregon governorship since 1862 but had no obvious candidate in 1870. There is no record of what advice, if any, Simpson provided. In the 1870 gubernatorial election, the Democrat Grover defeated the Republican candidate Joel Palmer, an 1847 emigrant and former Indian commissioner in the Cayuse War. A year later, Palmer would succeed Ben Simpson as Indian Agent at Siletz and Governor Grover would appoint Simpson's son Sylvester to state office.

Siletz after 1865

Benjamin Simpson's tenure at Siletz had been marked by the opening of 200,000 acres of reservation lands to settlement and a dramatic decline in the number of Indians living on the reservation. According to a census conducted by James Nesmith, the number of Indians living on the Coast Reservation had declined from 4164 in 1864 to 2000 in 1867.[161] Despite the declining population on the reservation, there were still tense moments for the Indian Agent. In September 1868, there was a rumor that Indians on the reservation were planning an uprising in retaliation for the murder of an Indian near Corvallis. Women and children from the agency were evacuated. Ben Simpson met with the Indians to explain that a Mr. Ballard had been arrested and would go to trial. The Indians were impatient with the process and skeptical that a white court would convict a white man for killing an Indian. Ben Simpson explained the judicial process and offered to accompany a group of Indians to observe the trial for themselves. Mr. Ballard was convicted and sentenced to prison. The crisis had been averted by Ben Simpson's intervention.[162]

Simpson had successfully expanded agricultural production on the reservation but had made little progress on education. His superiors seem to have been uniformly satisfied with what he had been able to accomplish in eight years as Indian Agent. An official report in 1870 described Benjamin Simpson as a "very efficient agent".[163] The best testimony to Simpson's character and performance may have been that of his successor at Siletz Joel Palmer. Palmer was a Republican with long experience in the politics of Indian Affairs in Oregon. Palmer expressed admiration for what Simpson had accomplished at Siletz, "During his term nearly all the improvements now on the reserve were made".[164]

During the spring of 1871, Benjamin Simpson planted 400 acres of vegetables and grains and prepared to leave the reservation. On May 1, 1871, after eight years as Indian Agent at Siletz, he transferred the Agency's livestock, equipment, tools and food supplies to his successor, Joel Palmer. Palmer reported that about 700 Indians were listed on reservation rolls but that half of them were not on the reservation at any given time. The Siletz Agency had a staff of 18 white male adults including a physician, several farmers and mechanics as well as one or more teachers. Palmer inventoried the Agency's property and found 42 work oxen; 19 milk cows; 34 beef cattle; eleven horses; five mules; seven wagons; five carts; two blacksmith shops; one flour mill; one sawmill, tools and food supplies (wheat; barley; potatoes).[165]

Yaquina Bay Lighthouse

Pacific Coast shipwrecks, like that of the Brother Jonathan in 1865, attracted the attention of the United States Lighthouse Board to the dangerous conditions on the West Coast and the need for navigation aids along the north coast. The Board began a large scale construction program that included lighthouses at Cape Arago in 1866, Cape Blanco in 1870 and at ten other locations by 1894. In February 1870, the Lighthouse Service approved construction of a light at the entrance to Yaquina Bay. The Congress appropriated $20,000 for the Yaquina Bay light and the Lighthouse Board assigned Col. Robert S. Williamson of the U.S. Army Corps of Engineers in San Francisco to locate a suitable site and design a building that could serve as a lighthouse as well as a residence for the keeper and his family. Colonel Williamson purchased a 36-acre parcel on a bluff overlooking the entrance to Yaquina Bay for $500 in gold coin and designed a two-story, four square building to serve as lighthouse and residence. Colonel Williamson selected Ben Simpson, the retiring Indian Agent at the Siletz reservation, to supervise construction.

On May 1, 1871, Simpson retired as Indian Agent and began building the lighthouse on a 120-foot bluff overlooking the entrance to Yaquina Bay.[166] As designed by Colonel Williamson, the lighthouse was a clapboard structure with four bedrooms and a 51 foot tower with a fifth order Fresnel lens. The light, powered by a whale oil lamp, could be seen by ships twelve miles away. The lighthouse design was unusual with living quarters for the keeper and his family in the same building as the light. By October 1871, the carpenters, masons, painters and laborers had completed their work leaving only the installation of the light. The construction contract had specified that the assembly and installation of the lantern and lens would be the responsibility of a Lantern Machinist from Portland. Ben Simpson had never seen a Fresnel lens before but, rather than delay waiting for the lampist to arrive from Portland, he assembled and installed the French-made light himself without assistance. The Yaquina Bay Lighthouse became operational November 3, 1871. The construction and furnishing had required $17,067 and six months.[167]

Colonel Williamson selected Ben Simpson to supervise construction of the lighthouse in 1871

The United States Light House Board had been established by the Congress in 1852 to advise the U. S. Lighthouse Service about where lighthouses were needed and to reduce political influence in lighthouse decisions. The board was composed of two naval officers, two officers from the Engineer Corps and two civilians and was responsible for the location of lighthouses and the modernization of the Lighthouse Service. The Lighthouse Board decided that the recently-constructed Yaquina Bay light was inadequate and persuaded the Congress to appropriate the funds to build a second and more powerful light three miles away at what was then called Cape Foulweather (now Yaquina Head).

The Yaquina Head Lighthouse was constructed in 1873 with a 93-foot conical brick tower, the tallest in Oregon, and a powerful light that was visible 22 miles at sea. Benjamin Simpson was operating his Yaquina Bay sawmill and transporting cargo between Oregon and San Francisco on his schooner the Louisa. As he explained, "...I delivered most of the material for building the light house at Cape Foulweather from San Francisco".[168] The schooner carried lumber to San Francisco and returned with 370,000 bricks to build the light tower. The bricks were manufactured in San Rafael, California and transported from San Francisco to Yaquina Bay. The brick was transferred to barges in Yaquina Bay and put ashore at Yaquina Head where it was hoisted to the building site by oxen and a derrick.[169]

The light at Yaquina Head was activated August 20, 1873. Within a few months, the Light House Board was inquiring whether the Yaquina Bay light was necessary any longer. On October I, 1874, the Old Yaquina Bay light that Ben Simpson had built was decommissioned after less than three years' service. The building at Yaquina Bay was used for a variety of temporary purposes until 1906 when it became a station for the U.S. Life Saving Service for 26 years. Ownership of the old lighthouse was transferred to the Oregon Parks and Recreation Department in 1934. The building was threatened with demolition before it was restored in 1974. After many years of neglect, the Lighthouse that Benjamin Simpson built in 1871 has been restored as a working lighthouse and is listed on the National Register of Historic Places. The light at Yaquina Head has been automated and continues to provide navigational assistance to ships along the Oregon Coast.

The Willamette Valley and Coast Railroad

Railroads were all the rage in post-civil war Oregon. Men who had walked across the continent with teams of oxen were fascinated by the new transportation technology and its potential. Promoters with bold plans appeared everywhere but railroads were expensive to build and dependent on massive amounts of capital which was not available in Oregon. As early as 1853-1854, the territorial legislature granted charters to four companies for railroads which were never built. A decade later, the state legislature offered a grant of $250,000 to the first company to construct I00 miles of track in the Willamette Valley. The grant was never claimed. The grand plan was to build a railroad connecting Portland and the Willamette Valley to California. The Oregon Central Railroad Company was formed in 1863, reorganized repeatedly before laying its first 23 miles of track in 1869. The railroad reached Salem in 1870 and the California border in 1887.

Ben Simpson was among the business and political leaders who saw the potential railroads offered and underestimated the amount of investment they required. The government opened Yaquina Bay to white settlement in 1865 and two years later the Willamette and Coast Railroad Company was formed to build a narrow-gauge railroad from the Willamette Valley to Yaquina Bay. The 1867 effort failed but a successor corporation was organized in October 1871. Ben Simpson, until recently the Indian Agent at Siletz, was among the directors of the second company along with Alfred B. Meacham, who had been his immediate superior as Superintendent of Indian Affairs in Oregon. The second company, like the first, failed before laying any rail. In October 1872, Ben Simpson was among the founding directors of a third corporation in which Col.T. Edgenton Hogg was the lead investor. Colonel Hogg was able to attract eastern capital while fending off control by larger railroads and their investors. Under Colonel Hogg's leadership, but without the participation of Ben Simpson, the Willamette and Coast Railroad was completed December 31, 1884.[170]

Oneatta

Benjamin Simpson completed his tenure as an Indian Agent in May 1871 and settled on a large piece of property on the Yaquina River upstream from Yaquina City (now Sawyer's Landing) where he established a town which he named Oneatta.[171] He built a steam-powered saw mill at Oneatta which, at its peak, employed fourteen men and cut 20,000 feet of lumber a day. By 1876, Oneatta was large enough to have its own post office. Simpson's schooner carried lumber, primarily fir, from his Oneatta mill down the Oregon and California Coast to San Francisco and returned with supplies and manufactured goods. In September 1871, the ***Elinora***, with Ben Simpson aboard, returned from San Francisco with supplies for the reservation and the new lighthouse. Two months later, the Superintendent of Indian Affairs contracted with Simpson to purchase 1000 sacks of potatoes and 100 barrels of flour in San Francisco and to be delivered to Siletz on the Elinora. The goods arrived in February 1872. Joel Palmer, the Indian Agent at Siletz, complained about the cost and quality of the flour and potatoes.[172]

After a few years in the coastal trade, Ben Simpson began to look for new opportunities. He had sold his first schooner several years earlier and, in 1874, he sold the Elinora in San Francisco for $10,000.[173] Years later, Ben Simpson recalled the asymmetrical trading relationship between Oregon and California and the resentment Oregonians felt about their colonial status:

> *For many long years [Oregon] served a bitter and harassing vassalage to California-drawing its supplies from San Francisco and shipped thither all its products which were either exported to the Eastern states or foreign countries wider the label of the Golden State...*[174]

Ben Simpson returned to Salem in 1874 in hopes of obtaining a government job. In 1878, Simpson sold Oneatta, with its sawmill, two stores, two saloons, post office and land to Allen Parker (1828-1905). Parker was an overland pioneer of 1852, former Sheriff of Linn County and former Mayor of Albany, Oregon. Parker represented Benton County in the Oregon legislature in 1880 and 1882. Parker operated the town businesses and sawmill for several years. The post office and stores closed and Oneatta was eventually abandoned. Today the site is unmarked.[175]

Corruption in Indian Agencies

Nineteenth century Indian Agents had a reputation, sometimes well-deserved, for corruption. Oregon in the 1860s and 1870s was no exception. Indian Agents were selected through a political process, assigned to isolated outposts and supervised at a distance. Benjamin F. Biddle (1808-1882), the Indian Agent who served at Siletz before Ben Simpson, had been fired after his supervisor found that he was neglecting the Indians for whom he was responsible, wasting government property, using government property for personal purposes and padding the Agency payroll with a nonexistent employee. Biddle had left 6000 pounds of potatoes in the ground to rot while Indians were starving and had failed to care for 15,000 fruit trees delivered to the reservation. Biddle had paid Indian women one pint of flour a day to carry the trees six miles and billed the government $1023.[176] Despite his egregious neglect of duty and outright fraud at Siletz, Biddle returned to his home in Corvallis where he was elected Mayor in 1864.[177]

Ben Simpson was an Indian Agent for eight years and had many opportunities for private benefit from his government job. Like all Indian Agents, he had been selected through a "political" process rather than an open competition based on merit. The Oregon Superintendent of Indian Affairs who fired Agent Biddle had recommended another candidate, but Simpson had the advantage of having served nearby as a temporary Indian

Agent at Grand Ronde. Whatever the nature of his appointment, Simpson seems to have had an unusually flexible work arrangement during the years he was the Indian Agent at the Siletz Reservation. While he was a full-time government employee (1863-1871), he used Indian labor to build a wagon road (1864-1866), invested in a woolen mill off the reservation (1864) bought a newspaper and ran for U.S. Senate (1866), built and operated two coastal schooners (1868; 1870), built a lighthouse (1871) and invested in a railroad through former tribal lands (1871-1872). These activities took him off the reservation and created situations in which his personal interest may have been in conflict with his government responsibilities or in which he used his office improperly. At a minimum, he appears to have taken a full-time salary but devoted some of his efforts to activities unrelated to his job. Was he just another in a long line of corrupt Indian Agents?

Ben Simpson's outside activities were no secret to his co-workers, supervisors or political enemies and most of them occurred after he had completed his service as Indian Agent. The newspapers of the time were outrageously partisan and would not have hesitated to attack Simpson had they considered any of his outside activities improper. Simpson's political enemies were, like the newspapers, silent on the issue. Simpson had his own resident scold in Royal A. Benson, the Army corporal who kept a diary at Fort Yamhill and the Siletz reservation. Benson expected Indian Agents to be corrupt. He believed "Indian Agents are a curse on the Indians and likewise the country".[178] After seeing an abandoned grist mill on the Fort Yamhill reservation, Benson observed "I was more than ever impressed... that all Agencies and Agents were swindles.··(sic)[179] The construction of the unused mill that Benson considered' a swindle" occurred before Benjamin Simpson became Indian Agent. From Benson's limited description and naive view, it is impossible to determine whether or not the construction of the mill was the product of corruption. It was certainly wasteful but was not a decision for which Ben Simpson was responsible.

Benson was specific in his criticism of Benjamin Simpson in 1864 when he noted in his journal: "B. Simpson, Ind Agt after a 4 weeks absence come in to find nearly every "Siwash" gone. His place is here instead of dabbling in politics outside."[180] Apart from the gratuitous derogation of Indians, the Corporal's observation was fair. Simpson was, at this time, involved in the ownership of a newspaper in Salem and the construction of the Military Road while also preparing for his 1866 campaign for the United States Senate. While Simpson was away, his resident staff of eighteen farmers, teachers and craftsmen would carry on in his absence.

Ben Simpson was a lifelong opportunist. He pursued business and political opportunities throughout his career and often exploited the relationship between the two. The period at Siletz was no different. The question is whether he made improper use of his position as Indian Agent to benefit himself. The most ethically murky episode occurred during the period he was supplying Indian labor for the construction of the wagon road in which he was both the construction contractor and an investor. As Indian Agent, he had responsibility for the well-being of the Indians under his protection. The road project offered an opportunity for the Indians to earn money after they had completed spring planting. Simpson had the authority to approve the off-reservation employment of each Indian. He also provided the foreman for the crew and appears to have set the wages. At some point, he also became an investor in the enterprise although be seems not to have received the investment return that he had expected. The road scheme was a pyramid of frauds and Benjamin Simpson appears to have been one of the victims. The Indians were dissatisfied about pay rates but appeared to have received their pay. Soon after starting work on the contract, Simpson concluded that it was unworkable and withdrew.

While he was Indian Agent at Siletz in 1863, Benjamin Simpson was part of a group of six investors, one of them a former Superintendent of Indian Affairs, who acquired the ***Oregon Statesman***. Three years later, Simpson bought out the other investors and appointed two of his sons to edit the paper during his unsuccessful 1866 campaign for the United States Senate. The Senate campaign and the newspaper were unusual activities for someone serving as an Indian Agent but neither involved any impropriety or neglect of duty. Late in his period of service at Siletz, Simpson built schooners which transported lumber to California, from a mill he had built near Yaquina Bay, and returned with cargo including some destined for the reservation. After he completed his term as Indian Agent, he continued to transport supplies for the reservation in his boats. Simpson was using his own schooners to transport supplies the Agency had ordered or purchased in San Francisco. The relationships seem, by today's standards, to have been somewhat cozy but they were widely-known at the time and were not considered improper. His successor at Siletz, Joel Palmer, was quick to register a complaint when there was a question about the cost or quality of the goods Simpson was providing the reservation.

To the casual observer, the lighthouse projects at Yaquina Bay may seem suspect. Benjamin Simpson received a contract to build a lighthouse in 1871 about the time he was completing his service as an Indian Agent. The lighthouse he built was abandoned after less than three years and replaced by another lighthouse nearby, for which he transported building materials. The Indian

Agency was not involved in either of the lighthouse projects. Neither of the lighthouses were erected on tribal land and Simpson had left the Indian Agency shortly before the construction began. The problem was not corruption in the Indian Agency but errors of judgment by the United States Lighthouse Board where the decisions were made about the location of the first light and the need for a second light. The Lighthouse Board approved the construction of the second light at the time they were proceeding with the construction of the first light.

Ben Simpson was also an investor and director of the second and third companies attempting to build a narrow-gauge railroad from the Willamette Valley to the coast at Yaquina Bay. Railroad construction in the West was often riddled with corruption, but the Willamette and Coast Railroad was something of an exception. The railroad was built without land grant subsidies. Like other railroads of the time, the Willamette and Coast enticed investment from small investors and local residents. These small investors, subscribers as they were called, lost all the money they had invested in the first two railroad companies. The Willamette and Coast Railroad did not create a conflict of interest for Ben Simpson. He had been the Indian Agent in the area, but the proposed route of the railroad was across lands that had been removed from the Siletz reservation in 1865. Simpson's involvement in the railroad occurred in 1871 and 1872 after he had completed his term as Indian Agent. There was nothing improper about his participation in the building of the railroad to Yaquina Bay.

Nearly 150 years later, it is possible to assess Ben Simpson's eight-year stewardship of the Siletz Reservation. The most important fact is Joel Palmer's observation that Simpson left the reservation better than he found it. He successfully improved the agricultural productivity of the reservation but failed to improve the educational progress of Indian children. At great personal risk, he defended Indian oyster beds against well-connected poachers. Although he was involved in several off reservation activities, there is little evidence that he neglected his Indian Agent duties as Corporal Benson charged or that he had used his position for improper personal benefit. The strongest criticism of Simpson's performance is his somewhat ambivalent involvement in the decision to reduce the size of the reservation and allow settlement. Attempting to satisfy all parties, he chose a moderate position which satisfied no one and contributed to a major reduction in the size of the reservation.

Ultimately the job of the 19th century Indian Agent was to protect the settlers from the Indians. This entailed confining Indians on the reservation and preventing any resumption of the bloody warfare of the 1850s. By these minimalist standards, Simpson was successful. He may have neglected his position on occasion to pursue political or business opportunities off the reservation, but he maintained order. He was severe in his punishment of Indian misbehavior, but he protected the settlers. His responsibilities to the Indians were secondary. Beyond confining the Indians and preventing violence, the purpose of the reservation system was to transform Indians into self-sufficient farmers. The assumption was that the white culture was superior, and that education, religion and farming assistance would enable Indians to become more like white people. As Simpson learned during the oyster controversy, there was little to be gained from defending Indian property rights. The settlers wanted the land. There was little the Indian Agent could do to prevent the settlers from displacing the Indians.

The 1872 Legislature

By 1872, Ben Simpson and his family had been living in Salem in Marion County for several years but he was spending most of his time at Oneatta in Benton County where he had a $22,000 contract to build a schooner and several employees. He had been an early booster of Yaquina Bay where he had built a lumber mill and a coastal shipping business. Like many politicians, Ben Simpson was a storyteller. Fifty years after the event, be recalled running for office in Benton County in 1872 as a Republican for the first time. He "had no trouble in getting the nomination" but found himself in what he later characterized as "the fight of my life". His former colleagues in the Democratic Party attacked him for being a "carpet bagger", which be certainly was. The day after the election, he traveled to the court house in Corvallis where the election results were being compiled and found that he had won by 60 votes. A supporter suggested facetiously that "... if you had really been a resident of the county you would have beat'em by at least four hundred."[181]

Ben Simpson, the new Republican from Benton County joined a legislature in which two of his sons had prominent staff positions. His son Sylvester, a Democrat, had recently served sixteen months as State Librarian of Oregon and was in his third term as Chief Clerk of the State Senate. In the 1872 House of Representatives, the Republicans held a 32-17 majority and, no doubt at the urging of the new Republican, the Speaker appointed Ben Simpson's younger son Sam to his first and only term as Assistant Clerk of the House.[182] In addition to changing political parties, Ben Simpson had also changed his legislative interests. In his previous years in the legislature, he had taken a somewhat parochial approach to the issues he addressed. He represented his constituents in their narrow interests leaving the broader issues of public interest to others. Representing Clackamas County, he had introduced bills to clarify land title in Oregon City, obtain charters for a church and a school and promote land grants for Oregon Trail widows. Representing Marion County, he worked to remove Indian names from places in his district.

Still ambitious, Ben Simpson had changed in other ways. He knew that he was unlikely to run for office again from Benton County and he may also have been positioning himself for an appointment to a government job like the one he received later that year. He also may have simply been doing a favor for Ben Holladay, the powerful Oregon transportation tycoon. Whatever the motivation, Ben Simpson became the advocate for complex legislation involving the operation of locks and dams at the falls of the Willamette. A previous legislature had granted a concession to a private company to build and operate the locks and dams on state-owned land. The revenue from the land leases had previously been dedicated to public education but had been diverted by the legislature to pay for the construction of the locks and dams. The legislation Simpson proposed would authorize the state to lease the locks and dams from the private company for ten years for $50,000 annually. At the end of ten years, the state would be authorized to buy the locks and dams for the actual cost of construction less $200,000. After years of attacks by Oregon newspapers, Simpson suddenly found himself receiving the approbation of the press in his new role as a Republican. The Portland newspaper reminded readers that Republicans had opposed the diversion of school funds in the first place and concluded that Simpson's proposal to bring the locks and dams under state control was the best way to proceed now that the money was spent.[183]

The 1872 legislative assembly was Ben Simpson's last in elective office but far from the end of his political career. He had used political connections to obtain the sutler's job at Fort Yamhill and the Indian Agent position at Siletz. By the Fall of 1872, he had been in the private sector a year and a half and was actively pulling political strings to secure another government job. Simpson asked his friend Matthew Deady to write U.S. Attorney General George H. Williams urging Williams to appoint Simpson as sutler at Camp Harney in southeastern Oregon.[184] Williams had been Deady's colleague for six years on the Territorial Supreme Court. Williams had also been an investor with Ben Simpson in the ***Oregon Statesman*** in 1863. Camp Harney, also called Camp Steele and Fort Harney, was a military fort constructed in 1867 to suppress Indian uprisings in south-eastern Oregon. The fort was located about twelve miles northwest of Burns, Oregon. Despite the lobbying by old friends, Williams did not appoint Simpson to the position at Camp Harney.

5 Oregon in Transition

For more than thirty years, Ben Simpson was enmeshed in Oregon politics. The seven terms he served in the territorial and state legislatures were only part of his political involvement. He was continuously active offering advice, promoting and opposing candidates and seeking favors for himself, his sons and his political cronies. He was more of a political operative than a leader. He offered no particular vision for Oregon but was adept at the process of politics with its emphasis on personal relationships and trading favors. In 1852, he explained his political philosophy to Judge Deady "***I go the whole hog for the old maxim that is to make one hand wash the other***" [185] What he meant was that when he did a favor for another person, it was with the expectation that sometime in the future he would be able to call on that person for a similar, but unrelated, favor. It was a politics of cronyism, personal obligation and reciprocity in which the insiders benefited while the broader society and the common good were too often neglected.

Simpson enjoyed the process of politics, the scheming, manipulation and negotiation, as well as the influence it gave him over people and events. He organized, connected and coerced. He rewarded those who assisted him and never forgot those who had opposed him. His role was often in the background trying to persuade others to act. As early as 1849, he was encouraging Samuel Thurston to run for territorial delegate in order to block James Nesmith's candidacy. A decade later. Nesmith was in the U.S. Senate and Simpson was appealing to him, without success, to protect the job of an Indian Agent at Siletz and to obtain a military commission for his protege Rodney Earhart. He used his influence to get his son Sylvester appointed Chief Clerk of the State Senate for six terms from 1868 to 1878 and his son Sam as Assistant Clerk of the House in 1872. By 1872 he had become a Republican, but his methods were unchanged. He was instrumental in the successful nomination of Joseph Wilson as Republican candidate for Congress. According to Judge Deady the other two candidates did not have a chance because "Ben Simpson had... been championing Wilson for the past 6 months".[186]

At the time Oregon was preparing for statehood, David Newsome had described Oregon politicians as "an overreaching, grasping set of swindlers, in whose vicinity honest people would be unsafe" but, he hastened to add, that not all Oregon politicians were corrupt.[187] He was writing at a time when issues like slavery and statehood commanded political discussion. There were strongly-held opinions in Oregon for and against each issue, but the decisions were free of the corrupting influence of money. Within a decade, this all changed as the state legislature became the focus of entrepreneurs and promoters seeking public subsidies for railroad construction. The political stakes were suddenly raised as the opportunities for private benefit increased beyond imagination.

The turning point came in 1868 when Ben Holladay arrived in Oregon loaded with cash and prepared to invest in building a railroad from Oregon to California. Holladay (1819-1887) had made a fortune in the stagecoach and freight business before coming to Oregon and was prepared to go to any lengths to acquire political power. The flamboyant Holladay spent lavishly in a brazen and successful effort to influence political officials and monopolize the nascent transportation industry. H. H. Bancroft described the process:

> *On the convening of the (1868) legislature, Holladay established himself at Salem, where he kept open house to the members whom he entertained royally as to expenditure and vulgarly as to all things else.*[188]

Holladay persuaded the legislature to revoke the land grants made to a competing railroad two years earlier and to reassign the grants to his railroad. Holladay took over the Oregon Central Railroad Company and reorganized it as the Oregon and California Railroad. He acquired monopoly control over shipping on the lower Willamette and started a newspaper in Portland. The stakes were enormous. The Oregon and California Railroad was subsidized by 3.8 million acres of land grants.[189]

Oregon had never seen anyone quite like Holladay. He was rich, cunning, vengeful and without scruples. He was generous to those who did his bidding and merciless to those who did not. Oregon business leaders had repeatedly organized railroad companies but had been unable to assemble the technical capacity and capital to actually lay track. Holladay, for all his ethical limitations, could raise the money and get the job done. He sold deeply-discounted bonds to German investors. He used bribes, threats and lawsuits to overcome obstacles. He lathered politicians with favors and built a Republican political machine in alliance with U.S. Senator John Mitchell. By 1873, the Oregon and California Railroad was operating freight and passenger service between Portland and Roseburg.

Over ten years, Holladay and his henchmen thoroughly corrupted the political process in Oregon. Ben Simpson became en-snarled in Holladay's schemes. Joseph Wilson, the Republican congressman who Simpson had championed, turned out to have been a former Holladay employee. In 1872, Ben Simpson approached Judge Deady on behalf of Holladay offering to help the judge get a much-desired salary increase. Simpson reported that Holladay was in favor of the raise and ready to assist the judge to travel to Washington, D.C. to make his case. Simpson offered to provide his old friend a free railroad pass for roundtrip transportation and a loan to cover other travel expenses. Despite his need for more income, Judge Deady wisely declined Simpson's offer and avoided becoming indebted to Holladay.[190]

Matthew Deady was an astute observer of Holladay and his schemes. Writing about the 1872 Locks and Dams bill in the legislature, he confided to his diary:

> *People will always be governed by railway and other corporate Kings until they learn sense enough to select, educate and maintain a legitimate King whose interest is necessarily the public good and who has a sufficient inherent power to curb the selfish and extravagant ambition of these vulgar adventurers.*[191]

The Judge was not proposing a monarchy but was musing about how conditions would have to change to restrain free-wheeling tycoons like Ben Holladay.

The following year, Holladay escalated his campaign to achieve control over Judge Deady. Holladay was irritated that Deady's criticism of Holladay's ally John H. Mitchell could influence voters in a close Congressional election. Mitchell was a recently-elected U.S. Senator and the leader of the Holladay faction of the Oregon Republican party. He was also the subject of articles in the Portland Oregonian reporting that the Senator was a bigamist who had changed his name, stolen from his law firm and abandoned women in three states. Ben Simpson was assigned the unpleasant task of persuading Judge Deady to withhold his criticism of the ethically-challenged Senator during the special congressional election to replace Holladay's candidate Joseph Wilson, who had died. Deady recorded the encounter in his diary:

> *... Had a talk with Ben Simpson in which I told him it was foolish for him or any of his crowd to think of coercing me on this Mitchell matter or any other by threats of abolishing my office or anything of that kind. Denied that he [emphasis in the original] had ever said or thought such a thing but admitted that Denny and some others had.*[192]

Holladay's efforts to ingratiate himself with Deady the previous year had failed so the transportation tycoon changed his strategy and attempted to threaten the Judge.

Deady confronted Simpson about the threats. Simpson admitted they had been discussed but only by other people. As it turned out the 1873 special Congressional election was thick with fraud. James Nesmith, the candidate of the Democratic Party, won but Holladay and Mitchell bought sufficient votes in Portland to make the outcome close. The alleged fraud resulted in proceedings in federal court. Holladay's captive newspaper called for Deady to be replaced. Holladay's agents packed the grand jury process to prevent an indictment and persuaded U.S. Attorney General George H. Williams to replace the United States Attorney in Oregon and block any prosecution.[193]

The Holladay period, although it only lasted ten years, thoroughly corrupted Oregon politics. Holladay successfully built a railroad where others had failed but he used his money and his power to subvert the political process. Judge Deady displayed his wise judgment by refusing Simpson's offer of free railroad transportation and a loan to cover expenses. He showed his courage by standing up to the threats to his job. Ben Simpson, on the other hand, was drawn into Holladay's corrupt schemes. At best, he was a well-meaning messenger offering assistance and advice to an old friend. At worst, he was attempting to bribe and threaten a federal judge. Ben Simpson had demonstrated his loyalty to the Republican Party and could expect the assistance of Senator Mitchell in securing a patronage job in Oregon.

The Panic of 1873 ended Holladay's free-spending ways. Banks failed and credit dried up. Holladay was ruined and his railroad was unable to make interest payments on its loans. In April 1878, the Oregon and California Railroad was taken over by representatives of its German bond-holders and Holladay was fired. Holladay was finished but the railroad to California was not.[194] The new owners stopped construction for several years before finally completing the rail connect1on to California in 1887. Holladay was gone but his associates remained influential in Oregon into the 20th century.

Siletz Revisited

The population of Oregon grew rapidly in the years after statehood. During the 1860s, the state populations increased by 73 percent to 91,000. Two-thirds of the residents were in the Willamette Valley where the most desirable land had long been claimed. Settlers looked covetously at Indian lands which they considered underutilized. Not satisfied with the 200,000 acres taken from the middle of the Coast Reservation in 1865, settlers and promoters wanted more. They were particularly eager to obtain property near the Oregon Coast where they had heard that fishing and timber were abundant. In 1870, settlers and promoters began a petition campaign to close the Coast Reservation, relocate the Indians to eastern Oregon and open the entire area to settlement. The Oregon legislature passed resolutions urging the Congress to close the reservation.[195]

The Congress and the federal office of Indian Affairs paid little attention to the petitions and resolutions from Oregon until 1873 when newly-elected Senator John Mitchell arrived from Oregon and began advocating annexation of the reservation. Mitchell argued that existing land policies were unfair to settlers. As he calculated it, each Indian at Siletz had more than 800 acres while settler families were limited to 160 acres under the 1862 Homestead Act. A Republican, Mitchell had come to Oregon as a political ally and business associate of Ben Holladay. Mitchell had overcome rumors of a sordid past to win the 1873 Senatorial election in the Oregon Legislative Assembly. The rumors persisted but Mitchell would go on to serve part or all of four terms in the U.S. Senate. At the time of his death, he was in the Senate while appealing a conviction for land and timber fraud.

Ben Simpson completed his term as Indian Agent at Siletz in 1871 but remained in the Yaquina Bay region where he built a lighthouse, operated a sawmill, engaged in the coastal trade, invested in railroad companies and was elected to the legislature as a Republican. During his eight years as an Indian Agent, Simpson had a mixed reputation, protecting Indians and punishing them. He defended Indian oyster beds against poachers and urged restraint in the transfer of reservation lands to settlers. He also was strict in punishing Indians for infractions on the reservation and in pursuing and capturing those who had escaped from the reservation. As a businessman and elected official who had only recently become a Republican, Simpson's view of the role of government was evolving. He was increasingly becoming a proponent of public policies encouraging and enabling private development like the Military Road across Oregon and the lighthouse at Yaquina Bay. In the 1872 legislature, he introduced a measure for a creating a public private partnership to own and operate locks and dams on the Willamette River. By 1873, Simpson was seeking appointment to a federal job, and he knew that the support of Oregon's new Republican Senator would be essential.

Senator Mitchell was part of a younger generation of Oregon politicians. In contrast to the pioneer farmers who had controlled Oregon politics during the period before statehood, Mitchell was a relative newcomer to Oregon and an urban lawyer. Mitchell saw Simpson as someone whose familiarity with the geography, residents and timberlands of the Siletz Reservation would be useful. Late in 1873, Mitchell met with Simpson to discuss closing the reservation and opening the area to settlement. Simpson supported development but was careful to balance the expansion demands of the settlers with the Indian needs for a place of their own. Simpson thought he had persuaded the new Senator to preserve part of the reservation for use by the Indians. Soon after his meeting with Simpson, Mitchell introduced legislation reducing the size of the Siletz reservation by more than half. Mitchell's plan was to preserve the central part of the reservation while opening the area north of the Salmon River and south of the Alsea River to settlement. The plan would require the relocation of the Indians from the northern and southern parts of the reservation into the central area.

As he had in 1865, Ben Simpson supported a compromise in which each of the parties received less than it had wanted. The settlers got some, but not all, the land they had wanted while the Indians lost part, but not all, of the reservation. Simpson justified this false equivalency as benefiting the settlers without harming the Indians. He explained to Mitchell:

> *To move the line five miles below the mouth of the Alsea River will not affect the Indians but will greatly accommodate the whites as they can use the timber which the Indians have no use for.*[196]

Whatever the rationale, the fundamental fact was that the United States was, for the second time in a decade, taking land that the Indians had been led to believe was theirs forever. A month after Ben Simpson endorsed Mitchell's Siletz proposal, President Grant appointed Simpson Surveyor General of Oregon.

The Congress approved Mitchell's proposal in March 1875 but added a last minute amendment: "Provided that these Indians shall not be removed until their consent has been obtained".[197] The consent provision was intended to complicate and delay the land grab in Oregon. For the Indian Affairs officials who had to administer the law, it was a bureaucratic formality which could easily be satisfied. For the Indians of Siletz, it was a different matter. Most of them had been forcibly moved onto the reservation twenty years earlier and most of them were strongly opposed to another move. The responsibility for explaining the new law and obtaining consent fell to the resident Indian Agents at the reservation. John Fairchild, the agent at Siletz, convened a council among the Tillamook in the northern part of the reservation on June l and George Litchfield, the sub-agent at Alsea convened a similar council in the south on June 17. In each case, the Indians refused to consent to relocation.

For the administrators of Indian affairs, refusal was not an acceptable response. It was the wrong answer. The Indians needed to be persuaded that the loss of land and relocation were in their best interests. In July, Edward P. Smith the U.S. Commissioner for Indian Affairs, most likely at the urging of an impatient Senator Mitchell, appointed Ben Simpson to be a special agent to obtain the necessary consent. Smith's orders to Simpson were clear: consent was not to be coerced but the Indians were "expected to comply".[198] Simpson correctly decoded this bureaucratic double talk to mean that he should obtain consent using any means short of force.

Simpson selected three Indian leaders he knew at Siletz and sent them south to prepare the Alsea residents for a discussion of relocation. Simpson convened a two-day council at Alsea in August where he distributed beef and tobacco to those attending. A month later, he convened a similar council at the mouth of the Salmon River where he promised the Tillamook that each Indian family would receive 40 acres on the Siletz reservation along with farm equipment, construction assistance and the materials to build a house. Participants at the Tillamook Council deliberated for three days. In each case, the reported outcome was the same. The Indians had consented. No record of proceedings was maintained at either council. The only reports of what had transpired were those of the Indian Affairs staff with vague evidence that the Indians had agreed to relocate.

Two days after the council at Alsea, Ben Simpson wrote Commissioner Smith in Washington reporting that opposition to relocation was "milder than before".[199] On the same day, Subagent Litchfield, who opposed the relocation, wrote Smith to discredit Simpson who he called a "Political Demagogue" and strong friend" of Senator Mitchell. Litchfield was no doubt irritated that Simpson had been appointed to get a second opinion. Agent Fairchild did not attend the council at Alsea but, relying on the three Indian leaders Simpson had dispatched, concluded that the Indians "expected" to relocate.[200] Neither Simpson's report of declining opposition nor Fairchild' second-hand report of Indian expectations was actual consent, but they were sufficient to satisfy the Commissioner of Indian Affairs that the necessary consent had been obtained.

The situation in the northern part of the reservation was somewhat less ambiguous. After three days of deliberation, the Indians agreed to relocate in exchange for a package of inducements Simpson had offered. Simpson reported the details of the agreement to the Commissioner of Indian Affairs in Washington:

> *On the third day however, after repeated meetings, they consented to abandon their country at once, and locate on the Siletz reservation... To accomplish this result they were promised assistance from the Government... allotted forty acres of Land... [materials and assistance in constructing] houses... plow and teams... seed potatoes for the first years planting...*[201]

Benjamin Simpson had obtained sufficient consent to satisfy the Commissioner that the statutory requirements had been satisfied. The government opened large parts of the reservation for settlement but never delivered the land, houses and farm equipment Simpson had promised. For the second time in twenty years, the Indians at Siletz lost land and were not compensated. Simpson's shameful collaboration with Sen. Mitchell resulted in the removal of 737,000 acres including 60 miles of Oregon Coast from the once-grand reservation. Large areas at the northern and southern ends of the reservation were opened for settlement. Indians who had lived in those areas were relocated into the remaining Siletz reservation, now one-sixth of its original size, without any of the assistance Ben Simpson had promised.

Surveyor-General for Oregon

Ben Simpson had no particular surveying skills or experience in April 1874 when he took office as the federal Surveyor-General of the Public Lands in Oregon. His primary qualification appears to have been the assistance he provided Ben Holladay and Sen. John Mitchell over the two previous years. In 1872, he had sponsored legislation for Holladay and interceded on Holladay's behalf with Judge Deady. In 1873, he advised Senator Mitchell about land at Siletz. Simpson replaced W.H. Odell who soon became the owner of the ***Oregon Statesman*** in Salem, which Simpson had previously owned. The newspaper provided Odell a platform for his vicious criticism of Ben Simpson's son Sylvester, the Oregon Superintendent of Public Instruction.[202] Ben Simpson worked out of an office in Eugene for a year. In April 1875, he moved to Portland where his office was in the United States Court House on SW 5th between Morrison and Yamhill where he had a staff of five clerks and draftsmen. In a time before restrictions on nepotism, Ben Simpson employed his friends and family. He hired his son Sam as Transcribing Clerk from April to June 1874. Rockey P. Earhart, his protege from Fort Yamhill, was hired as Chief Clerk and his teenage sons William M. (1856-n.d.) as a clerk and Grover B. (1858- 1934) as a messenger.[203]

The Surveyor-General was part of the U.S. General Land Office and was responsible for the survey of public lands and their orderly disposition. Simpson's predecessors had administered the Oregon Donation Land Act of 1850 from which Simpson and many of his relatives had benefited. The Surveyor-General for Oregon had a budget to engage contract survey crews and the responsibility for administering federal land laws including those designed to stimulate settlement and those intended to result in the reclamation of marginal lands. By the time Simpson was appointed Surveyor -General, the Donation Land Act work was largely completed and the office administered other federal land programs like the Homestead Act and the Swampland Act. The Homestead Act of 1862 offered 160 acres of public land to anyone willing to live on the land for five years and make improvements. The Swamplands Act of 1850 was originally designed for conditions in Arkansas but was amended in 1870 to include Oregon. Like the Desert Land Act of 1877, the Swamplands Act offered cheap land in exchange for draining wetlands and irrigating arid lands. Each of these early conservation programs was vulnerable to abuse by speculators obtaining cheap federal land by misclassifying productive lands as substandard or hiring bogus claimants to acquire large tracts of land.[204]

In 1877, Ben Simpson prepared a report to the Commissioner of the United States General Land Office. The report was a typical account of the advantages of Oregon with virtually no indication of what the Surveyor-General for Oregon had actually accomplished during the year. The report, sounding more like a Chamber of Commerce brochure than a government report, described the climate ("soft and gentle"), agriculture ("the Arcadia of the thrifty husbandman"), and industry. Simpson proudly reported that Oregon grows fruit "in magnificent profusion" and that the state has "inexhaustible forests of the finest timber known". Ben Simpson included statistics from his son's 1875-1876 report of the Oregon Superintendent of Public Instruction. None of this had much to do with the responsibilities of the Surveyor General.

Ben Simpson summarized a year of Oregon survey activity in one vague sentence in the passive voice ("Some work was and is now being done... " at three locations). complained about delays in the federal appropriation process and criticized the federal land programs his office administered. He reported that the Desert Land Act had little applicability to situations in Oregon and that there was a risk that perfectly good agricultural land would be misclassified as desert to qualify under the act. He saved his most scathing comments for the Swampland Act which, according to Simpson, did not fit the situation in Oregon at all but nonetheless,

> *The number and extent of filing under the swamp land laws inspire the belief that the state is just emerging from the primal flood.*

Simpson never used the word "fraud" in his report, and he never provided a specific example of abuse, but he made it clear that he believed that "the reckless pursuit of gain" had resulted in widespread abuse of federal land programs.[205]

Ben Simpson served four years as Surveyor General until 1878 when he was succeeded by J.C. Tolman. Tolman was a Republican legislator who narrowly lost the 1874 Oregon Gubernatorial election to Lafayette Grover. In 1878, Simpson's assistant. Rockey Earhart, was elected Secretary of State, the second highest position in Oregon at the time. Earhart served two terms as Secretary of State.

Postal Inspector

When his four-year term as Surveyor-General expired in 1878, Ben Simpson was able to use his political connections to secure an appointment as United States Postal Inspector for Oregon. In 1882, his quiet sinecure in the post office suddenly turned controversial. A package addressed to a woman in Independence, Oregon had been delivered instead to the woman's husband. The husband promptly returned the package to the sender C.O.D. The package had contained copies of The New Northwest, a feminist newspaper published from 1871-1887 by Abigail Scott Duniway (1834-1915). Duniway was an Oregon Trail pioneer of 1852 and the leading advocate for women's rights in Oregon. Mrs. Duniway was outraged. She charged that there was "Crooked Business in this Post Office".[206] The mistaken delivery, in her view, was part of a conspiracy to interfere with the distribution of the newspaper and its feminist message.

The postal service responded by sending Benjamin Simpson, in his role as Postal Inspector, to investigate. Simpson held a public hearing and prepared a report of his findings. He confirmed Mrs. Duniway's basic charge that the postmaster had delivered a package of newspapers to Mr. J. W. Vau rather than his wife. Ben Simpson characterized the error as "inexcusable".[207] Mrs. Duniway was not satisfied. She accused Simpson of "conniving with a corrupt postmaster and a corrupt postal ring"[208] and expressed surprise that the postmaster had not been fired.[209] A letter to the editor in The New Northwest signed by "A Suffragist" criticized Simpson for the lack of decorum at the public hearing and suggested that, despite ruling in favor of the women, Simpson's sympathies were actually with the men.[210] It was a no-win situation but Simpson appears to have managed it fairly and with respect for the parties involved. There was no corrupt postal ring but there was a husband who disagreed with his wife about women's issues and a postmaster who was reprimanded for delivering a package to the wrong person.

Nancy Simpson

There was something special about ***Nancy Cooper Simpson***. She was a child of the frontier, but she also had dreams far-beyond the hard-scrabble frontier life she had grown up in. She was born in a family fort in the Boonslick region of Central Missouri and grew up surrounded by cousins and uncles who were Indian fighters, Santa Fe Trail pioneers and frontiersmen. Her grandfather ***Col. Benjamin Cooper*** (1756-1841) fought in the ***Revolutionary War*** in Kentucky, was the leader of the settlers on the Missouri frontier during the ***War of 1812*** and the captain of the second successful trading expedition on the Santa Fe Trail. Her father William Cooper (1797/8-1848) had fought Indians as a teenager at Coopers Fort, participated in a wild adventure to recover hidden furs on the Arkansas River in 1815, accompanied his father on the Santa Fe Trail in 1822 and fought in the ***Black Hawk War*** of 1832. One of her cousins served on an exploratory expedition with John C. Fremont in 1845 and another relative was the legendary frontiersman ***Kit Carson.***[211] While she was little, her family moved from Howard County, Missouri to nearby Cooper County (named for a great uncle killed defending the settlements in 1815) and Saline County.

Nancy Cooper Simpson

With the opening of the Platte Purchase in 1838, William Cooper and his Higgins and Smelser in-laws acquired land in western Missouri. The Cooper land was adjacent to property owned by Alvis Kimsey, a Simpson in-law, and about a mile from land owned by William Simpson. On June 8, 1843, Nancy Cooper married her Platte County neighbor Benjamin Simpson. Simpson was a widower with a young son. His first wife, ***Eliza Jane Wisdom*** married Ben Simpson in 1839 and died in 1841 seven days after their son John Thomas Simpson (1841-1920) was born. Nancy and Ben Simpson had two additional children in Missouri, Sylvester born in 1844 and Sam in 1845. (Appendix IV) They passed over the names that were common in their families like Benjamin, Frank, Richard, Thomas and William as well as the uncommon names like Braxton and Sarshel to choose distinctive names for their two young sons: Sylvester Confucius and Samuel Leonidas. The names would set them apart for life.

In the spring of 1846, Nancy and Ben Simpson left Platte County, Missouri with their three young sons. They traveled in a large wagon train with three generations of relatives including several with children. Nancy Simpson would have been fully occupied on the overland journey caring for five-year-old John, two-year-old Sylvester and the infant Sam but she could count on the assistance of the six unmarried teenage girls and young married women without children who were part of the 47 member Simpson wagon train.

Nancy Simpson raised eleven children. In addition to her step-son John and the two boys born in Missouri, Nancy and Ben Simpson had an additional eight children, born between 1847 and 1865, after they arrived in Oregon. (Appendix IV) During their years in Oregon, they moved frequently as Ben Simpson launched new businesses or held government jobs. They lived at Oregon City, French Prairie, Waldo Hills, Fort Yamhill, Siletz Agency, Salem, Oneatta, Eugene and Portland. Throughout their years in Oregon, Ben Simpson had been away from their homes for extended periods, to punish the Cayuse, sell lumber in California, round up runaway Indians in southern Oregon and trade in San Francisco. Nancy Simpson was pregnant nearly every other year with children born in Marion County (1847), Clackamas County (1849), Marion County again (1852), Salem (1854), an unknown location (1856), Yamhill County (1858), Polk County (1862) and back in Salem (1865).[212]

With Ben Simpson occupied managing his stores, lumber mills and ships, advancing his political career and carrying out the responsibilities of his government jobs, the burden of child rearing fell heavily on Nancy. She cared for the children in the primitive cabins of the early years, reservation housing of the middle years and houses in Salem, Eugene and Portland during the later years. Although her own education had been limited, she was able to instill a love of learning in all of the Simpson children. They attended schools when they could and otherwise were educated by their mother. Despite their frequent moves and limited access to schools and libraries, several of the Simpson children were remarkably talented as writers, scholars and teachers. None of the eleven Simpson children followed their father into elected office (one ran for office and lost) and none emulated his risk-taking approach to business but six attended Willamette University and five graduated including three daughters.[213]

Of the eleven Simpson children, ***Francis*** did not live to adulthood. He died of a skull fracture at the age of twelve after being thrown and dragged by a horse.[214] The children who survived to adulthood were unusually accomplished. Two sons became lawyers and writers (one an essayist and one a poet), two became business executives with Wells Fargo Express in Chicago and Omaha (including one who wrote poetry as a hobby), and one sold real estate. ***John***, the child of Ben Simpson's first marriage, became a teacher and a successful cattle rancher. The four Simpson daughters all married and remained in Oregon. ***Louisa***, the oldest daughter, graduated from Willamette in 1866 in the class with her brother Sam and was a schoolteacher in Eugene, The Dalles and Portland. She married James A. Stowell, Jr., who was also a teacher, and they had a son.

Alice, the youngest daughter, married William Thomas Burney. Burney was born in Georgia and studied law at the University of Virginia. He moved to Oregon in 1878 and worked in the General Land Office in Oregon City and Portland and practiced law in Portland. W.T. and Alice Burney had four daughters and three sons before Alice died in 1892. Her brother Sam Simpson wrote a sad farewell to his beloved Alice:

No sweeter flower than thee can bloom
On this dark shore of sorrow-
Bid us good night in tearful gloom,
-. *And garland Death's to-morrow.*[215]

Elinora Simpson graduated from Willamette in 1869.[216] After Alice died, she married Burney and helped raise Alice's seven children. Burney and Nora had one son. With assistance from Nora, Burney collected and published a book of Sam Simpson's poems in 1910.

The fourth Simpson daughter, ***Isadora*** graduated from Willamette in 1872 and married ***William M. Killingsworth*** (1850-1915), a Portland businessman. Killingsworth was born in Missouri and crossed the plains to Oregon in 1853. He was a real estate developer in East Portland where a street is named after him. He was also involved in the first electric street cars in Portland and the establishment of the Portland Board of Trade. He was elected to the Oregon State Legislature in 1905 as a Republican. William and Dora Killingsworth had five daughters and one son and lived in a sixteen-room house on ten landscaped acres in East Portland.[217]

Old Oregon State Capitol and Willamette University in Salem.

The family legend, made true by repeated retelling, is that Nancy Simpson taught her children to read by the flickering light of the fireplace in whatever crowded log cabin they found themselves. Her son-in-law W. T. Burney turned the family legend into fact in the preface to the posthumous book of Sam Simpson's poetry he edited:

> *Sam Simpson... was taught the alphabet by his mother at the age of four years, from copies traced in the ashes on the hearthstone of their pioneer home.*[218]

Another author describes Nancy Cooper Simpson as "fierce in her intent that Sam get a good education, and she started early:"[219] Sam was the sensitive child who became the poet but there is no reason to conclude that his mother was not equally fierce about the education of each of her other children and her step-son John. Nancy Simpson, with her ten children and busy husband, had little time to develop her own artistic talents. Her daughter Eleanor Simpson Burney remembered, "... mother was a great reader. She also wrote poetry, though I don't think any of it was ever published. I think Sam got his taste of writing from mother."[220]

Nancy Cooper was also an enduring source of moral guidance to her children. Even her wayward son, Sam Simpson, for all his misbehavior, could not escape her influence. William Fidler, who had lived with Sam Simpson one winter, observed about the poet that:

> *The impress of a pious mother's training was something he could not thoroughly shake off, however else be might go astray personally.*[221]

Ben and Nancy Simpson attended the 5th annual reunion of Oregon Pioneers Association in 1877. The two-day celebration was held in Salem and featured a reading of their son Sam's short poem "An Oregon Pioneer" with its tribute to their generation and its:

Eighty years of sun and shadow,
Eighty years of smiles and tears![222]

The author was not present, and the poem was read by one of the Oregon Trail pioneers whose "long path" the poem celebrated.[223]

The long path ended for Nancy Simpson in 1882. She and Ben Simpson had been married forty years when she died. She was buried, with several Simpson relatives, in the Simpson family plot in Portland's Lone Fir Cemetery.[224]

6 A New Start

Ben Simpson was 65 years old in 1883 when Nancy Simpson died. He had lived in Oregon 37 years, operated numerous businesses and served in several elective and appointed positions. Rather than retire, he left Oregon to persue opportunities in Alabama. The Postal Department had employed him in Oregon, transferred him to Alabama where he worked as a federal Postal Inspector for one year. In 1884, he bought a 1300-acre cotton plantation four miles from Selma, Alabama which he operated for twelve years or more. The cotton plantation was a financial disaster. The value of the land, which had been $20 an acre at some point, perhaps when he bought it, had fallen to $7 an acre by 1897. Simpson had seven tenants farming 800 acres, but he estimated that he had lost $6000 over the previous three years. Despite the financial troubles he had experienced, Ben Simpson remained characteristically optimistic about the future. He had a plan to sell the 800 acres to the tenants and support himself off the remaining 500 acres. Ever the optimist, he expressed confidence that the economy would improve. As he explained, "I look for better times in the near future" with William McKinley, a Republican, as president. "I know him personally... he was my choice for president."[225]

Ben Simpson considered himself a Southerner. He had been born and raised in the South and had been sympathetic to the regional grievances of the South during the years leading up to the Civil War. However he saw himself, to Southerners, he was a northern Republican who had come south to pick over the bones of the old Confederacy. In short, he was a "carpet bagger". In his old age, he recalled his unpleasant experience in Alabama:

> *Nobody knows how bitterly the Southern people hated a Republican during the Reconstruction period unless by actual experience among them. I was ostracized and snubbed on every occasion and without cessation. There was nothing too mean or despicable to compare me with, to my disparagement but it had not been my nature to yield to unfavorable environments, and I usually had my say though it made existence miserable in the extreme.*[226]

Despite his social isolation as a Northerner among Southerners, the twice widowed, Ben Simpson married Caroline Gordon in Selma in 1884. Mrs. Gordon was the widow of P. B. Gordon who had died in 1874. She had previously been married to a Mr. Lilly from whom she separated about 1861. Little is known about Caroline Simpson except that she died August 2, 1902.[227]

The Coeur d'Alene Indian Commission

Ben Simpson was living in Alabama in 1889 when he was asked to lead a federal commission negotiating a treaty with the Coeur d'Alene Indians of Idaho. The Coeur d'Alene tribe had once spread over more than four million acres of land in the northern part of the Idaho panhandle but two executive orders, two previous treaty negotiations and Congressional inaction had reduced the size of the reservation. By the time the third Coeur d'Alene Indian Commission was formed in 1889, most of the members of the tribe were farming in the southern part of the reservation while homesteaders, mining concerns, a railroad, timber companies and others were coveting the resource-rich northern part of the reservation. The reservation had been established in 1867, when President Andrew Johnson, issued an Executive Order setting aside 250,000 acres of traditional tribal lands, within the four million acres, in far Northern Idaho. President Johnson acted without notifying the tribe that the reservation had been created or compensating the tribe for the loss of land outside the new boundaries. With its boundaries poorly defined and surrounded by forests, rivers and ore deposits, the reservation was under pressure from impatient settlers and enterprising companies demanding access to land they argued were empty and unused. In 1873, the Secretary of the Interior appointed commissioners to meet with the Coeur d'Alene tribe to renegotiate reservation boundaries. The 1873 commission recommended the expanding the reservation to 590,000 acres. On November 8, 1873, President Johnson issued a second executive Order establishing the expanded reservation.[228]

In 1887, a second federal commission negotiated with the Coeur d'Alene and persuaded the tribe to give up the four million acres of land outside the 1873 boundary in exchange for a one-time payment of $150,000. The United States Congress had not ratified the 1873 treaty expanding the reservation boundaries. In the Indian Appropriations Act of March 1889, the Congress authorized a third commission to negotiate with the Coeur D'Alene tribe. The mission of the Coeur d'Alene Indian Commission of 1889 was to acquire certain tribal lands that were not being used for agriculture. President

Benjamin Harrison appointed Ben Simpson, John H. Shupe and Napoleon B. Humphrey to be members of what was informally called the "Simpson Commission". Tribal leaders were opposed to another round of negotiations. They complained, with justification, that the tribe had already given up four million acres to the federal government and that they did not need a third commission reopening negotiations when the agreement from the second (1887) commission remained unratified and the $150,000 unpaid.

The Simpson Commission received its orders from the U.S. Commissioner of Indian Affairs in June 1889 and gathered in Portland, Oregon that August to prepare for meetings with the tribe. The Commissioners traveled by train and wagon to Idaho where they found the Coeur d'Alene leaders unwilling to negotiate anything until the 1887 agreement was ratified. The treaty process was stopped before it started. The Indians would not proceed without ratification and the commissioners could not guarantee that the Congress would ratify the treaty. Ben Simpson was experienced in working out political disagreements. He contacted the Bureau of Indian Affairs in Washington by telegraph and obtained authority to negotiate a treaty that would not go into effect until the Congress ratified the 1887 treaty. Negotiations with the tribe were interrupted for two weeks while the three Commissioners explored the resource-rich northern part of the reservation and identified boundaries that would accomplish the objectives of the government to acquire the so-called "unused" tribal land.

The negotiations resumed in late August after the commissioners returned from their investigation of the northern part of the reservation. Ben Simpson tried to persuade tribal leaders that the future of the Coeur d'Alene tribe was in agriculture and that the forests, rivers and mining lands to the north would be of little use to them. He blithely assured the tribe that the Congress would ratify the 1887 treaty, and he avoided persistent questions about compensatory payments to individual tribal members whose land lay outside the proposed reservation. By August 31, the negotiations suddenly took a positive turn. Andrew Seltice (1819-1902), the long-serving chief of the Coeur d'Alene, offered to sell tribal land in the North for $5 an acre if the previous agreement was ratified. Simpson was not satisfied. He thought the price was too high and he wanted additional timber land included in the treaty pointing out the obvious to the tribe, "the more land you let us have, the more money you will get".[229] The treaty negotiations moved to a speedy conclusion. On September 9, 1889, the chief and 143 other members of the Coeur d'Alene tribe signed a treaty in which the tribe ceded an additional 183,000 acres of reservation land to the federal government and the United

States agreed to pay $500,000 to the tribe for the land. The 1889 treaty would not be binding until the Congress ratified the 1887 treaty including the payment of $150,000 previously promised the tribe. The treaty stipulated that the federal payments would be distributed equitably among tribal members.

The Coeur d'Alene had successfully protected the valuable agricultural lands in the southern part of the reservation and had received assurances that the 1887 treaty would be ratified before they lost any additional land. Ben Simpson and his two colleagues had achieved their primary objectives by purchasing much of the timber land, mineral deposits and other property in the northern part of the reservation for the federal government. To the relief of everyone involved, in March 1891, Congress ratified the 1887 treaty as well as the 1889 treaty and also appropriated the $650,000 to be paid to tribal members. Within a year, 1000 homesteaders had filed land claims on the ceded land and by 1893, a fourth commission was dispatched to obtain additional land from the tribe to accommodate avaricious settlers who had encroached on the shrinking reservation.[230]

The Coeur d'Alene Indian Commission was Ben Simpson's last public service in a long career. The Commission had achieved the government objectives by obtaining land in the "unused" part of the reservation. The Commission also enabled the tribe to achieve its goals of protecting the agricultural lands in the southern part of the reservation and ensuring Congressional ratification of the 1887 treaty. The 1889 treaty did not resolve the problems faced by tribal members farming in the ceded lands. The 1889 treaty also appears to have been short-sighted. It consigned the tribe to a future of subsistence farming and enabled non-Indians to exploit the timber, ore deposits, water ways and other natural resources of the ceded territory. In retrospect, there does not seem to have been many alternatives. The United States neither had the means nor the inclination to expel squatters from reservation lands. To the squatters, the land looked "unused". The leaders of the Coeur d'Alene tribe were realistic about their choices and, like tribes before and after, traded one part of their traditional lands to protect another part. The tribe also obtained the assurance that the United States would ratify an earlier treaty.

The pattern was distressingly familiar. It had been replayed countless times along the frontier when settlers wanted lands that had been set aside for the Indians. The government promised land to the Indians and then reclaimed the land when settlers wanted the land for themselves. Rather than protect the Indians and the integrity of previous agreements, the government accommodated the settlers and squatters by arranging further cessions of land. Rather than enforcing the laws and resisting the settlers, the government-initiated processes to change the laws and placate the settlers. The process was a form of official extortion in which the threat of unlawful behavior by settlers was resolved by shrinking the size of the reservation and opening Indian lands to settlement.

Ben Simpson had seen this dynamic in the Platte Purchase in Missouri and had participated in it at the Siletz Reservation in Oregon. For him and for the Indians with whom he was negotiating, it was most likely perceived as a realistic response to a recurring phenomenon. The Indians were reluctant to give up ancestral lands but recognized that they could not hold back the flood of settlers. Giving up some of the land seemed a reasonable compromise if it would protect other land. With 183,000 acres of the reservation opened for settlement and industrial development, the Coeur d'Alene farms were protected, and the tribe was assured that the government would ratify its previous agreement with the tribe. The Simpson Commission had achieved its objectives and obtained the northern lands. In exchange, the Commission had to agree to a substantial payment and to guarantee the ratification of the previous agreement. Their objectives achieved, the members of the Simpson Commission disbanded, and Ben Simpson returned to private life on his Alabama plantation.

The Return to Oregon

Sometime between 1897 and 1902, Ben Simpson sold his Alabama cotton plantation. His last business venture had been a failure. He returned to Oregon soon after the August 1902 death of his third wife and retired in Portland. His son Sam Simpson, the pioneer poet, may have been thinking of his father when he wrote "An Oregon Pioneer" with his "eighty years of love and duty... eighty years of hopes and dreams"

Cherished, honored, slowly passing
To the dim and mystic shore,
Loving life, yet blandly listening
For the silent boatman's oar.[231]

Ben Simpson, the Oregon Pioneer was more than eighty years old when he returned to Oregon. He had lived in Alabama for nearly twenty years and had been unable to attend the annual reunions of Oregon Trail veterans with their bands, banquets, speeches and triumphal processions through downtown Portland. He had missed the reunions of 1883, 1888 and

1889 at which old-timers read selections from his son's long poem "The Campfires of the Pioneers".[232]

By the time of the 31st annual reunion in 1903, Ben Simpson was back in Portland. With his oldest son John, he joined more than 1000 pioneers who had arrived in Oregon before 1859 including 41 other old-timers who marched behind the 1846 banner. If he stayed to the end of the festivities, he heard the principal speaker close the meeting with "a few lines from our own Sam Simpson".[233] In his retirement, Ben Simpson attended several annual gatherings of the Oregon Pioneer Association including the 33rd reunion in 1905 attended by nearly 1400 pioneers. The 1905 reunion was the largest ever held but, for the first time, the program did not include a procession of pioneers. The reunion report described a grand celebration marked by "the uncertain steps of men and women of the ranks of the battle-scared veterans of life's campaign".[234]

Ben Simpson died May 17. 1911 after a fall at 229 Alberta Street, the East Portland home of his daughter Dora S. Killingsworth. He was 92 years old. He had outlived three wives, four children and most of the people who had traveled across the plains with him more than sixty years earlier. The Portland ***Oregonian***, often critical of him, in his lifetime, described him in a headline as "Distinguished in Military, Political and Industrial Life of Community".[235] He was buried in the Simpson family plot at Lone Fir Cemetery in East Portland.

Ben Simpson had led a full and complicated life. He had been captain of a wagon train on the Overland Trail at the age of 28 and in public life in Oregon for more than forty years. He had been an Indian fighter, an Indian Agent and an Indian treaty negotiator. He bravely did his duty and protected Indian oyster rights against poachers at the same place he later connived with others to take Indian land. He was elected to seven terms in the territorial and state legislatures, representing four counties and two political parties. Despite extensive legislative experience, his legislative record was, at best, undistinguished. He seemed to have no particular vision but was swept along by the popular issues of the day. He sponsored legislation to assist Oregon Trail widows and orphans (1851), placed unachievable conditions on proposals for statehood (1852) and competed with other legislators to remove Indian names

Benjamin Simpson's gravestone in the Lone Fir Cemetery in Postland, OR

from Oregon towns (1853). He ran unsuccessfully for the U.S. Senate offering platitudes about moderation in 1866. By his final legislative term(1872), Simpson was a Republican and a foot soldier in Ben Holladay's schemes to build a transportation empire in Oregon.

In contrast to his modest legislative record, Ben Simpson was a remarkably responsible civil servant. He served more than sixteen years between 1863 and 1884 in federal appointive positions (Indian Agent; Surveyor General; Postal Inspector). These were patronage jobs which, as often as not, were neglected by appointees or used for private benefit. In each position, Ben Simpson faced challenges and acted on principle. As Indian Agent at Siletz, he protected Indian oysters against well-connected poachers. As Surveyor General, he warned against fraud in federal land programs. As Postal Inspector, he investigated and confirmed feminist claims of discrimination.

The two most troubling episodes in Simpson's career in Oregon were his attitude toward slavery and his involvement with Ben Holladay. The defense of slavery was not unusual for the time. It was an ugly concoction composed of loyalty to the South, self serving observations about wages and labor supply and racist assumptions about the need to control black people. His beliefs, although strongly held, changed abruptly when the southern states seceded from the union. For Simpson, and for the federal job he held at the time, preservation of the union was more important than states' rights. In his mind, regional differences did not justify armed rebellion.

The most unpleasant episode of Simpson's career was his involvement with Ben Holladay and his minions. Holladay was rich, powerful and unscrupulous. His influence resulted in Ben Simpson's appointments as Surveyor General and Postal Inspector but they came at a price. Simpson conspired with Holladay's crony Senator Mitchell to eviscerate what was left of the Siletz Reservation and he abused his friendship with Judge Deady in an unsuccessful attempt to bring Deady under Holladay's influence. Simpson served honorably in the appointive jobs, but his integrity was severely compromised by his association with Ben Holladay. He lost much of his fortune but returned to Oregon as a respected pioneer. At the time of his 92nd birthday, the Portland ***Oregonian*** called him "A pioneer of prominence in Oregon's up-building" and summarized his long career, "In industry, Indian fighting, politics and common-wealth building, General Simpson left his mark on the affairs of Oregon".[236]

7 The Scholar in Oregon

Sylvester Confucius Simpson (1844-1913) was a man of great early promise.[237] A school mate remembered him as "a man of brilliant intellect... and a man of great learning."[238] Despite a fragmented primary and secondary education, he had earned a Master's degree from Willamette University by the time he was 20 and studied law while teaching Latin and Greek to college students. Before his 25th birthday, he had been appointed Chief Clerk in the State Senate where, according to a prominent Oregon historian, he was "the best clerk the legislature ever had."[239] His father, Ben Simpson, was a widely-known politician and businessman. His mentor, federal judge Matthew P. Deady, was the most respected legal mind in Oregon. Sylvester Simpson was in demand as a writer and public lecturer. Before he was 35, he had served as State Librarian, State Superintendent of Public Instruction and executive assistant to the Governor. But something was missing. He attributed it to a lack of burning ambition. By his 35th birthday, he was ready to leave Oregon and start anew in California. At his death, the historian who had called him the best clerk in Oregon Senate history described his career in California as that of a "legal hack writer".[240]

The oldest son of Ben and Nancy Cooper Simpson, Sylvester Confucius Simpson was born March 21, 1844, in Elm Grove, Platte County, Missouri. He was a two-year old toddler in 1846 when he crossed the plains to Oregon in a wagon train with his parents, two brothers and more than 40 other relatives. He grew up in the crude log cabins of the Willamette Valley learning to read by the light of the fireplace. He was encouraged to read by his mother and enrolled in subscription schools with poorly-trained teachers, few textbooks and no coherent curriculum. His older brother John described the subscription schools the children of the pioneers attended:

> *... we had not sufficient books, in fact we had to dig out everything we learned in any way we could find. On those days we had no public schools, but they were all private schools...* [241]

When Sylvester was very young, his family lived in Oregon City, the largest town in the territory, and the only one with a library. In later years, he attended the Dallas Academy near Salem. Whatever the source, Sylvester Simpson had a life-long love of learning that carried him through college and shaped his early career in Oregon and later California.

Education in Oregon

Sylvester Simpson was an anomaly. He was an educator in a state where education was not highly valued. He was a college graduate in a state where the public remained unconvinced that high school education was necessary. He was passionate about the importance of education in Oregon but too sensitive to criticism to be effective in the bitterly partisan and personally damaging battles of Oregon politics. Public education was one of the areas in which the innate conservatism of the 19th century Oregon residents was most evident. Most residents, like Simpson's parents and grandparents, had attended schools with untrained teachers, ungraded classrooms, chaotic curricula, substandard buildings and brief terms. Many of the pioneers in Oregon were complacent about education and satisfied that the education they had received a generation earlier would be adequate preparation for the future in Oregon. They envisioned a life for their children very much like the life they had lived and saw little need for education beyond the basics.

Peter Burnett (1807-1895), an emigrant of 1843, recounted his experience as a student in a frontier school in Missouri;

> *... we had too much hard work to admit of attending school except at intervals during the summer. At school I learned to spell, read, write, and cipher so far as the rule of supposition, and learned English grammar so far as to be able to parse and punctuate with tolerable accuracy. This was the sum total of my school education.* [242]

Burnett was involved in the provisional government in Oregon in 1844. At the time of the Gold Rush, he went to California where he was elected the first governor.

NOTE *From Wikipedia:* **While in Oregon politics, Peter Burnett pushed for the total exclusion of African Americans from the territory. He authored the "-Burnett's lash law" that authorized the flogging of any free blacks who refused to leave Oregon. He wanted to exterminate all the American Indians too.**

For many of the Oregon pioneers, the sort of education Peter Burnett described was all that was expected and all that was necessary. Other pioneers had higher expectations for their children and, like Simpson's parents, sent their children to whatever subscription school or public common school was available and to the private secondary schools known variously as academies, colleges, institutes or seminaries.

Peter Hardeman Burnett *(1807–1895) Supreme Judge of the Provisional Government of Oregon.*

Elementary Education

The compact creating the 1843 provisional government had pledged that education would be "forever encouraged" in Oregon but establishing schools was more forever than encouraged. Public schools, the so called "common schools" depended on private initiative. Parents, many of whom had attended similar schools in Missouri or other frontier states, paid teachers to operate three-month subscription schools for their children. Missionaries, religious organizations and private individuals created numerous private educational institutions, but Oregon was slow in developing statewide public education. Settlers attempted to establish public schools in several locations but found them difficult to sustain. Residents established short-lived common schools in Polk County in 1846, Tualatin County in 1847 and Portland in 1851 and 1853. The schools operated briefly but were soon closed for lack of money. Portland ran out of money for education in 1857 and closed all public schools in the city for a full year.[243]

The public was generally supportive of the idea of public elementary education but was opposed to the idea that public education might continue beyond the elementary years. The early secondary schools in Oregon were entirely the result of private initiative, religious denominations or a combination of the two. Mrs. N.M. Thornton opened a ladies seminary in Oregon City in 1847. Catholics established a school for boys in French Prairie and one for girls in Oregon City. Under various auspices and for varying periods of time, private secondary schools provided high school instruction in Dallas, Portland, Santiam, Sheridan, Sublimity and other communities. The first public high school in Oregon opened in Portland in 1869, a full decade after Oregon became a state.[244] Progress was slow. With the exception of a popular spelling book which an enterprising Oregon printer republished in 1847, there were few textbooks available. During the territorial period, the only library in Oregon was the one opened in Oregon City in 1847. The library had a total of 500 books.[245]

The delegates to the Oregon Constitutional Convention of 1857 discussed education. They correctly anticipated that the federal government would grant 500,000 acres of public land to Oregon to create an endowment for public education. The constitution that Oregon voters approved included a common school fund to support schools and libraries as well as a university fund. The constitution authorized the legislative assembly to "provide by law for the establishment of a uniform and general system of common schools" and directed the legislature to distribute the proceeds of the common school fund among the counties using a formula based on the proportion of children in each county between the ages of 4 and 20. The constitution created a separate fund for higher education but prohibited use of the fund or its proceeds for ten years. The 1857 constitution provided for a superintendent of public instruction but assigned the duties of that office to the governor for the first five years.[246] The Delegates to the Constitutional Convention intended to draft a document which, apart from the divisive issue of slavery, would be widely-acceptable to Oregon voters. The compromise on education was to authorize the state to capture federal funds for education but to postpone decisions about the structure, financing, teacher qualifications and curriculum of a public education system in Oregon. As it turned out, the five-year moratorium incorporated in the 1857 constitution continued fifteen years.

Higher Education

Until 1862, when the Morrill Act made federal land grants available for public higher education, most colleges and universities in the United State were private in origin and governance. There were exceptions, like the University of North Carolina which had operated as a public university since 1795, but most states, relied on religious denominations and private initiative for their higher education. In Oregon, several denominational schools established as academies during the Territorial period evolved into private colleges. The earliest of these was the Methodist missionary school which became Willamette University in 1853. A second school was established by Tabitha Brown, a widow who traveled the Overland Trail in 1846. Mrs. Brown was concerned about children whose parents had died on the Overland Trail. She opened an "orphan school" in 1847 which became Tualatin Academy in 1849 and, with support of the Congregational Church, Pacific University in 1863. The Disciples of Christ established Bethel Collegiate Institute in 1853 and Monmouth University in 1855. The Baptists founded Baptist College in McMinnville in 1858. The Methodist Episcopal Church, South sponsored Corvallis Academy (later Corvallis College) in 1858, Presbyterians formed Albany College in 1866, and the United Brethren established Philomath College in 1867. Several of these pioneer institutions have survived to become distinguished private colleges and universities including Lewis and Clark College (formerly Albany College), Linfield College (formerly Baptist College), Pacific University and Willamette University.[247] By 1876, when the University of Oregon enrolled its first students, there were eight denominational colleges and 28 academies operating in Oregon.

Oregon was slow to respond to the incentive provided by federal land grants for higher education. The state was entitled to 60,000 acres of federal lands under the1862 Morrill Act. The land grants were intended to support education in science and agriculture. Despite the incentives, Oregon delayed developing public higher education until 1876 when the University of Oregon opened with five faculty members, 80 college students, 97 students preparing for college and no library. In 1883, the Methodist College at Corvallis became the Oregon State Agricultural College.[248] Other states emphasized teacher training by creating two-year "normal schools"' to train public school teachers. Michigan opened a normal school in 1853 followed within five years by Illinois, Minnesota, Missouri and Rhode Island. California established a normal school in 1862. Oregon followed in 1882 opening normal schools at Ashland (now Southern Oregon University) and Monmouth (now Western Oregon University). The state's commitment to teacher training was short-lived. In 1909, the state legislature abolished the three normal schools then operating in Oregon and conducted a referendum on which school should survive.[249]

Willamette University

Truly the "Pioneer University", Willamette was the first university established west of the Rocky Mountains and one of the first in the nation to enroll both women and men.[250] Located in Salem, across the street from what would later be the Oregon state capitol, Willamette trained the children of the pioneers to be the teachers, lawyers, doctors, ministers and other leaders the developing state would need. Methodist missionaries who came to Oregon in 1834 had established a training school for Indians in 1842. After it became evident that the Indian training school was not serving its intended purpose, the missionaries re-branded it as the Oregon Institute in 1844 and began enrolling emigrant children. In 1853, the Oregon Institute obtained a charter from the territorial legislature as "Wallomet" University for instruction in "principles of virtue and the elements of liberal knowledge". The new university graduated its first student, a woman, in 1859 and a second student, also a woman, in 1862. The Willamette class of 1863 included twelve students including one who would be a justice of the Oregon Supreme Court and one who would be Superintendent of Schools in Portland.

During the 1860s, Willamette operated a large preparatory program and a small college-level program. In 1864, the year Sylvester Simpson graduated, Willamette enrolled 264 students of whom 40 were in the four-year baccalaureate program. Collegiate students could choose between classical studies leading to a Bachelor of Arts degree and scientific studies leading to a Bachelor of Sciences degree. The classical course required higher mathematics, natural science, Latin, Greek and at least one foreign language. The scientific course was similar but required less Latin and no Greek.[251] Students were required to pass examinations at the end of each term and in preparation for graduation. All courses were graded on a ten-point scale with the expectation that the highest score would be awarded rarely in cases of exceptional performance. Students averaging five or less over a term would not be promoted.

Willamette was established and governed by Methodists but was explicit, as early as 1865, that it was "by no means a sectarian institution". Like many colleges of the period, Willamette required all students to attend prayers each morning and "some place of divine worship, and a lecture on the Scriptures"" each Sunday. Students who failed to attend the daily chapel or Sunday services received demerits like those for poor performance in classroom recitation. The academic calendar of the 1860s would be familiar to any student of the semester system. The fall semester began in September, and a spring semester began in February with a short winter vacation and a long summer vacation. The only anomaly was that commencement ceremonies were in July. Students paid quarterly tuition of $7.50 to $10 in 1864-1865 with additional fees for music, art and modem language instruction. Men and women in the collegiate program took courses together but were assigned to separate study rooms and used separate entrances to the chapel.[252]

With 40 students in the collegiate program in 1864-1865, Willamette had a small faculty with instructors in moral philosophy, mathematics, natural sciences and ancient languages. Thomas M. Gatch (1833-1913) was president of Willamette during the period Sylvester Simpson was a student. Gatch was a graduate of Ohio Wesleyan and had studied at Lane Theological Seminary in Cincinnati. He was the grandson of a prominent Methodist evangelist but was not himself an ordained minister. Gatch was president of Willamette from 1860 to 1865 and again from 1870 to 1879. He later served as president of the University of Washington and Oregon State College. In 1866, an anonymous editorial writer, presumably Sam Simpson, assessed each of key members of the Willamette faculty. He found the new president "a man of extensive acquirements", the mathematics professor a "complete master of his particular branch" and his brother, S.C. Simpson, Professor of Ancient Languages, "young but capable". According to Sam Simpson, himself a recent Willamette graduate, "... there should be no reason why Willamette University should not become the Yale of the Pacific slope".[253]

Despite the tiny student body, Willamette students of the 1860s organized a variety of extra-curricular activities including literary societies and student publications. The literary groups, including the Hesperian Society and the Alka Society, provided a forum for students and Salem residents to present papers on a variety of subjects. During the period Sylvester Simpson was an undergraduate, some topic or opinion offended the Willamette administration. In 1863, the University adopted policies requiring that any paper presented at a literary society be reviewed and approved by the faculty before presentation. The following year, the University banned non-students from participation in campus literary societies. The policies were sufficiently flexible that Sylvester Simpson was able to participate in a debate at the Hesperian Society in 1867.

Student publications, like ***The Willamette Chronicle, The Gem*** and ***The Protean***, were an outlet for student humor and imagination. They were distributed in a hand written form and filled with puns, bad jokes, imaginary correspondents and unlikely events.[254] Sylvester Simpson was the editor of The Protean while he was an undergraduate at Willamette. In an eight-page, hand-written copy on lined paper, Simpson complained about the "affected, unnatural style" in which he was forced to write in order to amuse his readers. He included a poem by Charles W. Kahler of the Class of 1865, an essay on "Temperance", a short story, assorted jokes and a spurious letter from an information-starved reader in Salt Lake City requesting a dozen copies of the Willamette student newspaper.[255]

Charles B. Moores, a Salem lawyer and 1870 Willamette graduate, wrote many years later of the five Simpson children who graduated from the University. About Sylvester Simpson he observed, "No man of stronger intellect ever passed the portals of Willamette."[256] After his graduation, Willamette hired Simpson as a Professor of Ancient Languages. The little university was growing. Simpson was one of seven students graduating in the class of 1864. Two years later, the graduating class had nineteen students including Sylvester Simpson's future wife Frances McFarland and his younger brother Sam. Three of Sylvester Simpson's sisters, Louisa, Class of 1867, Eleanora. Class of 1869 and Dora, Class of 1872 also graduated from Willamette and became teachers in Oregon.[257] Pacific University in Forest Grove, the successor to Tabitha Brown's orphan school, graduated its first student, Harvey W. Scott, in 1863. Scott, the brother of feminist crusader Abigail Scott Duniway, went on to be the influential editor of the Portland Oregonian where he was a determined opponent to the suffrage his sister advocated and a fierce critic of Sylvester Simpson and his efforts to reform public education in Oregon.

Early in its history, Willamette began to hold annual alumni reunions. Beginning in 1866, the Willamette reunions featured brief and humorous reports on the events in the lives of the graduates of the tiny university. The reports were generally light in tone with puns, silly jokes, inflated rhetoric and classical allusions. As the years went on, the reports added somber reflections on the deaths of classmates while poking fun at lawyers, doctors and people's names. Sylvester Simpson was invited in 1866 to prepare the first of these reports which he chose to call "***Annals***". He set the tone for the ***Annals*** when he announced this is an ambitious narrative like the Annals of Tacitus, "telling of grand events in great swelling words".[258]

Simpson's ***Annals*** began with the earliest class. He reported "Since our last reunion, the whole class has got married and all to one man." He reassured the alumni that the class of 1859 had not taken up plural marriage but that it had but a lone graduate.[259] Simpson prepared the ***Annals*** intermittently for several years. He interjected opinions about certain professions like the graduate from the class of 1863 "who [was] contributing to the Polk County grave-yards... he is a "regular' practicing physician" or "the class of '65 is greatly afflicted, every man in it is a lawyer"[260] He conveyed attitudes like his comment about an 1869 graduate who "... is at some town in California whose name I can't pronounce".[261] He did not let family loyalty interfere with his barbs, reporting that his sister Dora of the class of 1872 was living in Eugene and "married to a man with the very ominous name of Killingsworth".[262] The Annals were inclusive and fun. They were an annual reminder of the special nature of that first generation of women and men who had grown up on the Oregon frontier and earned college degrees at Willamette.

Post Civil War Oregon Politics

Democrats, including particularly the "Salem Clique", had dominated Oregon politics through the territorial period but had splintered over slavery and related issues in the period leading up to the Civil War. With the Democratic Party split into two factions, Oregon voted narrowly for Abraham Lincoln in 1860.[263] In the period after the Civil War, Democrats regrouped and shared power with Republicans until about 1880 when Republicans began to take over. From statehood in 1859 to 1880, four of six Oregon governors and nine of fourteen Members of Congress were Democrats. The pattern shifted abruptly about 1880. During the last twenty years of the 19th century, three of four Oregon governors and all fourteen representatives elected to the House were Republicans.

Sylvester Simpson was 22 years old and recently out of Willamette University when he entered Oregon politics in 1866. After graduation, he had continued at Willamette teaching Latin and Greek while also studying law in a lawyer's office. By 1866, he had a law office at the Library Block in Salem when his father asked him and his brother Sam, neither of whom had any professional journalism experience, to edit a Salem newspaper supporting Ben Simpson's candidacy for the United States Senate. After the failed Senate campaign, Sylvester held a series of senior staff positions in the legislative and executive branches of Oregon state government. These positions coincided with a period of realignment in Oregon politics as power began shifting from the Democratic Party to the Republican Party.

Ben Simpson had been elected to the legislature in Oregon six times as a Democrat before 1870. During the Civil War, he had supported the Union faction of the Democratic Party but had found that the Republican Party was more aligned with his interests in business and economic development. By 1872, when he ran for the legislature from Benton County, he had completed the transition to the Republican Party. The Republican affiliation also assisted him in competing for appointments from Republican presidents to the salaried positions he later held as Surveyor-General and Postal Inspector. Sylvester Simpson was a Democrat, and his career depended entirely on appointments by fellow Democrats. Democrats held a 13 to 9 majority in the Oregon State Senate in 1868, when Sylvester Simpson was first elected Chief Clerk and continued to control the Senate to 1878 when he completed his sixth and final term as Chief Clerk. After 1878, Republicans maintained uninterrupted control of the Oregon State Senate for twenty years.

The Oregon Legislature met for six weeks in September and October in even numbered years. In the interstices between Senate sessions, Sylvester Simpson sought other jobs and sources of income. After the 1870 legislative session, Simpson accepted a chair in the Medical Department of Willamette University and "some little smatters of business"· which filled his time.[264] Lafayette Grover (1823-1911), a Democrat, was governor of Oregon from 1870 to 1877. In May 1871, Governor Grover appointed Sylvester Simpson to be the 14th State Librarian of Oregon. The state librarian was primarily responsible for maintaining legislative records as the state did not have a general-purpose library at the time. The State Library collected laws of other states, Congressional reports and federal laws as well as the records of the legislative Assembly in Oregon. In 1876, five years after Simpson was librarian, the state library had about 7000 volumes. Simpson served in the nonpartisan position until September 1872 when the legislative assembly reconvened and he returned to the Chief Clerk position in the Senate. In January 1872, Governor Grover appointed Simpson to be the first Superintendent of Public Instruction for Oregon. He served less than two years and resigned in September 1874 at the time of the biannual session of the legislative assembly.

Public Intellectual

In addition to teaching at Willamette and practicing law in Salem. Sylvester Simpson was busy early in his career as a public lecturer and writer on a variety of topics. He presented the first of his Annals for the Willamette University alumni in 1866. The following year, he debated the proposition that Congress should suppress polygamy in Utah. He argued that Congress did not have the authority to prohibit polygamy and that "religious heresies are not to be crushed by violence".[265] By the time he was 30, he had built a reputation in Oregon as a public intellectual. He wrote articles, debated and lectured on a wide range of current topics. Some of his speeches were ceremonial, like those prepared for the Fourth of July or a college commencement, while others were intended to be inspirational or motivational, Like those presented at temperance societies or promoting missionary work.

In one lecture, he advocated vigorously for the abolition of the death penalty which he described as "...a hideous, unchristian, inhumane thing".[266] He argued, in great detail, that the public hangings of his time had little deterrent value, prevented repentance and diminished the sacredness of human life. In a debate, he argued that executive pardons for convicted criminals were an anachronism and should be abolished. The pardoning power, in his view. "robs the law of its terrors by diminishing the certainty of its penalties".[267]

Simpson tried to select topics which would be interesting and uplifting for his audiences. He gave a long lecture to the Portland YMCA on the life and work of George Peabody (1795-1869), an Anglo-American financier and philanthropist. Simpson was intrigued by Peabody because he was "equally great in the accumulation of wealth and in the charitable distribution of it."[268] The lecture followed Peabody from modest origins in Danvers, Massachusetts to success as an international banker in London and his philanthropic investments in libraries and educational institutions in the United States (Baltimore; Kenyon College; Phillips Andover Academy; the Southern Education Fund; Yale). Simpson was prescient in his choice of topics. The education fund Peabody endowed became the first general purpose foundation in the United States and the model which Andrew Carnegie, John D. Rockefeller and others have followed ever since.[269].

The Peabody lecture had been well-received, and Simpson was exploring possible topics for his next YMCA lecture. He suggested the life of robber baron James Fisk, Jr. but was troubled that the story did not "point a moral". Fisk (1835-1872) was an unscrupulous but enormously successful New York financier who was murdered by a rival over the affections of an actress. The lurid tale failed to satisfy Simpson because, "Punishment with her lame foot did not overtake [Fisk)".[270] Judge Deady was not impressed with the proposed Fisk lecture and suggested that Simpson consider an alternative topic like the 1871 Geneva Peace Conference. Simpson replied modestly,

> *I am woefully ignorant on the subject. I know comparatively nothing about the treaty... Besides my knowledge of general history is neither very minute nor very accurate.*[271]

Despite his initial misgivings, Simpson accepted Judge Deady's advice and prepared a long lecture on the Geneva Conference.

Simpson's concluded that the international tribunal at Geneva was "a decided forward step in the march of Christian Civilization" because it provided a setting to resolve international disputes without warfare. The United States had claimed that it suffered damages when Great Britain violated the Neutrality Act by building ships for the Confederate navy during the Civil War. In 1872, the two countries agreed to submit their dispute to arbitration by an impartial panel composed of one representative from the United States, one from Great Britain and three from other countries. The Geneva judges found that the United States had suffered losses as a result of the neutrality violations and ordered Great Britain to pay the United States $15.5 million.[272]

Judge Deady attended Simpson's Geneva Conference lecture at the Portland YMCA with a lady friend. He did not comment on the substance of the lecture but was critical of the presentation. The Judge wrote in his diary that it was "A good lecture. Just made and a little ***raw*** [emphasis in original] yet, particularly in delivery."[273]

Despite his protestations of "ignorance", Simpson seemed to be able to make nearly any issue interesting and instructive. He wrote a particularly subtle speech on the true nature of charity in which he boldly examined the delicate issue of Indians in Oregon. He had grown up on Indian reservations and spoke from painful experience about "the degraded, diseased, dying remnants of the noble people that formerly possessed our country". Rather than blame the Indians, he emphasized the settlers' responsibility for the situation.

> *By conquering the Indians and circumscribing their territory, we have stopped their natural progress; we have destroyed their vitality as a people.*

He rejected current Indian policy explaining "We cannot force them to keep step in the march of civilization". He recalled observing the eloquence of chiefs preparing for battle and proposed an alternative approach based in Indian culture. He urged those intending to assist the Indians to "learn the language, find out their habits of mind..." Simpson's suggestions were a dramatic departure from the policies that had guided his father to confine tribes and attempt to transform them into farmers. Sylvester Simpson argued that true charity demanded Indian policies with far more respect for the Indians and their culture.[274]

In many ways, Simpson was least effective in the patriotic speeches he was asked to prepare for the Fourth of July[275] and the inspirational speeches he presented for temperance and missionary organizations. In one speech, he combined patriotism and temperance arguing that temperance was patriotic.[276] In another, he denied that the subject of temperance had been exhausted leaving nothing new to say.[277] In a third, he advocated the prohibition of liquor sales, as he put it, to "hurl King Alcohol out of the world".[278] In these statements to sympathetic audiences, he never explained that his interest in temperance was not entirely theoretical but based in concern about a close relative. In addition to his temperance work, Simpson also promoted missionary efforts, as he said, "to spread the light of the gospel among the heathen".[279] In contrast to the lectures which challenged his audiences to consider new ideas, the patriotic, temperance and missionary lectures offered few if any insights. They seem to have been intended to reinforce existing ideas rather than introduce new information or concepts. They offered few new ideas and reflected the attitudes of the times.

In contrast to the patriotic and inspirational speeches, Simpson engaged in public debates which allowed him to express controversial opinions without taking personal responsibility for them. In one such debate, he argued with great precision that the Mexican War was not a "just war".[280] In another essay, he relied on moral relativism to defend Brutus's assassination of Caesar.[281] Simpson wrote essays on many topics. Some were serious, like his critique of philosophical stoicism, in which he argued that contentment is neither attainable nor desirable.[282] Some of his essays were satirical and some were difficult to categorize. The "Farmers Movement" told of a populist uprising in which farmers organized against railroads, land speculators, bankers and others who oppressed them.[283] Was the essay predicting the future, reporting on the emergence of the Grange movement in Oregon or was it simply a fantasy? He left the question unanswered.

Sylvester Simpson had a fifteen-year career in Oregon. From his graduation from Willamette in 1864 to his departure for California in 1879, he was continually writing and speaking to various Oregon audiences. During this period, he was starting a family, beginning to practice law and scrambling for political appointments. He was located in Salem near the University and its library, and he was remarkably well-informed about current events and personalities. He knew about education reform in British boarding schools, the benefactions of obscure philanthropists and the downfall of wayward tycoons. When he did not know about the Geneva Convention, he promptly found out and turned it into a lecture for the YMCA. In some cases, like the speech about Indian policy, be spoke from experience but also displayed his awareness of emerging trends in national policy. Many of his speeches and essays were intended to introduce new ideas and challenge conventional thinking. He also used his rhetorical skills to motivate graduates, missionary gatherings and temperance organizations. For fifteen years, he was an intellectual celebrity in Oregon.

Sylvester Simpson and Education

Many of Simpson's best speeches and essays addressed issues in education. He had been thinking about education since he finished college in 1864. He was only 21 years old in 1865 when he prepared a "Course of Studies for District Schools in Oregon". He reviewed and rejected the approach used in other states because he felt it did not fit the attitudes and circumstances in Oregon. The curriculum he envisioned for Oregon would:

> *... be both preparatory and to a certain extent complete in itself. It would give the students a thirst for knowledge which would spur on those who had the means to still further attainments while it would fit those who can go no farther for entering immediately into active life.*[284]

He suggested that the Oregon common schools devote less time to geography because it relied excessively on memorization of facts and neglected thinking skills. He also suggested that Chemistry be introduced into the common school curriculum because of its practical application in agriculture.

In a lecture and newspaper article entitled "A Plea for Free Education", Simpson directly challenged those residents of Oregon who objected to tax-supported education. He asserted that public schools were "the proudest boast and glory of a state". He justified public education as a benefit for the society as a whole and an essential component of a democratic society. He argued that "The only safety is in the state taking the beginnings of culture by establishing a free system of popular instruction". He pointed out that the $150,000 the state currently allocated for public education each year provided less than $4 annually for each of 39,000 school age children in Oregon. He advocated for an increase in school taxes and an extension of the school year from three months to six months.[285]

As he had in his 1865 "Course of Studies" essay, he discussed the purpose of education emphasizing the distinction between "stuffing" the student with facts and learning how to think, what he called "drawing out". The idea that education involved "drawing out" has its origins in Plato's "Crito" written more than 2000 years earlier but was a fresh alternative to the rote memorization that passed for learning in 19th century pedagogy. Some years later, Simpson spoke to an audience of graduating college students, several of whom were likely to become teachers, and reiterated the distinction. As he explained to the graduates, the "aim of education is not knowledge but learning. The object is not to know things so much as to learn things"[286]

Sylvester Simpson went beyond ideas for incremental school reform in a provocative series of 1866 editorials he published in the Salem newspaper his father owned. The younger Simpson argued that public education was so important to national "growth and prosperity" that it should be part of a national system. He was critical of local school systems for diminishing the importance of education:

> *... in most of the States the instruction of the young has been deemed by a majority of the citizens to be a matter of merely secondary importance, always ranking after the ephemeral political issues which are in continual agitation before us; and that the school laws have been sadly neglected even by the mediocre men who generally compose our State legislatures.*[287]

He was vague about the details of a national system except that it would incorporate the successful models used in the New England states, would attract teachers of higher quality and would not necessarily increase the cost of education. He dismissed criticism that the idea was "utopian" pointing out that Scotland and Prussia had each established successful national education systems.

Simpson also used lectures to motivate teachers. In a lecture on "Arnold of Rugby", he used the example of the legendary British school master and educational reformer Thomas Arnold (1795-1842) to inspire teachers to "gain success and distinction". The lecture was based on the improbable assumption that public school teachers in Oregon would perceive commonalities with the headmaster of an ancient British boarding school. As Simpson explained, "ambition finds its surest stimulus in another's fame" and the Rugby School Headmaster was "one of the great heroes of our own profession".[288] Simpson, who was beginning to have his own doubts, may have been trying to locate a role model to stimulate his own ambition.

No topic seemed beyond his scope or interest, but education was a common theme throughout his essays and speeches. For him, education was the social mechanism through which individuals, groups and societies advanced. He talked about the purpose and importance of education in the graduation speeches he gave and in essays like "A Plea for Free Education" where he advocated for increased school taxes and an extended school year. He promoted education by attracting attention to educational reformers like "Arnold of Rugby" and philanthropists like George Peabody. His speech on the true nature of charity turned out to be a lesson in culturally-sensitive education. Most of all, he embodied the education he was promoting. He was the role model for the change he advocated and a logical candidate to reform the public education system of the state of Oregon.

A Man Will Do Much for His Brother

Sylvester Simpson's younger brother Sam was a talented but troubled soul. During his adult years in Oregon, Sylvester Simpson frequently spoke in public but rarely if ever mentioned his brother although there were many occasions when his brother's story might have added dimension or credibility to the lecture. Sam Simpson had been highly regarded as an undergraduate at Willamette and became prominent in Oregon after the 1868 publication of his poem "Beautiful Willamette". Sylvester did not mention Sam in his annual Annals of Willamette, and he did not talk about Sam in his lectures at temperance societies. Sylvester and Sam Simpson were nearly the same age. They had grown up together on the Indian Reservation, attended Willamette University at nearly the same time, worked together as editors of their father's newspaper and had each become lawyers at a young age. The similarities stopped with issues of personality and behavior. Sylvester was scholarly and sober. Samuel was clever, engaging and unable to hold a job because of his drinking problem.

Sylvester was deeply loyal to his younger brother and repeatedly tried to help him obtain jobs in the vain hope that steady employment would result in sobriety. He wrote:

> *... with all his weaknesses, my brother has many noble and worthy qualities and abilities of no mean order, and I would give my right hand to see him take the place among men he ought to occupy.*[289]

Sylvester used euphemisms like "habits" or "weaknesses" when discussing his brother's drinking but did not give up hope that his brother's behavior would change if he had the right job. He explained that there was a "fraternal feeling tugging at my heart" and that "A man will do much for his brother".[290] His feeling of obligation to his brother would eventually complicate his own career.

Oregon Code Commission

In 1872, the Oregon legislature created a commission to revise and reorganize the state legal codes. The legislature appointed Judge Mathew Deady to lead the commission. Deady was the obvious choice. He was widely-respected and had successfully undertaken a similar project at the time of statehood. Sylvester Simpson was elated when he was also named to the commission. For the first time, it would enable him to work with Judge Deady as a colleague, albeit one expecting deference. Simpson wrote the Judge, "I appreciate the unexpected and under-served honor of being associated with you in so important a trust".[291] The appointment also had a second attraction. It paid a stipend of $5 a day to commissioners.[292] Describing himself as an "impecunious fellow", Simpson admitted that the money would be important to him.

Sylvester Simpson had started to plan the work of the commission when Governor Lafayette Grover became aware that Simpson would be drawing two state salaries. The Governor offered Simpson the choice between serving as a Code Commissioner or as Superintendent of Public Instruction. The Governor explained that there was no legal obstacle to one person holding two jobs but that it would be politically untenable for Simpson to be paid two state salaries. Simpson was disappointed but he accepted the position of superintendent because, as he told Judge Deady, it offered a higher salary.[293] Governor Grover appointed Lafayette Lane (1842-1896) to replace Simpson on the Commission. Lane was the son of Oregon's first territorial governor. The younger Lane represented Oregon for one term in the U.S. Congress in 1877-1879.

Although he had started work as Superintendent in late January 1873, Simpson continued to complain about being forced off the Code Commission. He made high minded arguments like "I have an ambition to have my name associated in some way with the work... "which he undermined with schemes about how he might share in some of the salary of the clerk to the commission or collect pay for work he had done before becoming state superintendent. He lashed out at the people who he blamed for forcing him to resign from the Code Commission:

> *I owe it to Bush and Bill Watkins that I have been driven to this resignation. I don't care a fig for their opposition but I confess I don't understand it".*[294]

Asahel Bush was not a good man to antagonize. He had been the leader of the "Salem Clique" and most influential person in the Oregon Democratic

Party since 1850. He was the territorial and state printer from 1850 to 1864, founding editor of the ***Oregon Statesman*** and a successful banker in Salem. William H. Watkins (1835-I 889) was a saddle and harness maker who was active in the Democratic Party. He was appointed Superintendent of the Oregon State Penitentiary by Governor Grover. These critics were loyal Democrats and supporters of Governor Grover.

For someone who had been involved in Oregon politics, Simpson seems to have been surprisingly stubborn about his situation. His desperate efforts to increase his income blinded him to the obvious reality that the state should not be paying two salaries to one person however talented or hard working that person might be. The issue was not the intervention of political enemies but a simple matter of political realism which he chose to ignore. As time went by, Simpson ceased complaining that he was forced to choose between state jobs, but he persisted in his efforts to get money from the Code Commission. Three months into his work as Superintendent of Public Instruction, he requested payment "for services as Code Commissioner up to the time of my resignation" explaining, in plain English, "I am in need of money".[295]

A Growing Family

Sylvester Simpson was two years out of college in 1866 when he married Frances McFarland who had been one of his students at Willamette. Mary Frances McFarland (1848-1905), called Frances or Fanny, was born in Indianapolis, Indiana, the daughter of John Jacob Mcfarland (1802-1884) and his second wife Desidera Metzger McFarland (1806-1884), a milliner from Harrisburg, Pennsylvania. With her parents, Frances McFarland sailed to Oregon in 1851 and settled in Salem. She graduated from Willamette in 1866, in a class of ten men and nine women, and married Sylvester Simpson October 11, 1866. (Appendix VI) He reported the marriage to the Willamette alumni in the ***Annals*** of 1875. In an awkward attempt at humor, Simpson called his wife "Frank McFarland".[296] The two young Simpsons immediately began a family. Their son Ernest was born in 1867, followed at two-year intervals by Lynn in 1869, Frank in 1871, Myrtle in 1873, Dessie in 1875 and Ray in 1877. Three additional children were born in California after 1879. (Appendix IV).

With five young children, income was a nagging concern for Sylvester and Frances Simpson. The need to increase his income had led Simpson into the untenable situation in which he was drawing two state salaries and the unpleasant choice between the job he wanted and the job with the higher salary. Although he was only in his early thirties, Sylvester Simpson was nearing the top of the public sector salary scale in Oregon. In 1876, for example, the Governor, Secretary of State and Superintendent of Public Instruction were paid $1500 a year while the Governor's Private Secretary was paid $1200 and the State Librarian $500. Salaries were slightly better at Willamette in 1876 where the president was paid $2000 a year and professors $1400.[297] Simpson changed jobs frequently and worked at concurrent jobs to increase his income. He earned erratic fees from his law practice. There is no record whether he received honoraria for the many lectures and articles he prepared in the 1860s and 1870s. Whatever the sources and amounts of his income he earned, he found it inadequate to support his family.

Superintendent of Public Instruction

The choice between the Code Commission and the Schools turned out to be a choice between nonpartisan legal research with a respected federal judge and a partisan position battling political opponents, educators and newspaper editors objecting to every reform. Sylvester Simpson was taking on the responsibility for the creation of a uniform, statewide system of public education in Oregon. Public education in Oregon had been neglected. It was independently administered by 22 locally-elected county superintendents who supervised schools in 578 local districts. The state school fund had been poorly managed and provided support for about three months of instruction. Some districts had imposed taxes and subscription fees to extend the school year but most of the schools in Oregon had short school years and high teacher turnover. School buildings in Oregon reflected the pattern of neglect. The buildings were cheaply built and poorly maintained. One county superintendent appraised the school buildings in his district:

> *Some of them are bad; and some are worse; and many of them are a disgrace to the people of Marion County and an insult to the civilization of the nineteenth century..* [298]

County superintendents often held other, full-time jobs. They allocated funds among schools, certified teachers and too-infrequently visited the schools in their county. Local districts selected the textbooks to be used, often following the preference of the teachers. Parents provided the books.

Sylvester Simpson was a logical candidate for the superintendent position. He had been lecturing and writing about the purposes of education and the ways in which public education in Oregon should be reformed for several years. As early as 1865, he had proposed that Oregon schools should offer a uniform curriculum that would serve those students preparing for higher education as well as those for whom the common school would be the extent of their education. He had proposed specific curriculum modifications, reducing instruction in geography and increasing chemistry, to increase the practical value of the education and to improve critical thinking. In later years, he advocated for increased school budgets and an extended school year.

By the time he became State Superintendent, Simpson had concluded that the core problem in the Oregon schools was the chaotic curriculum and the absence of a uniform set of textbooks. He described the situation:

> *Diversity of textbooks has been the bane of the public schools of Oregon. Prior to the enactment of the [1872 school] law, this was a constant source of complaint from our teachers. They contended, and justly, that it was impossible to organize their schools or classify their pupils properly while this diversity existed. In some schools, owing to the diversity in textbooks, it was necessary to have almost as many classes as there were pupils.*[299]

While he was frank about the reforms he sought, Sylvester Simpson was also realistic about the attitudes of many Oregonians toward education and the nature of the opposition reformers could expect. In 1865, he had written that the frontier experiences of so many Oregonians had:

> *... given to our people a peculiar character... given them great strength of will and tenacity of purpose; hence, many of them will obstinately oppose any change in the system of education to which they have been accustomed.*[300]

He anticipated that there would be opposition to reform but he was unprepared for its persistence and the fierce personal attacks he would suffer. He assumed incorrectly that his critics were operating in good faith and would listen to reason. He was wrong.

The Oregon constitution of 1857 had placed the responsibility for managing the school fund and serving as school superintendent with the governor for the first five years of statehood. The Oregon legislature dithered an additional ten years before authorizing the transfer of the management of the schools from the governor's office to a new State Board of Education. The School Law of 1872 became effective January 29, 1873, and the following day Governor Grover appointed 29 year old Sylvester Simpson, the former state Librarian, to be Oregon's first state Superintendent of Public Instruction. The 1872 law specified that the State Board of Education would be composed of three state officials (Governor. Secretary of State;

Superintendent of Public Instruction) and provided for the appointment of educators, called "assistants" in the statute, to advise the board. The assistants appointed in 1873 included the presidents of Willamette University and Corvallis College, a professor from Pacific University; a representative from the Portland schools and the administrator of a seminary in Oregon City.[301]

The objective of the Oregon School Law of 1872 was to create an uniform, statewide system of common schools. This included the selection of a common set of textbooks for use throughout the state, the establishment of statewide teacher certification standards, increased school visitation and the adoption of "rules and regulations" for the schools. Each of these activities involved the expansion of the role of the state at the expense of the county superintendent. Simpson explained in his report to the legislature,

> *... it has been necessary to make many innovations upon the former state of things... The fact that I have had to bear the principal share of the disfavor with which many of these necessary changes have been received has not, to say the least of it, made the office a very pleasant one to me.*[302]

Much of the disfavor and unpleasantness arose in response to the selection of textbooks. What the reformers saw as "state uniformity" critics called the "school-book monopoly".

The legislature had anticipated the possibility that textbook selection might be a source of controversy. The 1872 school law attempted to mollify the county superintendents by requiring their approval of all textbooks recommended for adoption and by limiting the adoptions to four years. To encourage the use of the statewide approved texts, the 1872 law also provided that payments from the state school fund could be withheld from districts which refused to use the approved textbooks. The Board of Education reviewed books in use in Oregon schools and recommended the adoption of ten broadly available and familiar textbooks and copy books in arithmetic, geography, grammar, history, and penmanship for grammar schools and eight science, algebra and composition books for advanced grades. In addition, the state Board of Education recommended the selection of a new sequence of five readers and a speller called the Pacific Coast series which A.L. Bancroft & Co. of San Francisco was preparing.

In August 1873, Sylvester Simpson wrote the county superintendents requesting their approval of the readers and speller of the Pacific Coast Series. At the time of the county superintendents' decision, the Pacific Coast series was not complete. Bancroft had hired A. W. Patterson, a physician from Eugene, Oregon, to write the first three readers and the speller and

Sylvester Simpson's talented but troubled younger brother, Sam, to write the fourth and fifth readers. The county superintendents reviewed incomplete copies of the Pacific Coast series and voted in September 1873 to adopt the Pacific Coast series as Sylvester Simpson had recommended. The vote was sixteen for the Pacific Coast series, four for Harper's series and two for that of another publisher.[303] By September 1874, Simpson reported that 453 of the 578 school districts in Oregon were using the Pacific Coast readers and that no district had been penalized with the loss of school funds.[304]

There was no significant controversy about the adoption of the eighteen textbooks currently in use but there was wild and prolonged criticism of the Pacific Coast series. The initial reviews of the Pacific Coast readers had been favorable. Benjamin Simpson, by this time a Republican, but a concerned father, asked Matthew Deady to write a letter of support for the readers,

> *Will you be kind enough to write a correspondence to the Oregonian favoring the adoption of the series of readers now in course of compilation by Bancroft & Co. in San Francisco? My object is asking this favor is that Sam L. Simpson is doing the work... is conducting himself well at present... an endorsement from you would be a great favor.*[305]

In September 1873, a teacher in Oregon City and a reporter in the Portland Oregonian wrote favorable reviews of the new series. In January 1874, the ***Oregon Statesman*** and the ***Oregonian*** published reviews supporting the selection.

Meanwhile critics of the series were gathering momentum. They attacked the Pacific Coast readers in letters to the editor and editorials claiming that the selection process had been flawed and the books would cost too much. They also attacked the excessive attention devoted to regional writers and the inadequate ethical and religious content of the readers. The specific charges against the Pacific Coast series were the flawed selection process, the cost, the content and the involvement of Sam Simpson. The selection process was criticized as arrogant and high-handed. According to one newspaper editorial "The questionable manner in which the Pacific Coast Series were first adopted has been pretty thoroughly condemned by the entire public".[306] The --questionable manner" was that the speller and the fourth reader had not been completed at the time of the review and the fifth reader was missing entirely. The manner was that the review period was short, and the Superintendent recommended approval. In the hyperbole of the time, the recommendation to approve was described as:

> *... the heaviest artillery in the State [was] brought to bear upon the County Superintendents to induce them to adopt a series of readers...* [307]

It was true that the selection process was hurried and that the review copies were incomplete. The "heavy artillery' was a journalist's invention and explanation of why the County Superintendents, none of whom owed their jobs to the State Superintendent, voted 16 to 5 to accept Simpson's recommendation that they adopt the Pacific Coast Series.

The textbooks debate was asymmetrical. The newspapers printed whatever charges their readers submitted, most anonymously, while Simpson attempted, with little success, to keep the debate civil. He refuted the claim that the textbooks were too expensive by pointing out:

> *Many of these books were in use in the State previous to their adoption as parts of the authorized series and had regularly established prices which have not been varied from since... The Readers are actually cheaper than [the textbook] previously used, in proportion to the number of pages.*[308]

Simpson's argument would have been stronger if he had cited the prices of specific textbooks and if he had not allowed himself to be drawn into a comparison of the price per page.

Critics of the Pacific Coast series hammered away at process issues in textbook selection but generally avoided content issues. The one exception was the charge that the new textbooks were excessively regional because they included poetry and prose by western writers. The Fourth Reader included selections by westerners like Bret Harte and Mark Twain along with Lord Byron, Charles Dickens, Ralph Waldo Emerson, James Russell Lowell, Percey B. Shelley and Alfred Lord Tennyson. The Fifth Reader included speeches and essays by Oregon Civil War hero Edward Baker[309] and Judge Matthew Deady as well as Joseph Addison, Nathaniel Hawthorne, Thomas Jefferson, Abraham Lincoln, Henry Wadsworth Longfellow and Daniel Webster. Students recited western poetry like Sam Simpson's "Beautiful Willamette" as well as Samuel Taylor Coleridge's "Rime of the Ancient Mariner" and Edgar Allan Poe's "The Raven". [310] The classics of English literature were fully represented with relatively few western writers, but the critics were unsatisfied. Some critics simply felt that western writing was second rate and did not belong with the classics. Others argued that excessive regionalism was incompatible with the national unity necessary to heal the wounds of the Civil War. One critic worried that easterners would regard "the school authorities of this State a narrow minded and sectional set."[311] Sylvester Simpson, had strong feelings about the issue. He responded that the intent of the readers was to be national and asked rhetorically, "Who can claim that a series of Readers is national that absolutely ignores the whole country west of the Rocky Mountains?"[312]

The decision to hire Sam Simpson to edit two of the Bancroft readers was a mistake. Sylvester Simpson had made no secret of his willingness to do anything necessary to help his brother get and hold a job. Although Sam Simpson was fully qualified for the task, his involvement in writing textbooks that his brother would review and recommend for state adoption was bad judgment and exposed Sylvester to additional criticism. Critics charged nepotism and used Sam Simpson's involvement to explain the cost of the readers, delays in their production and the emphasis on western writers. As one critic wrote that it looked as though the decisions of those in power "were for the special benefit of Dr. Patterson and Mr. S.L. Simpson and to gratify a sectional pride".[313.]

The criticism dragged on in the newspapers and legislature long after Sylvester Simpson had resigned as Superintendent of Public Instruction. The Portland ***Oregonian*** and the Salem ***Oregon Statesman***, each with conservative new editors, led the attack on the Pacific Coast readers. Harvey Scott, the crusading editor of the Oregonian objected to the content of the Pacific Coast Series and its neglect of moral lessons. W.H. Odell of the ***Statesman*** used language like "swindle" and "fraud" to describe the textbook selection charging that the Pacific Coast series cost more than the eastern alternatives.[314]

In 1874, the Oregon Legislature considered repealing the 1872 School Law, abolishing the State Board of Education and the position of the State Superintendent and rescinding the uniform textbook requirements. A Republican member of the legislature from Manon County conveyed the tone of the debate:

> *If the Superintendent's office is to be prostituted, as it has been during the past two years, blot it from the Statute books.*[315]

The proposed repeal of the 1872 school law failed in 1874, but the superintendent's position was changed from appointive to elective. The opponents of the Pacific Coast series remained angry and continued to vent in the newspapers calling the series "positive frauds... trashy as some spurious novels" and urging the burning of the offending textbooks.[316] In 1878, the legislature amended the School Law of 1872 and directed the county superintendents to substitute another series for the controversial readers and speller of the Pacific Coast series.

Although he had resigned from the Superintendent's position in 1874, Sylvester Simpson remained the target of criticism. In 1876, his critics accused him of improper financial dealings regarding the controversial textbooks. One charge was that he had offered discounted prices to those county superintendents who adopted the textbooks he preferred. A second accusation was that he was profiting personally from the textbook sales. In contrast to his passive and pedantic responses to earlier charges, Simpson defended himself forcefully and promptly to these attacks on his integrity:

> *I see that your paper misrepresents me again this morning... I never wrote a line for any schoolbook nor owned a farthing"s interest in any such book in my life...I never had any interest whatsoever either direct or indirect in any of the books adopted for use in the State or in the proceeds of sales of any of them.*[317]

For once, he was fighting back and defending himself with unequivocal denials. He stopped short of attacking his accusers or even identifying them. If he had his father's political skills, he would have found ways to discredit those who opposed him.

At one level, the so-called textbooks scandal was simple politics. The effort to create a statewide education system was the idea of a Democratic governor and it threatened the authority of the county superintendents who had traditionally had a free hand in deciding who would be allowed to teach and what would be taught. The Republicans were concerned about the loss of local control and the prospect of higher school taxes. The textbook issue arose in a Democratic administration at a time when the Republicans were growing in popularity. At another level, the so-called scandal was a culture war between those who wanted moral lessons in grammar school and those, like Sylvester Simpson, who wanted the textbooks to reflect the lives of western children.

In his 1874 report to the Legislative Assembly, Sylvester Simpson was candid about the challenges he had encountered in his job as Superintendent of Public Instruction:

> *I have found the position a most laborious and vexatious one. Being the first incumbent of the office, I have had no precedents to guide me and, at the same time, have had many peculiar, difficult and invidious duties to perform... I have had to organize a new system... the different counties of the state were practically independent of each other in school matters... We really had no State school system.*[318]

Despite the bitter and prolonged textbook debate, Sylvester Simpson's twenty-month tenure as State Superintendent was a success. He accomplished his objectives of establishing state leadership in public education and adopting a statewide curriculum. He organized the new

State Board of Education, established teacher certification standards and conducted training institutes for teachers in Salem and four other cities. He left office with recommendations that the school year be extended, county superintendents increase school visits and that education be made compulsory once the school year reaches six months. His recommendations were ignored.

Although the textbook controversy was nasty and all-consuming, Simpson prevailed. The critics' focus on a specific set of readers diverted attention from the central issue, which was the principle that Oregon adopt uniform, statewide readers. Although the Pacific Coast Readers were eventually replaced, the principle of statewide uniformity remained intact. In 1874, when Simpson's term as superintendent expired, he did not run for election to the position he had held by appointment. Dr. L.L. Rowland, a physician, minister and rancher, was elected state superintendent and served four years. In his 1876 report to the legislature, Dr. Rowland did not mention his predecessor by name but acknowledged his accomplishment. He reported that 620 of the 755 school districts in Oregon were using the Pacific Coast Readers. According to Rowland, Oregon "took a gigantic stride in advance when she approved the principle of state [textbook] uniformity". Rowland also reported that the average school year was gradually increasing in Oregon, but that school attendance remained a problem. The average school year increased from 4.1 months in 1874-1875 to 4.9 months the following year. Of the children of school age in Oregon, 56 percent were enrolled in school but only 40 percent attended on an average day.[319] Rowland was a Republican and the first in a series of Republicans who served without interruption for more than a half century until 1926 when a democrat was briefly appointed state superintendent. Oregon did not elect a Democrat to the position of state superintendent until 1933.[320]

After his term expired as state superintendent in September 1874, Sylvester Simpson returned to his position as Chief Clerk in the Senate. In 1875, he moved to Portland and formed a partnership to practice law with John Waldo. Waldo was the son of Oregon pioneer Daniel Waldo and had grown up in the Waldo Hills east of Salem near the Simpson family. Waldo had been a year ahead of Simpson at Willamette and had gone to San Francisco where he read law with a prominent judge. The Simpson & Waldo firm rented offices in Room 12 of the Dekum Building at the corner of 1st and Washington in Portland.[321] In 1876, for the first and only time, Sylvester Simpson ran for election to the Oregon legislative assembly. He lost the election and returned to the position in which he had been most comfortable as Chief Clerk of the Senate. (Appendix VII) In 1877, the Simpson & Waldo law firm dissolved. John Waldo went on to serve on the Oregon Supreme Court in 1880 where he served as Chief Justice from 1884 to 1886.

Doubt and Insecurity

The textbook controversy was a turning point for Sylvester Simpson and his career in Oregon. He knew that the school reform he was proposing would result in criticism and opposition. After all, he was attempting to impose order on a system that had never been orderly. He knew that some of the county superintendents would object to their loss of authority to select textbooks or certify teachers, but he was not prepared for the sustained personal attacks that the opponents of school reform and others mounted. He was surprised by the vehemence of the opposition and its basic dishonesty. Disagreements about how to improve education had somehow become contorted into attacks on his integrity, character and worse. He was accused of nepotism, regional pride, swindle and fraud. The accusations were relatively minor (regional pride) or untrue (fraud) and all were unproven, but they seem to have deeply upset Simpson. He was hurt by the charges and unable to deflect them.

Through his father and his work in the Senate, Sylvester Simpson knew the members of the old political and judicial circles in Oregon. Through his relationship with Willamette, as a student, teacher and reunion speaker, he was at the center of the next generation of Oregon leaders. The new generation was better educated than their parents and better prepared for the challenges facing the state. Despite his accomplishments in the public arena while relatively young, Sylvester Simpson appears to have had long standing insecurities about what he could achieve. He shared these doubts in a revealing series of letters to his mentor, Judge Deady. In 1871, he denigrated his intellectual capacity: "... my mind is one of the dull, plodding sort and performs its labors slowly and with much toil"[322]. The painful experience as state superintendent propelled him into introspection and a melancholy assessment of his strengths and weaknesses. Simpson was barely 30 years old, and he had achieved public distinction in Oregon as a lawyer, appointed official, lecturer and writer. Outsiders considered him successful and had high expectations for him. Privately he was filled with doubts and insecurity. He mercilessly assessed his own limitations:

> *I know that I am too timid and ease-loving for my own good. Diffidence, or morbid self-distrust, has been the bane of my life thus far. If I had*

> *more aggressiveness and 'push' about me, I could easily have distanced some competitors whom I now see before me in the race of life.*[323]

He half-heartedly acknowledged that he might make a good judge but concluded that his lack of combativeness as a trial lawyer would make it impossible to ever become a judge:

> *It may be that I have some of the qualities that would make me a good judge while I lack some that are necessary to success in the arena before the bench! But then I am conscious that the only way to the 'bench' is through the 'arena'.*

He also considered and rejected other alternatives

> *I haven't enough piety for a preacher, and I have too much for an 'average' editor. And yet if I could get some such position... I would be strongly tempted to go into journalism. But here in Oregon such positions are rare if they exist at all and must be sought through an apprenticeship so rough that they will numb an ordinary man's mental, moral and physical constitution.*

He concluded sadly, "I seem to be tolerably good for so many things that I can't be very good for anything."[324]

When he was feeling sorry for himself or despairing about his career prospects, Sylvester Simpson blamed himself for his timidity and lack of ambition. He used a graduation speech, presumably at Willamette, to explore the paradox that life was not always fair and that the refinement of the educated individual might sometimes prove to be an obstacle to success. The audience of recent graduates and proud parents was expecting reassurance and commencement platitudes rather than the painful message that a college degree did not guarantee success:

> *There are some men and women of high culture who are too distrustful of their abilities and therefore too timid and unambitious to take their rightful place in the world... They have every quality that is necessary to win success, except the self-assurance that will enable them to push their way into the world's notice but lacking that, all the rest goes for naught.*[325]

Simpson may have been thinking of his father Ben when he described the success of the "boastful, brazen upstart" and the inability of the educated and refined individual to compete successfully against the vulgar self-promoter:

> *In too many cases, the man of fine ability and high culture who is too diffident to advertise his wares is permitted to trudge through life by some retired path while the boastful, brazen upstart struts along... with his impudent swagger.*

To achieve success, Simpson recommended that the graduates needed "a cheek of brass and a soul of flint".

The twenty months reforming the Oregon schools had been brutal. Sylvester Simpson had been the target of vicious personal attacks, and he had proven surprisingly ineffective in his own defense. Rather than directly refuting specific charges, his responses were too general or theoretical to be persuasive. He tried to reason with critics who were flailing away at the schoolbooks. He carried out his duties as superintendent, but he did not seem to have a taste for public debate. His self-criticism was accurate. He was far more comfortable with a contemplative and scholarly approach to issues than the mean-spirited bickering he associated with trial courts and public office. Whatever the cause, he was coming to the realization that he lacked the self-assurance and burning ambition that would be necessary to achieve prominence as an editor, judge or politician.

The Chadwick Administration

Lafayette Grover resigned as governor of Oregon in 1877 when he was elected to the United States Senate. Stephen F. Chadwick (1825-1895), the Oregon Secretary of State, succeeded Grover as fifth governor of the State of Oregon. Like his predecessor, Governor Chadwick was a lawyer and a Democrat. He served as governor from February 1, 1877, to September 11, 1878 while concurrently completing his term as Secretary of State. Governor Chadwick knew Sylvester Simpson from Simpson's time as State Librarian and had worked closely with him when they were both members of the state Board of Education. Governor Chadwick admired Simpson and invited him to return to Salem and serve as Assistant Secretary of State and the Governor's private secretary (today the position would be called chief of staff).[326] The position was an excellent fit with what Sylvester Simpson was learning about himself. He could spend his time on research and analysis while Governor Chadwick was the public face of the administration.

During his nineteen months as governor, Chadwick managed Indian Wars and a national economic slump along with the routine demands of state government like repairing the roof on the state capitol. The greatest challenges Chadwick faced were the Indian uprisings in 1877 and 1878. In June 1877, the Nez Perce led by Chief Joseph attacked isolated settlements in Idaho near the Oregon border but did not venture into Oregon. A year later, Indians from several tribes terrorized ranches in eastern Oregon, killing occupants and stealing livestock. The Governor visited Pendleton, Umatilla and other towns to deliver weapons, bolster morale and observe conditions. With the assistance of the army, the Indians were subdued and returned to their reservations. The national economic depression had little impact in Oregon, but Chadwick and his colleagues were concerned about the declining salmon harvest, the neglect of public harbors and the increasing number of vagrants appearing in Oregon (which they blamed on economic conditions in California). Governor Chadwick expressed pride in the growth of public education over the previous six years and the improvement in attendance, instruction and school supervision.

Chadwick did not run for election in 1878 to the position he had held since Governor Grover resigned to become a Senator. As he left office, he reported to the legislature that he had granted pardons to 21 inmates at the state penitentiary during his term in office and he urged the legislature to appropriate funds to repair the roof before it blew off the capitol. He recommended the creation of a state Fish Commission to regulate salmon fishing, a state Board of Equalization to increase uniformity in property tax assessments and a law prohibiting begging. Chadwick knew that the critics of school reform remained active. He did not mention any specific education issues but assured the legislators that the basic system of public education in Oregon was "excellent" and cautioned against "unwise or hasty" legislation that might "injure or destroy" that system. What he left unsaid was that the uniform textbook policy was the essential component of the system. The Governor's only recommendation for a new education law was to eliminate restrictions in the Swamp Land Act which delayed the sale of school lands.[327]

Sylvester Simpson's role in the Chadwick administration was, as he preferred, not immediately visible to the public. He advised the Governor and assisted the Governor, but he was not on the front lines and not the target of critics as he had been as state Superintendent. As Superintendent of Public Instruction, Simpson had been one of three trustees, along with the Governor and the Secretary of State, of the State Deaf-Mute School and the Oregon Institute for the Blind. The trustees appointed a superintendent to administer the school. Simpson was a trustee from October 1872 to September 1874 when he was replaced by Dr. L.L. Rowland, the newly-elected school superintendent. Each of the schools fell out of favor with the legislature and was denied an appropriation. The Deaf-Mute School was closed from 1878 to 1880, and the Institute for the Blind was closed from 1879 to 1883. During the period the 1878 legislature was in session, the Salem newspaper accused Simpson of..nibbling [sic] at the Blind School Fund" while he was private secretary to Governor Chadwick.[328] It is unclear what was going on. It may have been entirely innocent and part of the venomous partisanship the Salem paper had displayed since W. H. Odell had become owner in 1877. Odell's allegations were made late in the 1878 legislative session and did not prevent Simpson from completing his sixth and final term as Chief Clerk of the Oregon State Senate.

By 1879, Sylvester Simpson had a family to feed and declining prospects in Oregon. He was 35 years old and deeply depressed about his future. He had lost in his one try for elective office in 1876[329] and the Democrats who had appointed him to state positions had moved on. Governor Grover was now in the United States Senate and Governor Chadwick had retired. The Republican Party was growing in influence, and he had been worn down by criticism while serving as Superintendent of Public Instruction. The author of an article on the textbook controversy wrote "In the years following the adoption of the Pacific Coast series, both Simpson brothers had been discredited."[330] Her conclusion is far too harsh. The criticism of the Pacific Coast Readers intensified but there was little new information to discredit either of the Simpson brothers. After leaving the superintendent's office in 1874, Sylvester Simpson served in the Governor's Office and two terms as Chief Clerk in the State Senate. The explanation of his move to California was not that he was "discredited" but that he did not see any future for himself in Oregon. As he had confided to Judge Deady five years earlier, he had considered becoming a judge or editor and concluded that those careers required skills and personal characteristics which he simply did not have.

Sylvester Simpson was consumed by his personal ambivalence, but he was also aware that politics in Oregon were shifting. In 1878, a Democrat won the Governorship narrowly (by 61 votes out of 34,000 cast) but Democrats lost three of the five subsequent gubernatorial elections to the end of the century. Simpson's appointment as Chief Clerk of the State Senate depended on continued Democratic majorities in the Oregon State Senate. In 1880, the Republicans took control of the State Senate which they maintained without interruption until 1957. From 1880 to 1900, Republican candidates won all fourteen Congressional elections in Oregon.[331] The state that had been dominated by Democrats during its early days was rapidly becoming solidly Republican. The agrarian pioneers of the Democratic Party were rapid)y being replaced by the urban business interests of the Republican Party. Ben Holladay's political rampage was over, but the political restructuring of Oregon would continue. For once, Sylvester Simpson's political instincts served him well. It was time to consider opportunities outside Oregon.

8 The Scholar in California

Sometime during the summer or fall of 1879, Sylvester Simpson accepted a job offer from ***A.L. Bancroft and Company*** and moved to San Francisco with his wife Frances and their six children. Simpson had become acquainted with the Bancroft firm during the textbook controversy in Oregon. Bancroft & Co had been formed in 1870 when Hubert Howe Bancroft merged his history publishing company with the reference book and text book company operated by his brother Albert Little Bancroft. A.L. Bancroft and Co. published printed business forms, music books while also selling pianos and school furniture. Bancroft was the largest publishing company west of Chicago with annual sales of approximately $1 million, 250 employees and a five story, brick office building at 721 Market Street in downtown San Francisco.

Market St. near 5th St., San Francisco - 1865

A.L. Bancroft had added a law department in 1866 which published annual reports on decisions in the Supreme Courts of the western states and territories and the 9th U.S. Circuit Court of Appeals as well as legal reference books on mining law and water law. The law department had a staff of 50 editors, printers and salesmen.[332] By 1882, Bancroft had published 165 volumes of legal analysis including 57 volumes of state reports and 30 volumes of an ambitious, multi-year project called ***American Decisions***. Bancroft officials estimated that a total of 90 to 100 volumes of ***American Decisions*** would be necessary to cover the 1776 to 1869 period. The project was an enormous undertaking and would require at least fifteen years of research and editing. [333]

The Bancroft firm offered Simpson a salary of $125 a month to do legal research and editing on the American Decisions project in San Francisco. The prospect of a regular salary and opportunity to do legal research was attractive to Simpson. The decision to move to San Francisco involved more than salary and job description. It would also entail the first major separation in a closely-knit family. Sylvester and Frances Simpson had each lived in Oregon since they were children. Their parents, brothers and sisters, cousins and friends all lived in Oregon. They would be moving from the comfortable town of Salem, with a population of about 2500 people, to a city whose population exceeded that of the entire state of Oregon. They would also be moving to a place Sylvester Simpson had satirized, for an Oregon audience, as "The Modem Sodom". Tongue firmly in cheek, he had marveled at the "great advances in wickedness" in San Francisco.[334] His example of extreme wickedness was the "arch fiend" he had discovered who advertised funerals "at the shortest notice". Despite the San Francisco reputation and their ties to Oregon, Sylvester and Frances McFarland Simpson decided to move to San Francisco with their four sons and two daughters between the ages of two and twelve.

San Francisco

With a population of nearly 234,000 people, San Francisco was the largest city in the West and the ninth largest in the United States. It had a larger population than the 175,000 in the entire state of Oregon. San Francisco was the financial, manufacturing and cultural hub of the West. In 1880, San Francisco accounted for 99% of the imports on the Pacific Coast and 83% of the exports. Its banks and private investors provided financing for new development throughout the West and its industries produced cigars, clothing, furniture, lumber, mining machinery as well as processing numerous agricultural products. San Francisco had 43 breweries, as well as companies producing coffee, macaroni, pickles, spices and sugar. The city had 43 leather tanneries, 56 boot and shoemakers and 50 harness makers. There were 30 carriage and wagon makers, 18 furniture factories, 11 tool makers as well as boat builders, box makers, two windmill companies and a woolen mill.[335] The city was recovering from the national economic depression of 1870s and was poised to grow. The completion of the transcontinental railroad in 1869 had linked California to the rest of the United States and, along with the opening of rail service between San Francisco and Los Angeles in 1876, improved transportation was expected to bring growth and increased prosperity to San Francisco and the entire state.

The city was laid out as it is today with banks, offices, stores, theaters, hotels and restaurants concentrated along the Market Street corridor. In 1879, the population of San Francisco was crowded into the northeast quadrant of the peninsula. The tycoons who had grown rich building the transcontinental railroad or mining the Comstock lode had built showplace mansions on Nob Hill while middle class families were renting flats in surrounding areas and working-class families were living in tenements in the industrial areas south of Market Street. City growth had generally followed the path of least resistance with housing and light industry crowded into the marshlands of the South of Market, Mission and Potrero Districts and scattered development in the sand hills of the Western Addition area beyond Van Ness Avenue. In the mid-1870s, the invention of the cable car enabled middle class residents to consider houses and flats in the hills west of Kearny Street. By 1879, cable cars were operating on Clay Street, Sutter Street and California and the city had awarded 26 new franchises for additional transit lines. Within a few years, San Francisco would have 112 miles of cable car lines spanning the city and residential growth redirected westward into the Western Addition.

By 1879, the Palace Hotel had been in operation for four years on Market Street and passersby could enjoy the fountain at the intersection of Geary, Kearny and Market Streets that actress Lotta Crabtree had given the city in 1875. The city had an Art Association (1871), Academy of Sciences (1872) and 28 private libraries including those of the Mercantile Association, the Odd Fellows, Society of California Pioneers and the YMCA. The Mechanics institute had a reading room with approximately 30,000 books as well as the oldest chess club in the United States. The City of San Francisco hired its first municipal librarian in 1878, purchased 6162 books and opened its first public library June 7, 1879, in a large, rented room on the second floor of a building on Bush Street near Kearny. The new library was open from 9 in the morning until 9 at night except for Sunday. Within a year, the new public library expected to have 30,000 books in its collection and to have issued 10,000 library cards.[336]

It was a fine time to be in San Francisco. The economy was emerging from the national depression of 1873 and San Francisco was poised to grow. In 1879, the city had awarded the initial construction contract for a new city hall to be built at the southeast comer of McAllister and Larkin Streets replacing the "Old" City Hall in the Jenny Lind Theater on Kearny Street. The construction was estimated to require three years and $1.5 million.[337] Another civic project involved converting more than one thousand acres of sand dunes on the west side of the city into what would be Golden Gate Park. Work had been underway for a decade and in 1879, the completion of the first building, the Conservatory of Flowers, provided an indication of the wonders to come.

While residents awaited the completion of Golden Gate Park, they could enjoy Woodward's Gardens, a private amusement park covering four square blocks at Mission and 13th Streets. The gardens operated from 1866 to 1894 and offered attractions for all ages including a salt-water aquarium, and art gallery (with copies of famous paintings), a museum and a zoo with bears, monkeys, tigers and other exotic animals in cages. Tame animals wandered the grounds and there were boat rides, camel rides and goat carts for children as well as daily band concerts and dancing in the evening.[338]

San Francisco found it easy to spend money on graft-loaded civic monuments like the new City Hall but neglected its roads and schools. San Francisco had 63 schools, 637 teachers and 40,000 students in 1883. Spending on education was not keeping up with the increasing number of school-age children in the city. Between 1871 and 1883, the number of children in the public schools increased by 54 percent while the school budget increased 12 percent. The annual spending per student declined from $41.53 in 1871 to $25.66 in 1883.[339]

For all its external sophistication and cultural amenities, San Francisco politics retained ugly reminders of its rough and tumble origins. By 1879, the rabidly anti-Chinese agitator and sand lot orator Denis Kearney was at the peak of his influence. Kearney's grassroots movement had become the Workingman's Party of California. The Workingman's Party selected Isaac S. Kalloch and Charles de Young, co-founder and editor of the San Francisco ***Chronicle***, traded public insults which resulted in the newspaper editor shooting the candidate. Kalloch survived his wounds and was elected Mayor in 1879. The following year, the Mayor's son Milton retaliated by shooting and killing de Young. A San Francisco jury acquitted young Kalloch. For the next decade, San Francisco politics would be thick with corruption and cronyism.

Apart from its corrupt governance, the city that would be home to Sylvester Simpson's family for the next quarter century was cosmopolitan, tolerant and proudly eccentric. Few residents were more successfully eccentric than ***Emperor Joshua A. Norton***. Norton was a speculator who lost all his money investing in rice futures. In 1857, he declared himself Norton the First, Emperor of the United States and Protector of Mexico. The self-styled Emperor won the hearts of San Franciscans. He printed his own money (which was accepted by local merchants), issued Imperial proclamations (many of which were published in local newspapers) and was treated like a dignitary (theaters saved a seat for him; police saluted when he passed in his uniform). At the time of his death in 1880, city flags were lowered to half-mast and 30,000 San Franciscans lined the streets in tribute.[340] The idea that there were hidden celebrities among the common people was reinforced in 1883 when a mild-mannered San Francisco mining engineer was unmasked as Black Bart, the notorious stagecoach robber famous for eluding authorities and leaving poems at crime scenes.

NORTON I,
Emperor Of United States and Protector of Mexico.
BRADLEY & RELOFSON. SAN FRANCISCO

San Francisco loved its homegrown characters, but it also welcomed visitors from around the world. ***Robert Louis Stevenson***, who lived on Bush Street during the winter and spring of 1879-1880, described San Francisco as "the most interesting city in the union". In September 1879, former ***President Ulysses S. Grant*** stopped in San Francisco on his return from a two-year tour of Europe and Asia. The popular Civil War hero was greeted by large crowds, military bands and fireworks. ***President Rutherford B. Hayes*** visited San Francisco in 1880 followed by British poet ***Oscar Wilde*** in 1882.

The Simpson Family in San Francisco

San Francisco must have seemed exotic and overwhelming to Sylvester Simpson and his family coming from a small town where everyone knew everyone, where newspaper editors published outrageous articles but did not shoot politicians and where eccentric characters were not treated as civic celebrities. The Simpson family rented a flat at the southwest corner of Hyde and Turk Street in what is now the heart of the Tenderloin District. Their flat was on what was then the western edge of the city near what is now the Civic Center and a few blocks from the offices of Bancroft & Company on Market Street. The flat on Hyde and Turk was across the city from government offices near Portsmouth Square.

Sylvester Simpson was admitted to the California Bar December 5, 1879, and rented an office in the Montgomery Block at the southwest corner of Washington and Montgomery Street near Portsmouth Square. The Montgomery Block was the largest, safest and most grand office building in San Francisco in 1853 when it was built by Henry W. Halleck, later General-in-Chief of the United States Army in the Civil War. At the time it was built, the four-story Montgomery Block was the tallest building west of St. Louis and provided offices for law firms, mining engineers, bankers, newspapers and, beginning in 1880, Adolph Sutro's private library. The building had 175 rooms arranged around a central courtyard and was designed to be fireproof with thick masonry walls and iron shutters on the windows. More than fifty years after it was built, the Montgomery Block was one of very few downtown buildings to survive the 1906 fire. In later years, the building evolved into studios for artists, writers and political activists before it was demolished in 1959. The Transamerica Pyramid was built on the site in 1972.

The Montgomery Block was important for Sylvester Simpson because it was the site of the San Francisco law library. The law library had been organized in 1865 and was supported by subscription fees and by a docket fee on court cases. The library was located in rooms 27 and 28 of the Montgomery Block and contained more than 16,000 legal reference books, a full-time librarian (paid $200 a month) and extended hours (9am to 11pm).[341] Simpson rented room 40 for 1879. In 1880, he moved to room 34, presumably to be closer to the library, where he remained until 1883 when the San Francisco law library moved to the "New City Hall" which had been under construction for many years on former cemetery land in what is now the Civic Center area. Sylvester Simpson had an office in the new city hall law library in 1883 and 1884.

Life in California was a dramatic personal change for Sylvester Simpson. He could relax. For the first time in his adult life, he was not in the public eye, and he had a permanent job. He could devote his time to legal research and writing without having to worry about locating his next job and without the carping of political critics. He stopped giving public lectures and writing articles and concentrated on his legal research for the Bancroft firm. Perhaps this was what he had envisioned a few years earlier when he had criticized himself as "ease-loving". He was no longer feeling he had to take care of his brother or that he had to live up to the unrealistic expectations created by his early success or the example of his father. He stopped writing Judge Deady for advice and began a new life.

Beginning in 1885, Sylvester Simpson appears to have been less dependent on the San Francisco law library. From 1885 until 1889, the law library remained in the New City Hall, but Simpson had no office and must have worked at his residence or at the law library. He rented office space at two locations on Pine Street in 1890, 1891, 1893 and 1894 and worked at his Clay Street residence in 1892. In 1895, the nature of his law practice changed as he began working in law offices. That year, he was on the top floor of the Hobart Building at 532 Market Street in the law offices of Garber, Boalt and Bishop. In 1897, be formed a partnership with George B. Littlefield. Simpson and Littlefield opened an office on the third floor of the Mills Building on Montgomery Street where they remained two years. In 1899, the Simpson-Littlefield partnership dissolved. George Littlefield joined the Pacific Coast Automatic Sprinkler and Fire Extinguisher Company and Sylvester Simpson returned to the law offices of John H. Boalt in the Hobart Building where he remained the next five years. He worked at home in 1902 and retired in 1904 at the age of 60.[342]

During most of his twenty-five years in San Francisco, Simpson maintained his relationship as a research lawyer with Bancroft & Co. and its successor Bancroft Whitney. Late in his career, he was in a partnership for two years with George Littlefield and intermittently in the offices of John H. Boalt in the Hobart Building. He was restless in finding places to do his work. He rented offices in six different buildings but changed frequently. He had offices in the Hobart Building on Market Street for seven years with two interruptions. Apart from the five years he worked at home (1885-1889), his longest continuous stay in one place was the four years in the Montgomery Block (1879-1882). About half of the time he seems to have chosen offices that were near the San Francisco Law Library. At other times, he worked at home (seven years), on Pine Street (four years) and in the Mills Building (two years).

In contrast to the rich documentation of his public and private life in Oregon, Sylvester Simpson left little record of his twenty-five years in San Francisco. The family legend was that his career in San Francisco was entirely devoted to editing of the Bancroft-Whitney series ***The American Decisions: Cases of General Value and Authority Decided in the Courts of the Several States***. The series, which reached 85 volumes by 1911, reported and annotated decisions of state courts with extensive notes on each case. Simpson may have found his work in California valuable and satisfying but his he did not escape the expectations of his friends in Oregon who considered the work for Bancroft Whitney to have been a waste of his talent and no more than "legal hack writing"[343]

The 1870s and 1880s were a time of suburbanization in San Francisco as the proliferation of transit lines opened new areas for middle class residential development. Improved transportation made commuting practical from areas west of Van Ness Avenue including particularly the area called the Western Addition as well as the Upper Market and Mission District. The Western Addition had been part of the city since 1851 but had been considered too remote and too rural to be developed until the 1870s. Many of the Victorian houses for which San Francisco is famous were built in the Western Addition during this period as single-family cottages or multi-family flats. After living for a year at Turk and Hyde, the Simpson family moved to the first of a series of houses on the western edge of the Western Addition where they lived for one year each on Broderick, Pine and Turk. In 1883, they moved far across the city to the Mission District where they lived four years at 934 Dolores and two years at 703 Shotwell.

In 1889, the Simpson family moved back across the city to an area where the Western Addition and Pacific Heights neighborhoods overlap. They lived two years at 2503 California, three years at 2929 Clay and one year at 2115 Broderick in houses within a few blocks of one another near Alta Plaza Park. In 1890, two Simpson sons, Ernest and Frank, moved out (Frank returned in 1892 to live with his parents while he was a student) and the youngest daughter Avis died. Lynn, the second son, moved out in 1894 and Ray, the fourth son, died in 1897. In 1895, the Simpson family moved from the Western Addition to a series of houses on the western slopes of Nob Hill where they lived one year at 1325 Leavenworth, five years at 1408 Leavenworth, one year at 1225 Jackson Street and four years at 1227 Jackson. Of the thirteen San Francisco buildings in which the Simpson family lived between 1879 and 1905, only the flat on Shotwell survives unchanged in appearance. The building at 2115 Broderick appears original but has been modernized. The other eleven buildings were either destroyed by fire in 1906 (the four on Leavenworth and Jackson), demolished to be replaced by new buildings or torn down to build a school (934 Dolores). (Appendix VIII)

Burnbrae: The Mill Valley Cottage

Frances and Sylvester Simpson in Burnbrae (the Cottage) at the end of Cascade Dr. in Mill Valley, CA photo taken ≈1899-1903

Sylvester and Frances Simpson spent nearly twenty years in San Francisco where housing was congested and summers were foggy, before they began looking for a warmer place where they could spend summer months. Frances Simpson knew a Mrs. Barnard who lived in San Francisco and spent summers north of San Francisco in Marin County. In 1898, the two women crossed San Francisco Bay by ferry boat to Sausalito and rode the North Pacific Coast Railroad (later the Northwestern Pacific) to downtown Mill Valley. They went hiking along Mill Creek in Cascade Canyon. The area had been logged in the 1850s and had been subdivided in 1890. Most of Cascade canyon was outside the subdivided area. The two women followed a rough road to the end of the canyon where the local water company had built a

125-foot dam across the canyon in 1893 to hold water. The water company also constructed a smaller, covered reservoir about 400 yards downstream from the dam. Immediately downstream from the covered reservoir, Frances Simpson spotted an area with two large redwood trees which she found particularly appealing. She returned to the same place at a later date with her husband and teenage daughter Vera and camped out on the property for two or three weeks before deciding to buy.[344]

The Simpsons purchased one full acre on a steep slope for $500. The property was about a mile and a half from the railway depot in the center of Mill Valley and remote from the nearest house. Old Mill Creek crossed the bottom of the lot which was covered with ferns, huckleberries, second-growth redwoods, madrone, bay laurel and oak trees. In the spring of 1899, the Simpsons commissioned Harvey Klyce, (1867-1951) a Mill Valley architect and builder, to design and construct a summer cottage on the property.[345] The 517 square foot cottage was built for an additional $500 and was ready for use by the end of May 1899. It had a large central room, two small bedrooms and a tiny kitchen. The cottage was originally constructed with small porches at the front and back, a woodshed and a detached privy. Burnbrae, as it came to be called, had running water piped from a creek behind the house, a wood-burning cook stove and a fireplace in the living room for heating.

Sketch of the fireplace at Burnbrae, drawn in the guest book kept at the cottage.

Burnbrae was enjoyed over the years by five generations of Simpsons and their descendants. It was the scene of vacations, honeymoons, family picnics, potluck suppers, birthday parties, holiday celebrations and church outings. Children played in the creek and picked huckleberries to be used in pies. Everyone hiked the Tenderfoot Trail to the pipeline at the top of the ridge and Mountain Home. Energetic family members hiked the steep Zig Zag Trail to the top of Panoramic Ridge where trails led to Mount Tamalpais, Muir Woods or the ocean at Stinson Beach. Between 1913 and 1915, the small porches were extended around three sides of the cottage, a small bathroom was constructed in the back and a sleeping platform was erected uphill from the cottage for the noisy young. Family members maintained and improved the property regularly repairing and replacing the bridge over the creek, the porch around the building and the roof. In 1946, the candles and coal oil lamps that had provided illumination for 47 years were replaced when the cottage was electrified.[346] Burnbrae was sold in 1978 after a series of break-ins by burglars, vandals and squatters made the property impractical to maintain as a summer home.

The Next Generation

Of the nine children born to Sylvester and Frances Simpson, two died young. The youngest child, Avis (1887-1890), died of a childhood disease and Ray (1877-1897) died of a burst appendix as a young adult. The Simpson children grew up moving nearly every year from house to house in San Francisco. Some began careers in San Francisco, but all eventually moved out of the City. Three of the Simpson sons had long careers in journalism. ***Ernest Simpson*** (1867-1941) was 15 years old in 1882 when he began as a clerk with his father's publisher A.L. Bancroft & Co. He attended an academy associated with the College of the Pacific in San Jose where the president was a friend of the father's from the class of 1869 at Willamette. Ernest began his journalism career at ***Alta California*** where he was a reporter from 1889 to 1891. He joined the San Francisco Chronicle in 1892 as a reporter and was promoted to editor of the Sunday Supplement before serving as City Editor from 1895 to 1906. His wife Anna Pratt Simpson (n.d.- 1934) was Society Editor of the ***Chronicle*** during the same period. Soon after the earthquake and fire in 1906, the ***San Francisco Call,*** a morning paper and ***Chronicle*** competitor, successfully recruited Simpson to be Managing Editor. In 1913, William Randolph Hearst bought the Call and transferred Ernest Simpson to Chicago to be Managing Editor of the Hearst-owned scandal sheet, The Chicago American. Ernest Simpson left journalism in 1916 when he joined International Harvester in Chicago where he was director of Public Relations until his retirement in 1938.[347]

Ernest Simpson was the Editor of the San Francisco Chronicle at the time of the 1906 Earthquake. The following is an article he wrote just after the earthquake.

The Wisdom of the Dogs

By Ernest S. Simpson

BRUTE four-footed instinct triumphed over objective two-footed reason in that first moment of the Time of Terror.

It was the dogs, wild with fear, that gave me first the measure of our calamity. Sleep-dazed, with the "anguish of the beams' complaining," still in my ears, the air still quivering with the echoes of that stupendous noise, I looked out into as fair a morning as ever shone upon the world, calm fresh and smiling. Of the terrestrial tragedy there was no evidence because nightgowned, barefooted men and women [were] upon the curbs. They ran about aimlessly. Some knelt on the sidewalks as if praying; some rushed back into their houses and out again; some looked mutely at the serene sky. They wanted to know what had happened — what was to happen. Down across the dewy green of Duboce Park, a cloud hung housetop-high in the stirless air. It was not smoke but dust — the heavy dust of brick and mortar and concrete ground in the mills of the angry gods. That meant riven walls and crumbled chimneys. The houses, I could see, stood upright, after a fashion. Here was no sign of dire disaster. Walls could be made whole, chimneys and hearth could be piled brick on brick again.

But then came the dogs, couriers of the cataclysm — they had come far, for they ran slowly. Their jaws were dripping. They moaned and whined. All of them panted steadily up the steep hill. Then and thus I knew that, bad as it had been with us, on the hills, the darker chapters of the story of woe were to be read on the lowlands and in the valleys. We were shaken but safe; below us were nameless horrors, the dogs knew, and knowing, ran to the high places.

Soon, looming sinister and huge above the broken city, against the background of shining bay and Alameda's hazy purple hills, toward the pillars of smoke that heralded the coming of Catastrophe's twin sister, Calamity. I counted them — one far down toward the water end of Mission Street; one in the heart of the teeming southside; one across a spur of our hill in Hayes Valley. These pillars, lifting skyward, were solemnly significant. Destruction was upon us, desolation was to come.

When I had noted water flung from a bath tub to the ceiling; glassware and china tossed across rooms; double hung pictures neatly reversed; plaster of cross-walls scribbled upon fantastically with seams and cracks by the hand that had, for a moment, gripped us — when I rejoiced again for a house built upon the rock — I went down into the hall from which the dogs had so early fled. Ruin by ruin, disaster by disaster, I saw how truly they had told the story.

Spent with running, paralyzed by the terror, a little yellow fice, [mongrel] cowering on my lawn against a stout, unbroken wall. She snarled when I chirruped to her that it was all right now.

On an afternight a sleek cocker, very weary, called upon us in the hurly-burly of a great newspaper's army, called suddenly to fight the greatest of its battles. He was not hungry. What he wanted was human kindness. In his mouth he carried a big beef bone. When he lay down in utter weariness, he put his paw on it just as men with guns and clubs — on nearby streets — were standing guard over their little heaps of burnt and blistered, battered cans. I saw the Managing Editor reach down a grimy hand to pat the wanderer and was glad.

My friend's wise terrier, remote and safe from the shock or fire, began at once on the first day of the tragedy to forage and to conceal. She is still burying supplies in a back yard planted thick with her instinctive provision against the famine, that mankind, proceeding objectively, has averted.

Among the miles of smoking ruins dogs wander seeking masters, some of whom are here and some in the hereafter. They have come back from the hills.

Oh, yes — the dumb brutes knew first and knew best. I shall never forget how, in the fair, sweet morning, I saw them as they ran, moaning and whining, with dripping jaws, panting steadily up the steep hill.

San Francisco Chronicle

May 6, 1906

Anna Pratt Simpson (1866–1934) was the wife of Ernest Simpson and a prominent figure in San Francisco journalism and civic life. She served as Vice-President of the ***Woman's Board*** and Chairman of its Publicity Department for the ***Panama-Pacific International Exposition***. She was also the Society Editor for the Chronicle between 1895 and 1906.

In 1915, she wrote ***Problems Women Solved:*** *Being the Story of the Woman's Board of the Panama-Pacific International Exposition — What Vision, Enthusiasm, Work and Co-operation Accomplished*, published by the Woman's Board in San Francisco. The book is a historical account of the significant civic and logistical contributions made by women to ensure the success of the World's Fair, which was held to celebrate the completion of the Panama Canal and the recovery of San Francisco from its 1906 earthquake.

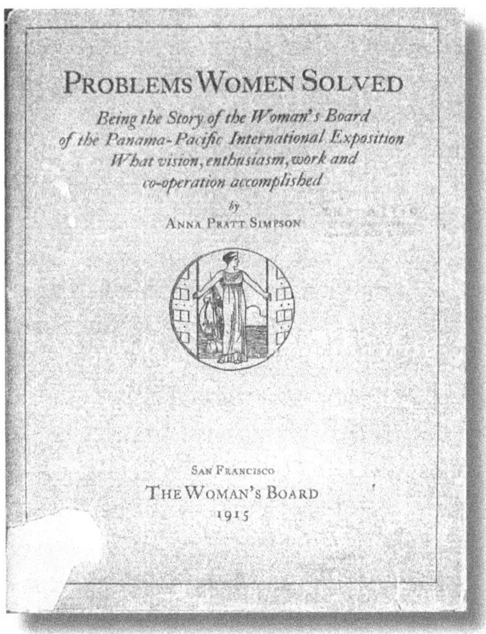

PROBLEMS WOMEN SOLVED

Being the Story of the Woman's Board of the Panama-Pacific International Exposition What vision, enthusiasm, work and co-operation accomplished

by

ANNA PRATT SIMPSON

SAN FRANCISCO

THE WOMAN'S BOARD

1915

The Woman's Board, also known as the Board for Lady Managers, provided women with a campaigning platform for discussing women's rights and social issues at the exposition. One technique it employed was the installation of numerous statues of women, such as the famous Pioneer Mother statue by Charles Grafly. The exposition also hosted the ***International Conference of Women Workers to Promote Permanent Peace,*** attended by pacifists from across the world in response to the First World War.

Lynn Simpson (1869-1944)

Lynn Simpson (1869-1944) the second of the five Simpson sons, followed his older brother into journalism. He graduated from the College of the Pacific in San Jose in1891 and was hired by the San Francisco ***Chronicle*** where he was telegraph editor from 1893 to 1913. He subsequently was the Publisher and Managing Editor of the ***Sacramento Union*** for five years. After stints at the ***Oakland Tribune*** and ***San Francisco Examiner,*** he moved to Santa Barbara in 1923 where he was Managing Editor of the ***Santa Barbara Daily News*** for nine years.[348] The third Simpson son, Frank (1871-1929) was a machinist at Union Iron Works before attending the University of California where he graduated as a mining engineer in 1906. Myrtle was the fourth oldest Simpson child and the oldest of four daughters. Before her marriage to Clarence C. Wilson in 1901, she had been citywide Superintendent of Christian Endeavor for San Francisco for five years. After her marriage, she lived at several locations in the Bay Area and one year in Los Angeles before moving in 1913 to the San Joaquin Valley town of Corcoran where she raised six children and was an active civic leader. She served as a trustee of the elementary school, founding president of the Corcoran PTA and Superintendent of the Primary Department of the local Presbyterian Church. Her younger sister, Dessie (1875- 1972), worked in the San Francisco office of the Northern California Congregational Church. In 1929, she married Leland D. Rathbone, a widowed Congregational minister. After Leland Rathbone died in 1938, Dessie Rathbone returned to Berkeley.

Kirke Simpson (1881-1972) was the first of the Simpson children born in San Francisco. He attended Trinity School and the Lick School of Mechanical Arts (now Lick-Wilmerding High School) in San Francisco before joining the Army during the Spanish-American War in 1898. He served as a bugler in Company D of the 1st California Regiment, U. S. Volunteer Infantry during the Philippine Insurrection.[349] After seventeen months in the army, he returned to the Bay Area and was taking courses at the University of California in Berkeley in 1904 when two of his older brothers, Lynn in San Francisco and Frank in Nevada, assisted him to get a job as a reporter with the

Daily Sun in the rough mining town of Tonopah, Nevada. By the time Kirke Simpson arrived in Tonopah, the editor of the Daily Sun had quit, and the inexperienced Simpson suddenly found himself both reporter and editor. After two or three years in Tonopah, he returned to the Bay Area where he was a part-time reporter for the Associated Press from 1908 to 1913 when he was transferred to the AP office in Washington, D.C. He was an AP reporter in Washington from 1913 to 1928 when he became a Washington columnist for the AP. He wrote "***The Washington Bystander***" column for seventeen years until his retirement in 1945. Kirke Simpson won the Pulitzer Prize for Journalism in 1922 for a series of articles on the burial of the ***Unknown Soldier of World War I***. He retired in 1945 and returned to California.

Kirke Simpson (1881-1972)

Tomb of the Unknown Soldier, Arlington National Cemetery, Virginia, near Washington, D.C.

"KNOWN BUT TO GOD..."–"Here rests in honored glory an American soldier, known but to God." So reads the inscription on the tomb of the

unknown soldier buried in Arlington National Cemetery. Kirke L. Simpson of the Associated Press won the Pulitzer Prize in 1922 for his story that day. It started this way, and it belongs in any history of the time:

> *Under the wide and starry skies of his own homeland, America's unknown dead from France sleeps tonight, a soldier home from the wars.*
>
> *Alone he lies in the narrow cell of white stone that guards his body; but his soul has entered into the spirit that is America.*

Kirke Simpson was an AP man in San Francisco and Washington for 37 years. His 1921 story on burial of the Unknown Soldier won the first AP byline and the first Pulitzer Prize ever awarded a news service man; still appears in journalism textbooks. For many years he was AP's Washington political columnist. He broke the news of Teddy Roosevelt's Bull Moose campaign, and made "smoke-filled room" a potent political phrase.

Note from Eleanor Roosevelt to Kirke - May 14, 1945

Hyde Park
Dutchess County, New York

May 14, 1945

Dear Mr. Simpson:

I have just retrieved your letter of April 26th, from the mass of mail which is piled around me here.

I saw your articles and liked them so much, but I will appreciate it if you will send me copies of all of them as I may have missed something.

It meant so much to Franklin to keep in touch with his old friends and he always loved his birthday parties, as you know. I knew you and all of the old friends would grieve. I think we can all be thankful, however, that he went without suffering. He would have hated a long illness.

With many thanks, I am,

Very cordially yours,

Eleanor Roosevelt

From 1928 until 1945 Kirke Simpson wrote the column "***Washington Bystander***" focused initially on national politics, then shifted to World War II interpretation through 1945. It appeared daily, leveraging his contacts in Washington, including friendships with ***FDR*** and ***Harry Truman***.

WASHINGTON BYSTANDER

By KIRKE SIMPSON

WASHINGTON, Feb. 9.—But for Postmaster General Walter Brown, January 14 would have gone down In 1932 political history only to democrats as a day of special note. Many things political happened that day; but they were all democratic happenings except for what Mr. Brown had to say.

KIRKE SIMPSON

Mr. Brown put President Hoover in nomination. He did it after a conference with the president and also in the light of the general expectation that Mr. Brown himself soon will take over the chairmanship of the republican national committee.

Now it is no news that Mr. Hoover will be a candidate. About the only thing on that subject Mr. Brown could have said. In itself constituting big news, would have been a declaration that Mr. Hoover would not run.

So the true significance of the Brown outgiving was that while he was careful to say he spoke only for the friends of Hoover, he was accepted as the voice of Hoover himself.

MONOPOLIZING THE NEWS

General Brown's strategy prevented a complete democratic sweep of the political news that day. Maybe that is what he had in mind.

With the democratic "victory dinner" in New York, with Governor Frank Roosevelt as headliner, a Boston party rally with Al Smith in action, an Ohio show with Senators Bulkley and Lewis sounding off, a Chicago gathering hearing a Jouett-Shouse's word of warning about over confidence, obviously it was going to take something right out of the main republican feed box to get any attention at all.

General Brown turned the trick.

That January 14 was a great day politically in even more ways than really started the Roseevelt-for-President drive for delegates, in-that, North Dakota democrats for-viting the New Yorker to get into the state primaries.

Up in Boston Al Smith's adherents called a similar "Come-on-in-the-water's-fine" invitation to him, evoking only his customary grin.

LITTLE JOY HERE

There was one happening that same day, however, which may have caused a considerable group of democrats very little joy. The friends so ardently urging Newton Baker's nomination got another evidence that Mr. Baker himself is still their greatest difficulty.

Writing to a League of Nations association convention in Philadelphis. Mr. Baker called again for American entry into the league "as a member on a 100 per cent basis."

That attitude only confirms what Mr. Baker has been saying early and late for years. In view of post-1920 political happenings, however, Baker men must have moaned to themselves when they read of it:

"Why bring that up now?"

Telegram ***President Harry S. Truman*** sent to Kirke as Truman returned to the US from the Potsdam Conference near Berlin - Aug. 3, 1945

Radio

TELEGRAM

The White House
Washington

AUGUST 3, 1945

KIRKE L. SIMPSON,
ASSOCIATED PRESS,
WASHINGTON, D. G.

HEARTY CONGRATULATIONS AS YOU ENTER INTO THE LEISURE OF A WELL EARNED RETIREMENT. YOU ARE ONE OF THAT GRAND COMPANY OF NEWSPAPERMEN WHO BRING IMAGINATION AND VISION TO THE DAY'S WORK AND TURN NEWS INTO LITERATURE AS YOU HAVE DONE SO MANY TIMES. AS YOU LEAVE THE SCENE OF SUCH LONG AND DISTINGUISHED SERVICE I WISH YOU THE BEST OF ALL THINGS — A LONG AND HAPPY MARRIED LIFE.

HARRY S. TRUMAN

In 1909, the Wright brothers gave demonstration flights at Fort Myer, Virginia. President Taft took Kirke to one of these events, and Orville Wright took him up for a flight. Sixty years later, in 1969, Kirke's great-nephew, Kevin Wilson, recalled Kirke describing the experience: "All I really remember is how cold it was up in the air—the wind came past my ankles, through my clothes, and out my collar."

Kirke was a member of FDR's, "*Cuff Links Gang*". This was a group of seven men that were assembled to help in FDR's campaign for Vice-President in 1920 and remained close friends. They would gather once a year near FDR's birthday, Jan 30. These gatherings occurred from 1921 until 1945. Below is a photo of a "To-ga! To-ga!" celebration. January 30, 1934. *NPx 47-96:1756.*

Kirke Simpson's great-nephew, Kevin Wilson recalls the following, *"Kirke was considered the nation's foremost civilian expert on the U.S. Navy. Supposedly, he could name every ship in the Navy by looking at its profile. One story he did tell me about the Navy in person: in the spring of 1942, he wrote a news story that predicted a Japanese attack on Midway Island. He used his interpretive naval map system and military knowledge for the prediction. He showed me a telegram from Bull Halsey, dated the day of the Battle of Midway (June 42), asking how Kirke could predict a battle that only a handful of top brass know about in advance. The navy had broken one of Japan's code in order to surprise them at Midway. Kirke was a good friend of Halsey's."*

Tiffany gold cufflinks that FDR gave to members of the Cuff Links Gang. This pair was for Renah F. Camalier, an original member of the Gang and one of the seven men on FDR's 1920 vice-presidential campaign staff. They also received a flask with their name on it.

NOTE **For more about Kirke Simpson see:**
https://bdhhfamily.com/kirke-larue-simpson/

For his article, ***Dedicating the Tomb of the Unknown Soldier*** (1921):
https://www.encyclopedia.com/history/dictionaries-thesauruses-pictures-and-press-releases/dedicating-tomb-unknown-soldier-1921-kirke-e-simpson

Vera Simpson (1884-1976) was the third of four Simpson sisters and the only one to attend college. She grew up in San Francisco where she attended Miss Hamlin's School. She graduated from the University of California with the class of 1908 and obtained a teaching position in the remote desert mining town of Johnnie, Nevada.[350] In 1913, she was teaching at Black Bear, a mining town in the mountains of Siskiyou County, where she met and married William D. Dickerson (1872-1921) a mining engineer with a twelve year old daughter, Mabel Dickerson (1901-1921). Will became ill and his family moved to Artesia in Southern California, Homitos in Mariposa County and the Bay Area in vain efforts to improve his health. He and his daughter both died in 1921. Vera Dickerson spent the rest of her teaching career in the schools of Vallejo and Oakland. About 1940, she and her sister Dessie bought a house at 26 Crystal Way in Berkeley where they lived the rest of their lives.

Retirement

In 1904, Sylvester Simpson closed his law office and retired. The following year, Frances McFarland Simpson died in San Francisco on July 13, 1905, at the age of 65. She was buried in the Simpson family plot at Woodlawn Memorial Park in Colma about eleven miles south of San Francisco.[351] After twenty-five years of legal research, it was no longer necessary for Sylvester Simpson to be in San Francisco. He lived briefly in Alameda before buying a large house at 2330 Russell Street in Berkeley where he lived the rest of his life. The Russell Street house is located just west of Telegraph Avenue south of the University of California campus. Russell Street was home for the unmarried Dessie Simpson and whichever other Simpson children were in the area like Vera who was a student at the University of California, Kirke who was a reporter for the Associated Press in San Francisco and Frank, a mining engineer. Sylvester Simpson died March I, 1913, at the Russell Street house in Berkeley and was buried in the family plot at Woodlawn. The San Francisco Chronicle reported that, as one of the chief editors of American Decisions, Simpson had "held a position of enviable eminence among the legal fraternity of San Francisco."[352]

Sylvester Simpson had been gone from Oregon for more than thirty years but he had not been forgotten. Joseph D. Lee, his school mate at the old Dallas Academy eulogized him at the 1913 Annual Reunion of the Oregon Pioneer Association calling Simpson "a man of brilliant intellect". George Himes, the historian, who had called him a "legal hack writer for Bancroft, San Francisco" recalled that Simpson had been "a thorough master of parliamentary rules" while he was Clerk of the Oregon Senate and added that former Governor and Senate President John Whiteaker had observed, "There was nothing the matter with Syl but the want of combativeness."[353]

The eulogists in Oregon persisted in measuring Sylvester Simpson against their expectations of him several decades earlier. They remembered the eloquent orator, the gifted professor and the capable administrator. Joseph Lee even remembered that he wrote poetry. They also remembered his hard-charging and eternally-optimistic father. They overlooked the fact that Sylvester Simpson had changed. As he admitted in his letters to Judge Deady, he did not have the personality for political intrigue or combat. He was not the same man who had left Oregon in 1879. He preferred job and income security for his large family and the calm of scholarly research to the rough and tumble of Oregon politics. Unlike his father, he was not comfortable with the competitive behavior required to become a judge, editor or public official. As State Superintendent, he had been doing work that he was passionate about, but he was not prepared for the personal toll it would take or the questions it would stir up. Rather than continue to be measured against the expectations of others, he moved to California and changed his life. He gave up public life for the anonymity and satisfaction of a private life of research, writing and family. He contributed analysis and editing to multiple volumes of Bancroft-Whitney's American Decisions and he raised a large and talented family.

9 The Pioneer Poet

When he was sober, he was a charmer but **Sam Simpson (1845-1899)** had a severe and persistent drinking problem throughout his adult life. He fought it, made fun of it and turned it into art. He wrote editorials and poems about it but was ultimately unable to control it. It took his ability to hold a job, his marriage and eventually his life.

Despite his drinking, he was able to produce an impressive collection of poems and achieve recognition among his contemporaries as a major regional poet.[354] One historian described Simpson as "... the poet laureate of Oregon and the singer of love songs to the state."[355]

Samuel Leonidas Simpson was an improbable poet. He was born in Missouri and raised on the Oregon frontier where education was sporadic, and books were few. His father, Ben Simpson, was a hard-driving pioneer businessman and politician with little formal education and little time or patience for contemplative activities like poetry. His mother Nancy Cooper Simpson had been born in a Missouri fort among veterans of frontier Indian Wars. She had little formal education of her own but inspired all eleven children she raised, ten of her own and a step-son, to lives very different from the one she had lived. At a time when very few people attended college, five of her children graduated from college and all of her children became lawyers, teachers or business executives. In a single generation, the Simpson-Cooper family advanced from log cabins and subsistence farms to city life and white-collar employment in Salem, Portland and San Francisco.

Born November 10, 1845, on a farm in Platte County, Missouri, Sam Simpson was a six-month-old infant in the spring of 1846 when his family started across the plains to Oregon. Mary Munkers, a ten-year-old girl and distant Kimzy cousin of the Simpsons, remembered taking care of little Sam on the trail when his mother was cooking or washing.[356] Like his older brother Sylvester, Sam Simpson learned to read at an early age from his mother, from whom, it is said, he also acquired his love of poetry. According to family legend, Dr. John McLaughlin, the retired Hudson's Bay Company official, gave Nancy Cooper Simpson a book of poems by the Scottish poet, Robert Burns which young Sam read as he grew up and influenced his sense of meter and choice of careers. Sam attended school in Marion County before moving with his family to the Indian Reservation at Fort Yamhill where he came under the influence of the military officers stationed at the fort. Lt. Philip Sheridan is said to have encouraged the teenager's interest in poetry and to have given him a book of poems by Lord Byron. In addition to Byron's poetry, Lieutenant Sheridan and the other young officers at fort Yamhill may also have introduced the future poet to the pleasures of drink.

There was little to do at the fort. Sheridan and his fellow officers gathered each evening at Ben Simpson's store where they drank and shared stories. The three oldest Simpson boys, John, Sylvester and Sam, were fascinated by these worldly young officers who invited them to listen and perhaps join in the drinking. John Simpson was impressed that the officers bought the most expensive liquor available and that Sheridan drank heavily but without any discernible impairment. "I never saw a man who could drink as much liquor as Sheridan without being affected in any way by it."[357] The three impressionable teenagers were learning about the wider world from military officers they knew and admired.

Following the example of his older brother, Sylvester, Sam Simpson enrolled at Willamette University when he was sixteen. By all accounts, he was popular among his schoolmates and began to publish poetry in the Pacific Christian Advocate. A classmate described him as tall and slender, of graceful carriage, brilliant of intellect and affable in manners".[358] He graduated from Willamette in 1865 at the age of nineteen and soon after began studying law with his father's friend Judge Riley E. Stratton in Corvallis. He passed the examination to become a lawyer in Oregon but was too young to be admitted to the bar.[359] In 1866, Sam Simpson's father Benjamin purchased the Salem ***Oregon Statesmen*** at which time he was a candidate for the United States Senate. The elder Simpson installed his sons Sam and Sylvester as co-editors. Four months later, after the Oregon legislature selected another candidate, Ben Simpson sold the ***Statesman***.

Sam Simpson published an editorial in the final edition announcing the demise of the venerable weekly:

> *With this issue terminates the existence of the Oregon Statesman, the oldest newspaper but one in the state... The Statesman is dead... A few months ago I mounted the tripod of the Statesman with many misgivings for the future and not little distrust for my own abilities for so arduous and exalted a work.*[360]

Sam was the primary editor of ***the Statesman***, and his brother Sylvester contributed lengthy editorials analyzing proposals for a national education plan. When the newspaper closed at the end of 1866, the two young editors returned to their previous jobs. Sylvester resumed his teaching at Willamette and Sam, now 21 years old, was admitted to the bar and began practicing law.

Beautiful Willamette

In the fall of 1867. Sam Simpson moved to Albany, Oregon to practice law. He entered a law partnership with J. Quinn Thornton in December 1867. Thornton (1810-1888) and his family had been on the Overland Trail in 1846 but far behind the Simpson McBride party. Thornton followed the new Southern Emigrant Road (Applegate Trail) into Southern Oregon where they experienced delays and other hardships. In 1847, Thornton served as Supreme Judge of Oregon under the Provisional Government. In April 1868, after working together for less than four months, Thornton and Simpson announced that they had dissolved their partnership. A week later, The Albany ***Oregon States' Rights Democrat*** published Sam Simpson's poem ***Beautiful Willamette***. The poem, titled ***Ad Willamette***, was buried on the third page of the newspaper between two advertisements and signed with the author's initials. Despite the inauspicious introduction, the poem and the 22-year-old poet were soon well known throughout Oregon. Everyone was familiar with the river and nearly everyone, it seemed, had read the poem. The river was dramatic and the poem about the river was memorable and widely reprinted throughout Oregon and adjoining states.

Beautiful Willamette follows the river from its origins in the mountains to its eventual release into the sea. In four stanzas, with compelling cadences and familiar images, the poem evokes the power of the river and its Heraclitean combination of the permanent and the transitory. The poem began:

From the Cascades frozen gorges,
Leaping like a child at play
Winding, widening through the valley,
Bright Willamette glides away;
Onward ever,
Lovely River,
Softly calling to the sea,
Time that scars us,
Maims and mars us,
Leaves no track or trench on thee.

In contrast to the pretentious displays of erudition that weakened much of his poetry and excluded the common reader, Beautiful Willamette was for everyone. It was a poem about a shared experience, and it was in a musical form that was appealing to casual readers.

The poem also rewarded those readers seeking a deeper meaning in the flow of the river to the sea. John B. Horner, author of ***Oregon Literature***, considered the poem to be an allegory of life. In his reading, the river began as a playful child, grew to maturity in the valley where it posed:

Life's old questions,
Sad suggestions,
Whence and whither? Throng thy stream.

In the fourth and final stanza, the river flowed into the "roaring waste of ocean" where it became indistinguishable from all the rest. [361]The ocean, as it would in other Sam Simpson poems, served as a metaphor for death.

Beautiful Willamette spread quickly. It was endlessly reprinted in newspapers and recited in schools. Simpson included the poem in the Fourth Reader he was editing for the Bancroft's Pacific Coast series for use in every classroom in Oregon. The poem even became a song when a Benedictine monk, set the verse to music. The song was performed by an Oregon chorus at the 1908 Alaska-Yukon Exposition in Seattle. The poem was a great success for Sam Simpson as well as a lifelong burden. At 22, he had written a poem that, in the view of the public, he never again matched. He was famous but he was also captive to his own achievement. Several years later, he admitted to a friend that ***Beautiful Willamette*** "has exercised a sort of tyranny over me".[362] For the rest of his life, Sam Simpson would be competing with himself and the poem he wrote when he was 22.

NOTE **Link for a video reading of the poem Beautiful Willamette: https://simpsonhistory.org/b_willamette/BeautifulW.mp4**

Changing Careers

After leaving the partnership with J. Quinn Thornton in 1868, Sam Simpson continued to practice law. That fall he married Julia Jeanette Humphrey (1848-1902). Sam had met Julia at Willamette where she studied for two years. She was from a large and prominent Portland family and was an accomplished singer. In his poem, ***Only a Feather***, Simpson called her a "sweet-throated thrush"[363]. They had two sons, Eugene (1869-1930) and Claude (1872-1932). Eugene had multiple careers in and near the water. He fished for oysters, crab and shrimp, was a tugboat captain in Puget Sound, a fish buyer at several locations and operated a glove factory in Canada where he eventually settled. He married and had two children and six grandchildren.[364] Claude, who never married, was a reporter for the ***Oregon Journal*** in Portland.

Sam Simpson was not satisfied with the practice of law. In March 1870, he used his savings and money borrowed from his father to buy the weekly ***Corvallis Gazette***. In his first issue as editor, Simpson boldly advised his readers, in what he called a "Salutatory", that the paper's editorial policy would be changing,

> *Temperance ceases to be the specialty of this paper as, in fact, it is not the forte of the present editor. Right here the bright habiliments of neutrality are laid aside forever, and wheeling into line the good champion of prohibition goes down in the smoke and fury of political war.*[365]

William B. Carter, the previous owner of the Gazette, was one of the pillars of the Grand Lodge of the Independent Order of Good Templars in Oregon. Carter was as devoted to prohibition as Sam Simpson was to drink. The editorial change Simpson announced was a fundamental switch from dry to wet.

Simpson immediately set out to make the Gazette distinctive and informative. In the inaugural issue, he declared that the weekly would be a Republican newspaper and criticized the Democratic Party as "a party without a soul and without a creed. It professes what it does not believe and believes what it does not profess...[366] He denied rumors that his interest in journalism was simply a temporary aberration and that he planned to return to the practice of law. In the same issue, he claimed that former governor Joseph Lane had (on three occasions) called him a liar and a thief and had offered to meet Simpson anywhere. Simpson declined the offer explaining that "it would doubtless be a dead issue on our side" [367]

The editorial content of the ***Gazette*** was deliciously provocative. Simpson wrote of a rival paper as "fictitious twaddle" and another competitor as"... a bold but indiscreet liar... a man cannot lie successfully unless he has brains".[368] Not satisfied with calling the rival a brainless liar, Simpson called him a "filthy spaniel". In addition to the colorful personal attacks on his competitors, Simpson wrote editorials about current issues. He championed the commercial prospects of Yaquina Bay, where his father was involved in schemes to open parts of the surrounding Indian reservation to settlement. Sam Simpson opposed proposals, like those his father supported, to close part of the Siletz Reservation. He wrote in the Corvallis Gazette that the Indians had already been shut-in upon a few half-productive acres" and that the existing treaty with the Indians should not be abrogated. He argued that the treaty with the Indians "ought to stand so long as the honor of a Christian nation is stainless and without reproach". [369] His father, the Indian Agent, was more flexible. He believed that the Indians could give up land for settlement without significant injury.

Despite the colorful language and straight-talking editorials, the Corvallis Gazette floundered under Sam Simpson's leadership. The paper consistently lost money before Simpson sold it in 1871. From all indications, Sam was drinking heavily during his year as editor and publisher of the Gazette. In January 1871, he visited family friend Matthew Deady in Portland asking for help getting a job with the ***Daily Oregonian.*** Judge Deady was fond of the young poet and agreed to put in a good word on his behalf but observed in his diary about Simpson "He is a genius, but as genius too often does loves whiskey too well."[370] In a March letter, Simpson acknowledged his struggle with alcohol to Judge Deady and pledged to reform himself

Since disposing of the Gazette, I have been so vexed and worried in the pursuit of other employment...I believe, withal it is better for me to begin life anew with loftier ambition and purer purpose. This dancing in the train of Bacchus is wearisome work to flesh and spirit and I will have no more of it.[371]

The poet and his battle with alcohol were in public view. He made no secret about the hold alcohol had over him and his despair about where it was leading. He wrote:

So, Bacchus, whither dost thou bear
What still is left of me,
Down to the valley of Despair,

Down to the wailing sea?[372]

In another poem, he wrote pledging abstinence:

I have banished the spectre of sorrow,
And conquered the dragon of drink;
I have tom a blank leaf from the morrow,
And fled from the Stygian brink.
There is death in the dew of the roses
That bloom in the blushes of wine;
There is danger where pleasure reposes,
Though we call her a goddess divine.

Simpson's family and friends were aware of the excessive drinking and went to great lengths to curtail it. As early as 1872, Sylvester Simpson was monitoring his brother's behavior. In a postscript to a letter to Judge Deady, be inquired "Sam has gone on the Bulletin. I wish you would ascertain for me, *sub rosa*, how he is getting on and let me know".[373]

After what must have been a public disaster in Corvallis. Sam Simpson's reputation made it difficult for him to obtain a newspaper job. As an alternative, he sought out short-term jobs where he could use his writing skills. His father, elected to the legislature for the seventh time, assisted Sam in getting a position in the House as Assistant Clerk during the 1872 legislative session. The following year, when his brother Sylvester was Superintendent of Public Instruction, Sam was hired by A. L. Bancroft & Co. of San Francisco to prepare the 4th and 5th level readers for the Pacific Coast series Oregon had recently adopted. The Bancroft Company later hired him at $150 a month for research and writing of H. H. Bancroft's ***The History of the Northwest Coast.***[374] Sam Simpson returned to journalism in 1874 when he was hired as an interim editor of the Oregon State Journal in Eugene while the editor was in Washington, D.C. Despite a new start and repeated pledges of abstinence, the drinking persisted. The editor he replaced reported "His writings were brilliant but irregular and could not be counted on".[375]

Sam Simpson remained unable to obtain or hold a long-term job but continued to seek short-term writing assignments. In 1877, a temperance advocate named Mrs. H.V. Stitzel was writing a novel when she suddenly died. Her husband hired Sam to complete the novel and prepare it for publication. Simpson, who had written short stories, somewhat disingenuously warned readers that "the book is the first effort of an unpracticed hand". The novel was 271 pages of Victorian melodrama with fainting women, scheming villains, misunderstandings, a faked death, coincidental encounters, wooden dialogue, and a happy ending. The characters were one-dimensional, and the plot was unconvincing. With Simpson's help. Mrs. Stitzel's posthumous novel ***What Became of It*** was published in 1878.[376]

By this time, Sam Simpson's marriage had collapsed. His drinking and erratic employment left Julia alone to support their two sons. At the urging of her Simpson in laws, his beloved but neglected Julia obtained a divorce in 1879. As he had with other painful events in his life, Sam Simpson turned his sorrow and guilt into poetry. He wrote of his lost love:

Adieu! No word can now be said
To wake a love forever dead;
Kissed for the last time, let it sleep
Where hopes repine and memories weep.[377]

In another poem, Simpson used drinking images to describe the marriage and divorce:

We did not drain the chalice,
But quaffed its rich bouquet
Maybe 'twas grace not malice,
That snatched the cup away.
You went your way serenely,
I went mine with blame;
Your brow was calm and queenly
And mine was red with fl(Sh)ame.[378]

After her divorce, Julia took a job teaching in a Portland elementary school to support herself and her two boys, now seven and ten years old. Three years later, Julia, then 34 years old, married Judge John Briscoe, who was twice her age. They lived in Oysterville[379] in southwest Washington where Briscoe (1813-1901) had served as Postmaster from 1874 to 1877. They had two children. After Judge Briscoe died, Julia returned to Portland where she died in 1902.

Poems for Special Occasions

Sam Simpson was already known as a poet while he was a Willamette undergraduate. Soon after his graduation, he was invited to contribute verse for college events like graduations, reunions and tree-planting ceremonies. In later years, he also wrote poems for the reunions of Oregon pioneers and the launching of a battleship. These poems tended to be long and celebratory in nature. The poems written for the university events were often pretentious, peppered with the obscure classical allusions that were considered evidence of learning at the time. Thee university poems evoked nostalgia for the college years and relied on conventional imagery to sharpen the contrast between the nurturing and protective mother university and the brutal and uncaring world outside.

The untitled poem he prepared for the 1873 Willamette reunion, urged his fellow graduates to defend their Alma Mater:

Plant thy lilies of light in the heart of her youth—
Her children that kneel at the altar of Truth!
And we who are facing the tempest of life,
Let us keep within hail and ye flit through the strife
With a stroke and a parry if foes should assail,
Let us fend our brave Mother through darkness and gale.
And return when we can to this classical grove
For a new pledge of friendship and promise of love.[380]

In "***Ashes of Roses",*** a poem he wrote for the Willamette Alumni Association, Simpson combined the seasons of the year and world travel to remind his audience that:

Wherever it reached us, in pleasure or duty,
The glamour of conquest or silence of woe,
The recall of our Mother, in accents of beauty,
Awoke our allegiance in love's overflow:--[381]

Sam Simpson also wrote the words for a class song for the Willamette graduating class of 1877 and a poem to celebrate the planting of the class tree in 1895.[382] In all his Willamette poems, Simpson evoked the memories of the college years to bolster the graduate as she or he faced the tempest of life.

In contrast to the academic pretension of the verses prepared for events at the University, the poems Simpson wrote about the pioneer experience were realistic and engaging. ***An Oregon Pioneer***, with its "eighty years of hopes and dreams", was a tribute to the emigrants, like his parents, who traveled to Oregon a generation earlier and built a state. Simpson wrote ***Campfires of the Pioneers*** during the winter of 1879 when he was living in a mountain cabin and not drinking. The poem followed the overland emigrants from the sad farewells leaving homes and families, across the lush spring prairies, through the monotony of the dusty trail and blazing sun over the mountains to Oregon:

And so the hearts and souls of men
Were darkly tried and tested then.[383]

Simpson's poems became a regular feature at the annual reunions of the Oregon Pioneer Association. The author was too shy or unreliable to attend but others, often the pioneers themselves, read ***The Oregon Pioneer*** at the 1876 reunion in Salem and selections from the ***Campfires of the Pioneers*** at the reunions in 1883, 1888, 1889 and 1903. Although he had been far too young in 1846 to remember anything about the wagon train experience, his poetry kindled memories of the overland trip among the aging pioneers.

A Productive Winter

Throughout the 1870s, Sam Simpson's friends and relatives were convinced that the way to stop his drinking was to find him a job that would engage his talents and take his mind off drinking. His brother Sylvester reflected this opinion in a letter, "I know that Sam is qualified for the position, and I believe that if he had it, it would be an incentive to keep him straight."[384] In the fall of 1879, some of Sam Simpson's former in laws devised an elaborate but successful ruse to lure him away from temptation. The scheme involved a camping trip into the mountains with a young relative to visit the recently discovered Oregon Caves. The campers stopped at a remote cabin in Jackson County where a Simpson admirer, William W. Fidler, invited Sam to spend the winter preparing a collection of his poems for publication. Fidler was a journalist and historian who had represented Josephine County in the Oregon legislature in 1876 and 1878. Simpson stayed sober all winter, read books from Fidler's extensive collection of poetry and classics and worked at chores. He kept busy at anything other than his own poetry.[385]

Fidler had a scrapbook with some Simpson poems and one of Simpson's sisters supplied others which could be included in a collection. At Fidler's urging, Simpson began working on new material for the collection. Released from the constraints of newspaper audiences, Simpson expanded his horizons. He composed "The Mother's Vigil", a moving poem about the lynching of an Indian that had occurred in Jacksonville, Oregon:

He was only an Indian, the son of Old Mary,
Swarthy and wild, with midnight of hair
That arose, as he sped to the Lethean ferry,
Like a raven of doom in the quivering air.
Ah, his crime? I've forgotten, --it was something or other

Judge Lynch's decisions were never compiled;
But we left him, at last, with his forest-born mother,
As she camped by the tree that had strangled her child.[386]

"The Mother's Vigil" was a dramatic departure from the many poems he had written celebrating the natural beauty of Oregon. It was about a real event and, unlike much of his work, it expressed a moral opinion.

Sober and suddenly productive, Simpson wrote at least eight other poems that winter in Fidler's cabin including his lengthy "***The Campfires of the Pioneers***" about the experience of the Overland Trail with its "A hundred nights, a hundred days" of fears and doubts of sun and dust. More than 500 lines long, this epic poem was a favorite at pioneer reunions.[387] Fidler was the only person who observed Simpson's creative process and wrote about it, even if it was 35 years after the event. He reported that Simpson recited his poems aloud before committing them to paper and rarely had to edit or rewrite. According to Fidler's account, once Simpson started writing, "He worked as I have seldom seen men work before or since, barely stopping long enough to eat..."[388]

That winter in Fidler's Jackson County cabin. Sam Simpson assembled a collection of his work for publication. According to Fidler's account, the book was never published because Simpson could not afford it. Ralph Friedman recounted the winter at Fidler's cabin in "High Tide for Sam Simpson" but added the information that the manuscript, entitled ***Dashings of Oregon***, was sent to a publisher who printed the books but went bankrupt before any were distributed. Whatever occurred with the publisher, no collection of Sam Simpson's poetry was published during his lifetime.

The Missing Decade

The 1880s were particularly painful and unproductive for Samuel Simpson. His older brother Sylvester moved with his family to San Francisco in 1879. His mother, Nancy Cooper Simpson, died in 1883 and his widowed father Ben Simpson moved to Alabama. Much of Sam Simpson's support system was no longer available to him.

From the winter of 1879 when Sam was in William Fidler's Josephine County cabin to 1893, when Simpson reappeared in Astoria, there was a period of more than ten years for which there is little record. Presumably, he was writing poetry, drinking too much and taking occasional jobs. Most of Sam Simpson's poems are undated so it is difficult to determine how productive he was during the missing decade, but it appears likely that the most of the poems which survived to be published were written before the 1880s.

The Battleship Oregon

Sam Simpson had a well-deserved reputation for unreliability. When sober, he remained productive, but he too often drank and missed deadlines. He was no longer welcome at the larger Oregon newspapers and was forced to seek work in smaller communities with smaller newspapers. In May 1893, Simpson was hired by the ***Astoria*** (Oregon) ***Weekly Budget*** as an editorial writer and staff poet. When the US Navy announced that it would name its newest battleship the ***USS Oregon***, civic leaders throughout the state immediately began competing for ways to participate in the celebration. City officials in Astoria asked Simpson to write a poem to be read at the launching ceremony and selected Narcissa White Kinney, the wife of a prominent Astoria businessman, to attend the launching and read the poem. Mrs. Kinney (1851-1901) had been a professional temperance lecturer before her marriage, and she would later serve as president of the Oregon state WCTU for six years. Simpson had several months to compose the poem but he procrastinated and eventually missed the deadline. Mrs. Kinney departed from Astoria empty-handed. The Astoria officials were embarrassed and angry to discover that there was no poem. The editor of the newspaper located Simpson in a local saloon, sobered him up and sat him down to write, ***The Launching of the Battleship Oregon:***

Be worthy of the mystic name
These matchless vales and mountains bear;
That in the tents of sunset Fame
May twine a wreath for thee to wear.[389]

Astoria residents took up a collection for the expense of telegraphing the 78-line poem to San Francisco where Mrs. Kinney waited anxiously. The following day, among a crowd of dignitaries, the retired temperance lecturer proudly read Sam Simpson's poem as the USS Oregon slipped into the waters of San Francisco Bay.[390]

The Astoria version of the making of the battleship poem is consistent with much of the story as told among Sam Simpson's descendants. In the alternate narrative, it seems that Sam Simpson was so drunk that his Astoria pals, acutely aware that their own reputations were at risk if there was no poem for Mrs. Kinney to read, dragged Sam to the town jail where they locked him in a cell to sober up and write the poem.[391] In each version, he amazed everyone present by batting out 78 lines of verse at the last moment.

U.S.S. Oregon in dry dock, Brooklyn Navy Yard; photo by Edward H. Hart Courtesy Library of Congress, LC-D4-20817

NOTE For the entire ***Battleship Oregon*** poem go to: *https://en.wikisource.org/wiki/The_Gold-Gated_West/Launching_of_the_Battleship_Oregon*

The incident in Astoria, presumably only one among a number of similar stories, curtailed Simpson's career in Astoria and propelled him to a smaller town and smaller paper in Ilwalco, Washington. For two years, Simpson was editor of the weekly ***Ilwalco Pacific Tribune***. During this period, he also contributed eight anonymous poems and a preface to a publication called ***The Guide*** which was published in September 1894.[392] Sam Simpson was painfully aware that he had squandered his talents and that his time was short. He wrote a poignant and revealing poem in 1896 at the time of his 51st birthday:

Time flies! And I all listless stand
With a rusted sickle and idle hand;
Soon must I face the gold-browned stars,
A beaten soldier in life's swift wars.[393]

He asked plaintively, "Have I been idle all these years?" He published the poem in the Albany Democrat where, nearly thirty years earlier, he had published the poem that made him famous and had been a burden ever since mocking his efforts and shattering his self-confidence.

Sam Simpson may have been thinking about himself when he wrote of a man in an ill-fated love affair:

He wandered aimlessly through life
Tho' his were talents rare;
He sometimes tried to baffle fate
But always met despair.[394]

By June 1899, Sam Simpson was living alone in the St. Charles Hotel in downtown Portland. According to one account, "when he came to Portland for the last time, he was a wreck."[395] On June 12, he left the hotel bar, fell on the sidewalk and severely injured his head. He died two days later in a Portland Hospital. He was 53 years old:[396]

The Portland Oregonian summed up Sam Simpson in a 1905 editorial:

> *... the fire of true poetic genius burned in the soul of Sam L. Simpson. His best endeavor, like that of many another man of genius (to use his own words) "failed of its prize" through the promptings of a restless and wayward spirit.*

An unusually candid newspaper eulogy described the grim last years of Sam Simpson's life:

> *Fame, as usual, found the poet after death. In life his treatment at the hands of mankind was miserable, in death he wears the amaranthine wreath. Those who applaud him most in death, while living, passed him by with a frown... He, with most uncommon talents, could hardly procure sufficient of life's necessaries to live from day to day. I opine the weakness which ruled, which ruined him.*[397]

For all the alcohol-induced disappointments and the waste of talent, Sam Simpson had a devoted following of friends and family who wanted to keep his memory alive. Members of the poet's family collected his poems for publication while groups in Salem and Portland initiated fund-raising campaigns to erect monuments. The June 1900 reunion of the Willamette University Alumni Association featured N. L. Butler of the class of 1877 who gave a memorial address about the poet and Mrs. Ida Vaughn of the same class who read a selection of Sam Simpson's poems.

Sam Simpson made no effort to keep copies of the poems he had written. He dashed them off, sent some to publishers, traded others for drink and lost or destroyed those that remained. When asked why he did not save his poems for publication in a book, he explained "I have never written anything that satisfied me". [398] The poet's sister Eleanor "Nora"· Simpson Burney had collected her brother's poems and, with the assistance of the poet's two sons and other admirers, assembled a representative group from which her husband, Portland attorney William Thomas Burney, selected 81 for publication.[399] The poems were arranged by category (nature; historical; poems of sentiment; patriotic, etc.) and published by J.B. Lippincott Company of Philadelphia in 1910, eleven years after the death of the poet. Burney contributed a preface in which he acknowledged gently that Sam Simpson, like Burns and Poe before him, "labored within the bonds of a habit" and concluded that "we who knew him best, know that he never reached the achievement that was possible to his talents'. [400]

Friends and admirers of' "Oregon's gifted poet" formed the Samuel L. Simpson Memorial Association in 1905 to raise funds for a monument to be erected in Salem on the Willamette campus or the grounds of the State Capitol.[401] The project, despite the participation of several of Salem's leading citizens, was never completed. Meanwhile, the Sons and Daughters of Oregon Pioneers raised funds for a monument in Portland. In 1927, nearly thirty years after the poet's death, the Sons and Daughters installed a large marble marker at Sam Simpson's grave in Lone Fir Cemetery.[402] The marker is inscribed with six lines from ***Beautiful Willamette***. The poem that had bedeviled him in life, followed him in death.

History has not treated Sam Simpson and his poetry kindly. His romantic style and insistent meter were slipping out of fashion at the time he was writing and have not experienced a revival. Simpson has been criticized for his reliance on Greek and Roman myth and his neglect of the people and places that surrounded him. Even his masterpiece ***Beautiful Willamette*** is no longer part of the elementary school curriculum in Oregon. Modernist critics rejected the entire body of Northwestern literature. In 1927, two young poets published a manifesto dismissing the literature of the Northwest as "... a vast quantity of bilge...an interminable avalanche of tripe."[403] In their diatribe, James Stevens of Washington and H.L. Davis of Oregon did not single out any particular writers for criticism but made it clear that, in their view, none was worth reading.

While his poetry may be mostly forgotten, the Sam Simpson story lives on in contemporary music. More than a century after Simpson's death, Portland folk rock musician Leigh Marble wrote and recorded "Inebriate Waltz". The song recounted the tragic story of an unnamed poet who complained bitterly about a particular poem but found some satisfaction in being remembered, if only as a footnote:

I wrote epics and sonnets and songs but dammit,
All they remember is Beautiful Willamette.

...

I gave it my life. It gave me my name.
I guess even a footnote is a measure of fame.

The poet without a name finds solace in the bar room and concludes "It was the river that killed me, sip by sip."[404]

Sam Simpson was not writing for posterity or to win the approval of literary critics a century later. His poems were often composed hurriedly but were intended for particular audiences. Many of his poems were intended to entertain or reassure newspaper readers. Others were written for specific audiences of Oregon Trail pioneers, Willamette graduates or for special occasions like the launching of a battleship or the planting of a tree. The poems Simpson prepared for specific audiences were intended to remind listeners of their shared experience and to strengthen their commitment to particular institutions. These poems were communications among contemporaries. They served their purpose and should not be evaluated as though they were attempts to communicate 19th century experiences across the generations to 21st century readers. For all the rhetorical flourishes, Sam Simpson was a poet of his time and place writing for audiences that he knew. And they knew him. A generation after his death, they were seeking ways to keep his memory alive. In 1950, the Portland ***Oregonian*** included Sam Simpson among the "***100 men of the Oregonian Century***". The newspaper, which had published many of Simpson's poems and stories during his lifetime, observed simply, "Oregon has always loved him".[405]

Samuel Simpson's gravestone in Lone Fir Cemetery, Portland, OR (Erected by the Sons and Daughters of Oregon Pioneers)

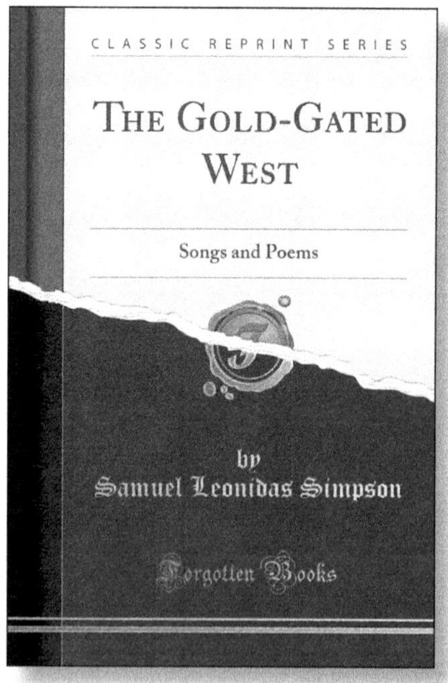

*"**The Gold-Gated West**" a collection of Samuel Simpson's songs and poetry.*

10 The End of the Trail

The map of the United States, which had been unrecognizable in 1845, was nearly complete three years later with the addition of Texas and the vast area west of the Rocky Mountains. The young republic formed along the Atlantic coast 75 years earlier had spread across the continent to the Pacific. Some attributed the growth to destiny while others credited the industry of the emigrants who had left homes in the settled areas and traveled by wagon 2000 miles to claim their share of the Oregon country. The changes in the national map were achieved rather quickly through diplomatic negotiations and military force but the changes on the ground in Oregon came more slowly. The three generations of the Simpson family in Oregon during this period were participants in the evolution of Oregon from the wild frontier of the provisional and territorial periods to the post Civil War attempts to transform the state with the development of railroads and the reform of the schools. The evolution is particularly evident in the changing role that land played in the lives of the Oregon pioneers and ways in which the modernization of Oregon released opportunities for social mobility.

Free land was the primary motivation of most of the early emigrants. Many of them were landowners in Missouri and nearby states but Oregon offered the possibility of larger parcels of new and productive land. Land ownership provided farmers with independence and the opportunity for self-sufficiency. There would be no one telling them what to do and no payments due the bank. The prospect of free land was appealing but there were significant risks. To begin with, the United States did not own the land in Oregon. Until late in 1846, Oregon was disputed territory governed by a joint-occupancy agreement with Great Britain. In the second place, the land distribution was no more than rumor and emigration bait until it became law in 1850. Finally, there were the costs and risks inherent in several months of overland travel through rough and hostile country. Thousands of early emigrants, like the Simpson family, calculated the risks and concluded the possibility of land was worth the risk of travel. As it turned out, the rumors they had heard in Missouri five years earlier about free land in Oregon eventually became law and more than 7000 pioneer families qualified for donation land.

The distribution of free land created thousands of independent farmers, but it also impeded the modernization of the Oregon economy. Rather than develop a diversified economic base, the Oregon economy remained dependent on small-scale agriculture and related industries like wool processing, cattle ranching, fish canning and timber cutting long after its neighboring states were building cities and diversifying their economies. As early as 1855, David Newsome recognized that Oregon did not have the skills, resources or political leadership to build a vibrant economy:

> *Oregon is far behind the times in enterprise and capital...cursed with bad legislation and bad laws. The laws here are made right under the fumes of the brandy bottle.*[406]

While the brandy bottle may have explained the "bad laws", the problem of capital aggregation was structural. The agrarian economy was one-dimensional. It produced products for local consumption but little for export. The structure of the economy made it difficult to aggregate capital within the state for investment. With inadequate local capital, Oregon was slow to develop the railroads that would link the economy to the rest of the country and vulnerable to control by investors outside Oregon. The agrarian tradition was also an obstacle to the modernization of the Oregon economy. Reform of public education, for example, was simply not necessary. As long as children were going to follow their parents as small farmers, the children did not need more education than their parents had received.

The Oregon pioneers had conflicting views about government. They wanted government to give them the land to which they believed they were entitled, protect them and their property, move the Indians out of their way and leave them alone. They resisted authority and taxation. A few pioneers, like Ben Simpson, saw government as a vehicle for personal advancement. He recognized that there were necessary government functions and that an enterprising fellow like himself could do as well or better than the next man while receiving a government salary. His government service was interwoven with opportunities for private benefit. The private benefit was not illegal but created situations that were ethically murky in which he represented several potentially conflicting interests. As an Indian Agent, he was firm in enforcing discipline and inconsistent in protecting Indian interests. As Surveyor General and Postal inspector, he appears to have been reasonably diligent about his job and, unlike some of his contemporaries, resisted using his position for personal gain.

After the Civil War, as his political views and affiliations evolved, Ben Simpson became increasingly aware that government had a role in stimulating private investment. He recognized that large projects like roads, locks and railroads were essential for Oregon's economic development but far beyond the capacity of private investors. Government subsidy was necessary to attract private investment into private enterprises.

Then as now, the distinction between politics and government was often blurred. While politics was the path to government, the rules of politics were different and blatant self-interest, lying, bribery and character assassination were common and expected. Ben Simpson was comfortable with these rules in ways that his sons were not. He understood the importance of reciprocity in politics (trading political favors), loyalty and political connections. He attacked political opponents and was the target of such attacks. Late in his career, he switched from the Democratic Party to the Republican Party where he was part of a thoroughly corrupt machine in which, common rules of honesty, loyalty and fairness did not apply. In order to advance his own career, Ben Simpson was involved in a scheme to entice a long-term friend into a corrupting relationship and was aware of plans to threaten his friend's job. The two strategies were heavy-handed and violated the long-term friendship with Judge Deady. The Judge quickly realized what was going on but did not seem surprised or outraged.

The role of government was different in each of the three Simpson generations. William Simpson expected little of government beyond approving his land claim. Ben Simpson had an expansive concept of government as a source of capital for economic development from which private individuals, if they were astute and politically connected, could benefit. Sylvester Simpson had a more modern view. For him, government was not to reward political winners with jobs and access to government contracts but to provide those basic services that individuals could not easily provide for themselves like education. Government provided such services because the services strengthened society as a whole and the people responsible for delivering the services should be trained, selected on merit and supervised rather than simply being rewarded for political loyalty. Sylvester was himself a political appointee, but he considered his positions to have been earned through merit rather than political patronage. He was only partially deceiving himself. His initial appointment as Chief Clerk of the Senate in 1868 was likely to have been the product of his father's connections but subsequent appointments, particularly as his father became a Republican, were based on performance. Sylvester was acutely aware of the income he could receive for government service, but his motivation was more the improvement of the service than using his position for personal benefit. His controversial term as Superintendent of Public Instruction would have been far less demanding if his objective had been to save his job rather than reform the system.

Ben Simpson may have been somewhat rough-edged and opportunistic, but he was also the person who propelled his family's social advancement. In one generation, he advanced from the fundamentalist preacher and farmer he might have been to the enterprising businessman and career politician he became. He was a frontiersman among the Indians, an entrepreneur in the logging and shipping business, an appointed, government official and eventually a carpet-bagging, Alabama plantation owner. When he accepted the Indian Agent position, Ben Simpson became the first member of his family ever to work for a salary. In the next generation, only his oldest son John, a cattle rancher, worked with his hands. The others became lawyers, teachers and businessmen.

Although he had been a leader as a young man on the Overland Trail, Ben Simpson was more of a follower in Oregon. He joined with others in business enterprises and political schemes. He maneuvered for government appointments. He was energetic, enterprising and thoroughly pragmatic. He considered the public good and his private benefit to be aligned in ways that might raise questions 150 years later but which, in his view, advanced each. His accomplishments are easy to underestimate because there were so many and seemingly so scattered, but they were the building blocks of a new state. The Portland ***Oregonian*** called him "a pioneer of prominence in Oregon's up-building".[407]

In the third generation, Sylvester and Sam Simpson were the privileged sons of a successful politician and businessman. Although they had come across the plains in an 1846 wagon train and lived in log cabins and on an Indian reservation, they were far from being frontiersmen. They were inheritors of connections, status and education. They had educational opportunities which their parents did not have but lived under the long shadow of the expectations created by their father's achievements. In each case, they suffered. Sylvester struggled with self-doubt in his public life in Oregon and moved to California where he could be the private, scholarly lawyer he wanted to be. Sam struggled with self-confidence his entire adult life. He was a celebrity at a young age but unable to shake off the demons that dragged him down. His poetry inspired Oregonians to appreciate the physical beauty and cultural history of their state. His chronic drinking ruined his marriage, destroyed his employment prospects and prevented him from attaining the levels of poetic artistry to which he aspired. Despite his limitations, he was widely known and admired in the Northwest as an Oregon poet.

The changes over three generations in the Simpson family show the social mobility that was occurring in the western states during the last half of the 19th century. Much of the motivation for the overland emigration was the acquisition of land and the Simpson families claimed all the land to which they were entitled under the Oregon Donation Land Act. William and Mary Simpson obtained 640 acres of land in Marion County, which they farmed and where they lived the rest of their lives. Ben and Nancy Simpson claimed their 600 acres but were not farmers and moved on to city life in Salem, Eugene and Portland. The irony is that Ben Simpson purchased land and returned to farming in his later years in Alabama. Sylvester and Sam Simpson were not adults during the early 1850s and consequently did not qualify for donation land. Since neither Sylvester nor Sam had any interest in farming, land ceased to be the critical factor it had been a generation or two earlier. Sylvester and Sam lived in towns in rented houses, apartments and hotel rooms through most of their adult lives. Sylvester lived for 25 years in San Francisco, all of it in rented houses. He only acquired real estate late in life such as the summer cottage at the end of Cascade Dr. in Mill Valley and the retirement house on Russell Street in Berkeley.

By 1875, land in Oregon had lost much of its importance and was an impediment to the emergence of the modern state. The availability of land had resulted in a proliferation of small and marginally productive farming units and delayed the consolidation of agriculture into larger units and migration from farms to towns. The irony was that the land which had attracted the settlers in the 1840s, proved to be an obstacle to the growth and modernization of the Oregon economy.

The story of three Simpson generations in Oregon is only slightly typical of the pioneers who settled in Oregon before statehood. The typical experience was that of William Simpson who farmed his donation land in the Waldo Hills the rest of his life. Ben Simpson claimed donation land but was far too restless and ambitious to confine himself to farming. He moved frequently, started multiple businesses and acquired others but rarely stayed very long with any project with the exception of the development of Yaquina Bay. He participated in many of the critical episodes in the development of Oregon including the pacification of the Indians, the creation of a governmental framework during the territorial period and the building of a modern transportation network. Throughout his long career, he was involved with the leading figures of his times including the members of the Salem Clique who dominated the territory in the 1850s, the Unionist factions of the Civil War period and the railroad promoters of the later period. For all of this, Ben Simpson was neither rich nor powerful. He did not have an independent economic base, like a bank or newspaper, on which he could rely, and he was never the leader of a political faction. He was less well-educated than many of the Oregon leaders of the time, but he gave witty speeches, prepared official reports and corresponded with some of the best-educated residents Oregonians of his time

Sylvester Simpson and Sam Simpson were also atypical pioneers. Their younger brothers and sisters were born in Oregon and were not technically pioneers, but they sustained the social and economic status their father had achieved. The daughters were well-educated and married well. The sons were successful in business but, in most cases, outside Oregon.

In his poem "Disillusion", Sam Simpson summarized the accomplishment and the frustration:

We won the bannered castles
Of the blue enchanted hills,
But, alas, we are the vassals
Of a fate that now fulfills;[408]

The long journey to Oregon had served its purpose. The extended Simpson family had prospered in Oregon but many of the family members and their descendants remained restless seeking the elusive bannered castles of their dreams beyond the boundaries of Oregon*.

** At last count, at least 17 relatives currently reside in the state.*

Appendices

APPENDIX I: Members of the Simpson Family on the Oregon Trail, 1846

The Simpson family on the Oregon Trail in 1846 was an extended clan of at least 47 people representing three generations and twelve households along with two or more single men. The family group was composed of William and Mary Simpson, their three unmarried children, seven of their married children with their families, at least ten Simpson grandchildren and various Simpson and Kimsey relatives:

William Simpson (53) and Mary K. "Polly" Simpson (49) with their unmarried children Martha Jane (16), James (12) and William Barnet (9);

James Anderson (36) and Eleanor Simpson "Ellen" (32) with their children Mary (13) John (11), Louisa (9), Benjamin (5) and James (3)

APPENDIX II: William and Mary Kimsey Simpson Family

William Simpson

Born: Rockingham County, North Carolina, June 27, 1793
Married: Warren County, Tennessee, April 13, 1813
Died: Marion County, Oregon, November 3, 1858

Mary (Polly) Kimsey

Born: July 7, 1797
Died: Marion County, Oregon, February 2, 1858

Children:

1. Eleanor (Ellen) (1814-1878), married James Anderson
2. Thomas K. (1815 1852) to Oregon in 1847
3. Benjamin (1818-1911)
4. Harriet (1820-1852) married Larkin Price
5. Cassia (1822-1846) married Alvis Kimsey, she died on the Oregon Trail
6. Mary Ann (1824-1849) married William Macklin (1824-1849)
7. Elizabeth (1826-1902) married N.B. Wisdom
8. David (1828-1906) married Julia Ann Haven, 1846.
9. Martha Jane (1830-1892) married Ninevah Ford
10. James (1833-1914) married Martha Jane Haven
11. (William) Barnet (1836-1925) married Melinda C. Haven

APPENDIX III: Simpson Family Oregon Donation and Land Claims

Claim	Claimant(s)	Location	Sections	Acres
263	**William & Mary K. Simpson**	T8S/R1W	19,20, 29	641.51
265	**David & Julia Simpson**	T8S/R1W	14, 15, 22, 2.	638.76
267	**James & Eleanor S. Anderson**	T8S/R1W	20, 21, 28, 29	639.34
332	**N. B. & Elizabeth S. Wisdom**	T8S/R1W	8, 9, 16, 17, 20, 21	640.42
553	**Duff & Mandana Kimsey**	T8S/R1W	7, 8, 17, 18	639 (1847)
694	**Larkin & Harriet S. Price**	T8S/R1W	15, 16, 21, 22, 27, 28	641.14
4492	**Nineva & Martha Jane S. Ford**	T8S/R1W	28, 29, 30	209
356	**Benjamin & Nancy Simpson**	T9S/R3W	9, 10	600
2012	**Elias (Majors) Magers**	T9S/R1W	13	160
3199	**Thos & Rosannah Simpson**.	T7S/R1E	18	316 (1851)

Source: Lottie L. Gurley, ***Genealogical Material in Oregon Donation Land Claims, Supplement to Volume I*** (Portland, Oregon, Genealogical Forum of Portland, 1975)

APPENDIX IV: Benjamin and Nancy Cooper Simpson Family

Benjamin Simpson

Born: Warren County, Tennessee, March 29, 1818

Married: 1839 **Eliza Jane Wisdom**, Platte County, Missouri, (she died 1841)

Children:

1. **John Thomas,**

   Born: Platte County, Missouri;, 1841

   Died: Sheridan, Oregon, 1920

Married: 1843, **Nancy Cooper**, Elm Grove, Platte County, Missouri, 1843

Nancy Cooper

Born: Coopers Fort, Howard County, Missouri, 1820

Died: Portland, Oregon, January 4, 1883

Children:

2. **Sylvester Confucius**

   Born: Elm Grove, Platte County, Missouri, March 21,1844
3. **Samuel Leonidas**

   Born: Elm Grove, Platte County, Missouri, November 10, 1845

   Married: 1868, Julia Humphrey (1848-1902); Divorced, 1879

   Died: Portland, Oregon, June 14, 1899
4. **Francis Marion**

   Born: 1847

   Died: 1859 (killed by horse)
5. **Louisa Ann** (1849-1888) Married: John A. Stowell, Jr.
6. **Elinora (Nora)** (1852-1925) Married: 1894 William Thomas Burney
7. **Isadora (Dora) Paradine** (1854-1932) Married: 1875 William Milton Killingsworth

8. **William Milton** (1856-n.d.) Married: 1879 Mary L. Dickinson
9. **Grover Benjamin** (1858-1934) Married: Alma C. Beasley (1864-1912); Mabel Manchester.
10. **Alice Blandina** (1862-1892) Married: William Thomas Burney.
11. **Clarence Wellington** (1865-1931) Married: 1893 Marion (May) Bailey.

Benjamin Simpson married **Mrs. Caroline Gordon** (widow of P. B. Gordon) 1884 in Selma, Alabama; Mrs. Gordon died 1902. They had no children.

APPENDIX V: Benjamin Simpson in Elective and Appointive Office, in Oregon

Elective Office:

Year County Party Legislature 1850 Territorial Legislature, 2'* Session Clackamas County Dem Territorial Legislature, 3d Session Marion County Dem

Marion County Dem

Marion County Dem

Dem

State Legislature, House Polk County Dem

State Legislature, House Benton County Rep

Source: H.R. Kincaid, "Officers of the Territory and State of Oregon", Biennial Report of the Secretary of State, (Salem, Oregon, State Printer, 1899), 36-74.

Appointive Office

Private, Company B, 1" Regiment, Oregon Mounted Rifles, Cayuse War, 1848
Postmaster, Fort Yamhill, 18xx
Acting Indian Agent, Fort Yamhill, 1863-1864
Indian Agent, Siletz Reservation, 1863-1871
U.S. Surveyor General for Oregon, 1874-1878
U.S. Postal Inspector, Oregon-Washington, 1879-1882
U.S. Postal Inspector, Alabama, 1883-1884
Chairman, Coeur d'Alene Indian Commission, 1889

APPENDIX VI: Sylvester and Frances McFarland Simpson Family

Sylvester Confucius Simpson

Born: Elm Grove, Platte County, Missouri, March 21, 1844
Married: Frances McFarland, Salem, Oregon, October 11, 1866.
Died: Berkeley, California, March 3, 1913

Mary Frances Mc Farland

Born: Indianapolis, Indiana, May 29, 1848
Died: San Francisco, California July 13, 1905

Children:

1. **Ernest Sylvester Simpson**
   Born: Salem, Oregon, August, 1867

Married: 1888 Maude Brown (she died 1900)
Married: 1903 Anna Pratt. d. 1934
Married: 1935 Eleise English
Died, Chicago, August 1941

2. **Lynn Carroll Simpson**
   Born: Salem, Oregon, January 25, 1869
   Married: 1891, Elizabeth Belle Van Eaton
   Died: July 16, 1944
3. **Francis (Frank) Marion Simpson**
   Born: Salem, Oregon, June 11, 1871
   Married: Hortense Burgess (1886-1938)
   Died: 1929
4. **Myrtle Una Simpson**
   Born: Salem, Oregon, July 1, 1873
   Married: 1901, Clarence C. Wilson, (1870-1962) San Francisco,
   Died: Berkeley, California, June 20, 1957
5. **Dessie June Simpson**
   Born: Portland, Oregon, June 26, 1875
   Married: 1929 Leland D. Rathbone (died 1938)
   Died: Berkeley, California, 1972
6. **Kirke Larue Simpson**
   Born: San Francisco, California, August 14, 1881
   Married: Ella May Field
   Married: Irene Lisherness
   Died: Los Gatos, California, August 1972
7. **Vera Nanette Simpson**
   Born: San Francisco, August 26 or 27, 1884
   Married: 1913, William Dickerson (1872-1921)
   Died: Oakland, California, February 29, 1976
8. **Avis Beryl Simpson**
   Born: San Francisco, August 27, 1887.
   Died: San Francisco, 1889

APPENDIX VII: Sylvester Simpson Appointive Offices

Professor of ancient languages and lecturer in mythology at Willamette University in Salem, Oregon. He taught while he was a student there in the early 1860s.

Chief Clerk, Oregon State Senate: 1868, 1870, 1872, 1874; 1876, 1878;

Oregon State Librarian, 1871-1872

Oregon Code Commission, 1872

First Superintendent of Public Instruction, 1873-1874

State Board of Education, 1873-1874

Trustee, Oregon Deaf Mute School, 1872-1878

Trustee, Oregon Institute for the Blind, 1873-1874

Private Secretary to the Governor, 1877-1878

Assistant Secretary of State of Oregon, 1877-1878

APPENDIX VIII: San Francisco Residences of Sylvester and Frances McFarland Simpson, 1879-1905

1879:	S/W corner, Hyde and Turk
1880:	1617 Broderick
1881:	2623 Pine
1882:	1426 Turk
1883-1886:	934 Dolores (4 years)
1887-1888:	703 Shotwell (2 years)
1889-1890:	2503 California (2 years)
1891-1893:	2929 Clay (3 years)
1894:	2115 Broderick
1885:	1325 Leavenworth
1896-1900:	1408 Leavenworth (5 years)
1901:	1225 Jackson
1902-1905:	1227 Jackson (4 years)

Sylvester and Frances Simpson built a summer cottage in Mill Valley at the end of Cascade Drive in 1899. In 1905, after the death of his wife and his retirement Sylvester Simpson bought a house at 2330 Russell Street In Berkeley.

APPENDIX IX: **Family Tree (Partial)**

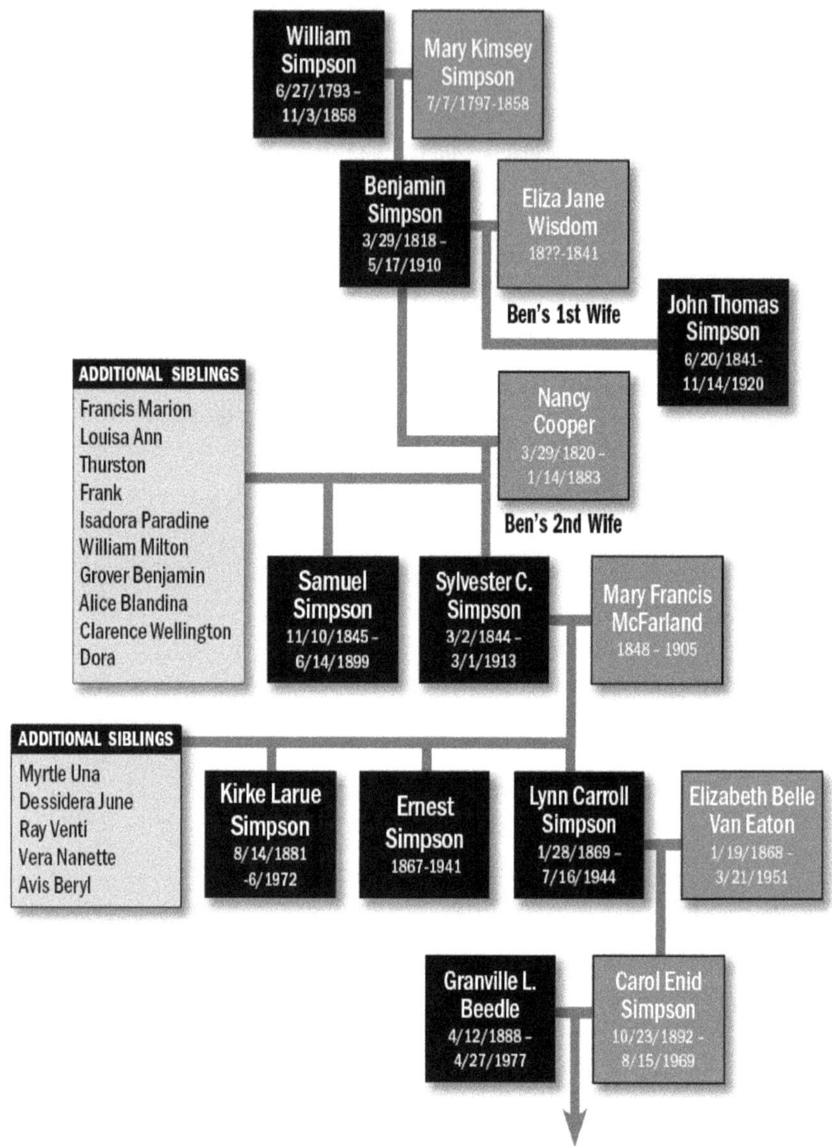

APPENDIX X: Simpsons in the Newspaper Business

Members of the Simpson family were involved with 13 different newspapers not including Kirke Simpson's work as an AP reporter and his column, "***Washington Bystander***" which appeared in many papers nationwide.

Benjamin Simpson (1818-1910)

11/26/1863 Ben became part owner of the ***Oregon Statesman***. In August of 1866 Simpson acquired the paper and installed his sons (Sylvester C. and Samuel L.) as editors/managers. Ben sold the Statesman 12/31/1866

Sylvester Simpson (1844-1913) *Benjamin's son*

1866 Editor/Manager, ***Oregon Statesman***

Samuel Simpson (1845-1899) *Benjamin's son*

1866 Editor/Manager, ***Oregon Statesman***. Sam also wrote for the ***Albany Democrat***, the ***Portland Oregonian***, and the ***Morning Oregonian***.

Ernest Simpson (1867-1941) *Sylvester's son*

1889-1891 Reporter, ***Alta California***

1892-1895 Reporter, ***San Francisco Chronicle***

1895-1906 Managing Editor, ***San Francisco Chronicle***

1906-1913 Managing Editor, ***San Francisco Call***

1913-1916 Managing Editor, ***Chicago American***

Anna Pratt Simpson (1866-1934) *Ernest's wife*

1895-1906 Society Editor, ***San Francisco Chronicle***

1915 Anna wrote the book, ***Problems Women Solved*** It is a historical account of the Woman's Board of the Panama-Pacific International Exposition (PPIE), which was held in San Francisco that year.

Lynn Simpson (1869-1944) *Sylvester's son*

1893-1913 Telegraph Editor & News Correspondent, ***San Francisco Chronicle***

1913-1918 Lynn purchased the ***Sacramento Union*** and was Managing Editor

1919-1922 Member of the Editorial Staff of the ***Oakland Tribune*** and ***San Francisco Examiner***

1923-1932 Managing Editor, ***Santa Barbara Daily News***

Kirke Simpson (1881-1972) *Sylvester's son*

1907-1908 ***Tonopah Daily Sun*** *(Nev.)*

1908-1945 ***Associated Press*** journalist who wrote key dispatches and columns over decades, most famously his 1921 coverage of the Unknown Soldier's burial, which earned him the Pulitzer Prize.

1912 Kirke was the sole journalist on ***Teddy Roosevelt's 1912 Bull Moose campaign*** tour throughout the US.

1928-1945 Kirke wrote the column "***Washington Bystander***" focused initially on national politics, then shifted to World War II interpretation. It appeared daily, leveraging his contacts in Washington, including friendships with FDR and Harry Truman.

Footnotes

Abbreviations

GGW *Gold-Gated West: Songs and Poems by Samuel L. Simpson*
OHS *Oregon Historical Society Research Library*
OHSQ *Oregon Historical Society Quarterly*
OOHS *Quarterly of the Oregon Historical Society*
SPL *Hugh Morrow Collection*, Salem, Oregon Public Library
SSP *Sylvester Simpson Papers*. Possession of the author
TOPA Transactions of the *Oregon Pioneer Association*

Footnotes

1 James K. Polk, "Inaugural Address", March 4, 1845.

2 John Quincy Adams in David W. Parker, ed., Calendar of the papers in Washington relating to the territories of the United States (Washington, D.C., 1911), 47. Adams served as President from 1825 to 1829.

3 John L. O'Sullivan, "The Spirit of Manifest Destiny", originally published Democratic Review, July August 1845, in Martin Ridge and Ray Allen Billington, ed., American's Frontier Story (New York, Holt, Rinehart and Winston, 1969), 491.

4 John L. O'Sullivan, New York Morning News, December 27, 1845.

5 Kirke Wilson, The Platte Purchase: The Simpson and Cooper Families, 1836-1846 (San Francisco, 1999), 11-15, 29n.

6 Kirke Wilson, Sweet Horizons of Dreams: The Simpson-McBride Wagon Train on the Oregon Trail, 1846 (San Francisco, 2006), 135-136.

7 T. T. Geer, Fifty Years in Oregon (New York, Neale Publishing Company, 1912), 489. Theodore Thurston Geer (1851-1924) was born in the Waldo Hills east of Salem and served as Governor of Oregon from 1899-1903.

8 H.O. Lang, ed. History of the Willamette Valley (Portland, Oregon, Himes & Lang, 1885), 561-562; Howard McKinley Corning, Willamette Landings (Portland, Oregon, Binfords & Mort, 1947), 97; Gunter Barth, ed., Al Quiet on the Yamhill: The Civil War in Oregon (Eugene, Oregon, University of Oregon, 1959), 128n.

9 Elizabeth French McLench Odell, A Semi-Centennial Offering to the Members and Friends of the Methodist Episcopal Church (Portland, Oregon, Swope and Taylor, 1884), 40-41.

10 W. Barnet Simpson interview with Fred Lockley, "The Impressions and Observations of the Journal Man", Oregon Daily Journal, March 18, 1925.

11 Ibid., March 20, 1925. The Simpsons had traded surplus food supplies at Fort Hall for credits with Hudson Bay Company in Oregon.

12 T.T.Geer, Transactions of the Twenty-Third Annual Reunion of the Oregon Pioneer Association, 1895, 45. David Simpson was later a prominent local official in Marion County where he served as county assessor for nine years and was elected to the Oregon legislature in 1868 and 1874. He was one of the founders and president of the Salem Electric Railway.

13 John T. Simpson, in Shirlie Simpson, The Oregon Pioneer: Benjamin Simpson and His Wife Nancy Cooper Simpson (Palatine, Illinois, 1982), 16. Shirlie Simpson was the wife of Grover Simpson II, a great grandson of Benjamin Simpson.

14 John Simpson, Ibid.

15 Barnet Simpson in Lockley March 18, 19 and 20, 1925; Sam L. Simpson, Five Couples (Masset, Queen Charlotte Islands, British Columbia, 1981), 15. Samuel Leonard Simpson of Canada (1906-2000) was a grandson of Sam Simpson the poet. To distinguish between

the two, "Sam Simpson" is the poet and Sam L. Simpson is the grandson.

16 John Simpson, in Shirlie Simpson, Oregon Pioneer, 16-17.

17 The denomination is generally referred to as "Primitive Baptist" today but preferred to be called "Old School Baptist" during the period before the Civil War. J. Orin Olephant, "The Rise of the Old School Baptists in the Oregon Country", Pacific Northwest Quarterly, Vol. 20, No. 2 (April 1949), 124.

18 Sam L. Simpson, Five Couples, 20-24.

19 Oliphant, "Old School Baptists", 132.

20 Ibid., 131-133.

21 Elder John Stripp to Elder Gilbert Beebe, August 4, 1851, Ibid., 138-139.

22 Sonora A. Hess to the Baptists of Oregon and Washington, January 7, 1906.

23 Sam L. Simpson, Five Couples, 23

24 Clifford R. Miller, "The Oid School Baptists in Early Oregon", Oregon Historical Quarterly (hereafter OHQ) December 1957, 313.

25 Ibid., 324-321.

26 Sam L. Simpson, Five Couples, 23.

27 Hawaiian workers had been imported by Hudson Bay Company for work in the fur trade.

28 The 1851 treaty negotiations are described in greater detail in Wilson, Horizons of Dreams, 104-108.

29 Benjamin Simpson, Report of the Surveyor General for Oregon, 1877.

30 Genealogical Materials in Oregon Donation Land Claims, Vol. I (Portland, Oregon, Genealogical Forum, 1957), 11.

31 David Simpson to Sylvester Simpson, March 26, 1897, possession of the author.

32 "Oregon Donation Land Claims Obtained by Simpson and Related Families", Wilson, Sweet Horizons, 137-138. William Simpson appears on the 1847 tax list in Yamhill County, the 1849 census in Champoeg (later Marion) County, the 1853 census in Marion County and the Marion County assessment rolls from 1854 to 1858.

33 Lottie L. Gurley, G*enealogical Material in Oregon Donation Land Claims*, Supplement to Volume I (Portland, Oregon, Genealogical Forum of Portland, 1975), 18, 22, 24, 58, 124.

34 Sylvester Simpson, "The Old Arm Chair", undated manuscript in the possession of the author, hereafter, Simpson Collection.

35 "92nd Year Reached", Portland ***Oregonian***, March 29, 1910.

36 William Barnet Simpson interview in Fred Lockley, "Impressions and Observations of the Journal Man", Oregon Journal, March 20, 1925.

37 Oregon City had a population of 697 at the time of the 1850 census.

38 Frances Fuller Victor, The River of the West: The Adventures of Joe Meek, Vol. I (Hartford, Connecticut, R.W.Bliss, 1870; republished Missoula, Montana, Copper Mountain Books, 1985), 148-149. 39 Rachel Fisher to her parents, March 13, 1848 in Kenneth L. Holmes, ed., Covered Wagon Women : Diaries and Letters from the Western Trails, 1840-1849 (originally published 1985, republished, Lincoln, Nebraska, University of Nebraska Press, 1995)105-106.

40 Undated article, c. 1880 in Shirlie Simpson, Oregon Pioneer, 22.

41 Spain and Russia also had had claims to Oregon. Spain dropped its claim in 1819 and Russia in treaties of 1824 and 1825.

42 Frederick Merk, The Oregon Question: Essays in Anglo-American Diplomacy and Politics (Cambridge, Massachusetts, Harvard University Press, 1967), 51-56, 178.

43 "Address of the Canadian Citizens of Oregon to the Meeting at Champoeg, March 4, 1843" In Victor, River of the West, 84.

44 First Organic Law or Constitution of Oregon, July 5, 1843 in H. R. Kincaid, Biennial Report of the Secretary of State of the State of Oregon, 1897-1898 (Salem, Oregon, State Printer, 1899), 113-117. (Hereafter Biennial Report). There was some confusion in Oregon when a copy of the 1843 revised Iowa statures appeared in Oregon. The 1843 Iowa laws replaced the 1839 Iowa laws in Oregon in 1849.

45 Provisional Constitution of Oregon, July 26, 1845, in Kincaid, Biennial Report, 118-123.

46 Hubert Howe Bancroft, History of Oregon, Vol. I, 1834-1848 (San Francisco, The History Company, 1886), 299, 310. Although Bancroft listed himself as the author of the two volume History of Oregon, Frances Fuller Victor did most of the writing of these and two other Bancroft northwest histories.

47 Frances Fuller Victor and Frank C. Baker, The Early Indian Wars of Oregon (Salem, Oregon, State Printer, 1891; facsimile edition, Nabu Public Domain Reprints, n.d.,), 77.

48 An Act in Relation to Land Claims, Legislative Committee of Oregon, June 25, 1844 and December 24, 1844 in Peter H. Burnett, Recollections and Opinions of an Old Pioneer (New York, D. Appleton and Company, 1880; republished Da Capo Pres, 1969), 172, 200-202.

49 James K. Polk, Inaugural Address, March 4, 1845,

50 The details of the United States-Canada border in the Puget Sound region were not resolved until 1871.

51 Bancroft, Oregon, Vol. I, 669-749. Clifford M. Drury, Marcus and Narcissa Whitman and the Opening of Old Oregon, Vol. II (Glendale, California, The Arthur H. Clark Company, 1973), 201-319; Ray Heard Grassley, Pacific Northwest Indian Wars (Portland, Oregon, Binfords & Mort, 1953), 20-33; Lang, Willamette Valley, 305-318; William A. Mowry, Marcus Whitman and the Early Days of Oregon (New York, Silver, Burdett and Company, 1901), 219-222; Victor and Baker, Indian Wars, 94-226. Marcus Whitman, a physician, and his wife Narcissa were volunteers for the American Board of Commissioners for Foreign Missions (Congregational, Dutch Reformed and Presbyterian) assigned to the Cayuse Indians at Waiilatpu near Walla Walla in what is now southeastern Washington.

52 Victor and Baker, Indian Wars, 132.

53 Alvis Kimsey married Ben Simpson's sister Cassia in Missouri. She died crossing the plains in 1846.

54 At the time of the 1850 census, Marion County, Oregon had a population of 2749.

55 "Indian Wars, Claims of Soldier for Service Pension", Military Pension Papers, Claim #7073, Dallas County, Alabama, August 14, 1902.(The pension was granted May 2, 1903). Muster Rolls, Cayuse Indian War, 1847 and 1848" in Victor and Baker, Indian Wars, 508, 518; Bancroft, Oregon, Vol. I, 702; Lang, Willamette Valley, 313-314. Ninevah Ford married Ben Simpson's youngest sister Martha Jane in Oregon and settled on a 209 acre donation land claim in the Waldo Hills.

56 Bancroft, Oregon, Vol. II, 644n.

57 John Simpson in Shirlie Simpson, The Oregon Pioneer, 11.

58 Victor and Baker, Indian Wars, reports 537 officers and men in twelve companies. Lang, Willamette Valley, 313-314 lists fourteen companies and their officers. Bancroft, Oregon, Vol. I, 671-683-685,702- 703, 727, 730 lists sixteen companies. Companies were designated variously by number, letter or Captain's name. In one case, a company complained that the number assigned to it was wrong and resulted in short rations and marching in the dust at the rear of the regiment.

59 There are inconsistencies in the number of person killed at the Whitman Mission and the number of captives released. Thirteen people were killed at the mission. A fourteenth escaped but died later. Ogden ransomed 47 captives from the Cayuse and evacuated an additional six adults and three children from the Spaulding mission. Drury, Whitman, Vol. II, 289-290; Lang, Willamette, 311; Mowry, Whitman, 3i5-316.

60 Drury, Whitman, Vol. II, 289. Ogden also paid a smaller but similar fee to the Nez Perce for the safe evacuation o f the Spaulding Mission at Lapwai.

61 Ibid., 296.

62 Victor and Baker, Indian Wars, 165.

63 Bancroft, Oregon, Vol. I, 704; Lang, Willamette, 514; Victor and Baker, Indian Wars, 172.

64 Ibid., Vol. I, 703, 711. The canon was the property of Oregon City.

66 Ibid., 710-715; Lang, Willamette, 314-315; Victor and Baker, Indian Wars, 172-179.

66 Victor and Baker, Indian Wars, 189. It appears that Captain English's company had lost only two men to injury, illness, battle wounds or defection since the initial enlistment.

67 Benjamin Simpson to T. A. Wood, April 20, 1903. OHS MSS. Collection. Woods was a Portland lawyer.

68 Oregon Spectator, April 6, 1848. Victor and Baker, Indian Wars, 190. Major Henry A. G. Le was appointed to succeed Colonel Gilliam.

69 Ray Hoard Glassley, Pacific Northwest Indian Wars (Portland, Oregon, Binfords & Mort Publishers, 1953), 12-35.

70 Benjamin Simpson to T. A. Wood, April 20, 1903.

71 Hubert Howe Bancroft, History of Oregon, Vol. II, 1848-1888 (San Francisco, The History Company, 1888), 91-98. Drury, Whitman, Vol. II, 321-332. Glassley, Indian Wars, 47; Victor and Baker, Indian Wars, 248-251.

72 Victor and Baker, Indian Wars, 252.

73 John R. McBride, "Gold in California", Mss. # xxx, 3, OHS Mss. Collection.

74 Oregon Spectator, July 25, 1850. Barnet Simpson, Lockley Interview, March 18, 1925. "General Ben Simpson Dies as Result of Fall", Portland Oregonian, May 18, 1910. Simpson had been called "General" since serving as Surveyor-General for Oregon, 1874-1878.

75 Orville Pratt quoted in E. Kimbark MacColl and Harry H. Stein, "The Economic Power of Portland's Early Merchants, 1851-1861, Oregon Historical Quarterly, Summer 1988, 120. Pratt was an Associate Justice of the Territorial Supreme Court from 1848 to 1853.

76 An Act Creating the Territory of Oregon, August 14, 1848 in Kincaid, Biennial Report, 124-125.

77 Samuel R. Thurston to Elizabeth McLench Thurston, June 15, 1850 in James R. Perry, Richard H. Chused and Mary DeLano, "The Spousal Letters of Samuel R. Thurston, Oregon's First Territorial Delegate to Congress, 1849-1851", Oregon Historical Quarterly, Spring 1995, 40.

78 Geer, Fifty Years in Oregon, 491. James W. Nesmith went on to represent Oregon in the United States Senate and the House o f Representatives.

79 Kincaid, Biennial Report, 36.

80 Benjamin Simpson to Samuel R. Thurston, March 28, 1850. [sources]

83 Ibid., March 28.

84 Statutes of a Local Nature and Joint Resolutions of the Legislative Assembly of the Territory of Oregon (Oregon City, Oregon, 1851)

85 Benjamin Simpson to Samuel R. Thurston, December 9, 1850. Thurston (1816-1851) died at sea while returning from Washington.

86 Journal of the House of Representatives of the Territory of Oregon, Second Session of the Legislative Assembly (Oregon City, Oregon, 1851).

87 Charles Henry Carey, The Oregon Constitution and Proceedings and Debates of the Constitutional Convention of 1857 (Salem, Oregon, 1926), 9.

88 Undated clipping, 1851, Oregon Historical Society, Scrap Book 112, 31.

89 Journal of the House of Representatives of the Territory of Oregon, Special Session, 1852 (Oregon City, Oregon, 1852), 120.

90 Carey, Oregon Constitution, 11-12. Oregon voters rejected the proposed constitutional convention in 1854, 1855 and 1856.

91 Charles H. Carey, General History of Oregon (Portland, Oregon, Binfords and Mort Publishers, 1971), 662-663.

92 Benjamin Simpson to Matthew Deady, November 17, 1852. Marysville was an early name for the town that became Corvallis.

93 Corning, Willamette Landings, 93-94; Leonard C. Hosford, History of Stern and Sidewheel Steamboats on the Columbia, Snake and Willamette Rivers, 1835 to 1847 (Portland, Oregon, Oregon Historical Society, n.d.), 6. Randall V. Mills, Stern-Wheelers up Columbia: A Century of Steamboating in the Oregon Country (Lincoln, Nebraska, University of

Nebraska Press, 1947, reprinted 1977, Bison Press), 199.

94 John T. Simpson, Lockley interview in Shirlie Simpson, Oregon Pioneer, 21.

95 Ibid., 22.

96 David G, Lewis and Robert Kentta, «Western Oregon Reservations: Two Perspectives on Place", Oregon Historical Quarterly, Winter 2010, 476-485; Charles Wilkinson, "Reflections on Writing a Siletz Tribal History", Oregon Historical Quarterly, Winter 2010, 462-464. The Grand Ronde Agency was merged into the Siletz Agency in 1908 and closed in 1925. Federal recognition of the Confederated Tribes of the Grand Ronde Community was terminated in 1954 and restored in 1983.

97 Absalom F. Hedges served as Superintendent of Indian Affairs for Oregon from June 1856 to May 1857.

98 W. T. Burney, ed. The Gold-Gated West: Songs and Poems by Samuel L. Simpson (Philadelphia, J. B. Lippincott Company, 1910), 7-8.

99 During the Fort Yamhill period, Sheridan gave Ben Simpson a sword which, remains in the possession of the Simpson descendant, David Healy. The story of Sheridan's sword was a family myth which proved true.

100 Barth, Quiet on the Yamhill, 201,201n.

101 Gordon B. Dodds, **Oregon: A Bicentennial History** (New York, W. W. Norton & Co., 1977), 89, 98. The law excluding blacks from Oregon was repealed by mistake in 1854.

102 Nathaniel Ford of Polk County should not be confused with Ninevah Ford of Marion County who married Ben Simpson's younger sister Martha Jane.

103 R. Gregory Nokes, Breaking Chains: Slavery on Trial in the Oregon Territory (Corvallis, Oregon, Oregon State University Press, 2013), 90-96.

Dred Scott v. Sanford, 60 U. S.3ains: Slavery on Trial in the Oregon Territory

104 Dred Scott v. Sanford, 60 U. S. 393 (1857).

105 Benjamin Simpson to Matthew Deady, June 22, 1857.

106 David Newsome to the Illinois Journal, March 4, 1957, in David Newsome, The Western Observer, 1805-1882 (Portland, Oregon, OHS, 1972), 68.

107 Ibid., October 5, 1855, 61.

108 Matthew Deady to Benjamin Simpson, July 28, 1857.

109 Nokes, Breaking Chains, 134, 142. John McBride, who later served as a Congressman from Oregon, was the author of the reminiscent account of the Simpson-McBride trip across the plains in 1846.

110 Charles H. Carey, General History of Oregon (Portland, Oregon, Binfords & Mort Publishers, 1971),

111 Special Election, Nov. 9t A.D. 1857, Poll Book of Douglas Precinct, Simpson, Five Couples, 28.

112 In 1926, Measure 3 repealing the exclusion provisions in the constitution passed 108,332 to 64,954

113 Benjamin Simpson to Matthew Deady, March 29, 1865.

114 Barth, Quiet on the Yamhill, 38

115 Ibid., 6, 38.

116 Ibid., 78-79.

117 Benjamin Simpson to J. W. Nesmith, June 14, 1862. Nesmith represented Oregon in the United States Senate from 1861 to 1867. He was influential in the 1865 decision to open part of the Siletz Reservation to settlement.

118 Bancroft, Oregon, Vol. I, 640-646.

119 Ben Simpson letter, June 14, 1862.

120 A. B. Meacham to E. S. Parker, September 30, 1869. Meacham letters, Coe Collection of Western Americana, Yale University, Vol. II, Box 3. Meacham (1826-1882) was Superintendent of Indian Affairs in Oregon from 1869 to 1872.

121 Daily Statesman, February 25, 1863, in Oregon Historical Society, Scrap Book 112, 31

122 Benjamin Simpson to J. W. Nesmith, November 28. 1861.

123 Charles Wilkinson, The People are Dancing Again, (Seattle, University of Washington Press, 2010), 144-145; Lewis and Kentta, "Western Oregon Reservations", 476-485;

Wilkenson, "Reflections", 462-464. Barth, Quiet on the Yamhill, 199n. Schwartz, "Sick Hearts", 230, 234. At the time, Grand Ronde and Siletz each had an Indian Agent and Alsea had a sub-Agent. The Siletz Agency was closed in 1925. Federal recognition of the Confederated Tribes of Siletz Indians was terminated in 1954 and restored in 1977.

124 Superintendent of Indian Affairs, Second Annual Report, September 21, 1870.

125 Superintendent of Indian Affairs, Third Annual Report of the Condition of Indians in Oregon, October

126 Barth, Quiet on the Yamhill, 167-173, 173n.

127 Benjamin Simpson, Third Annual Report, Siletz Agency, October 3, 1865.

128 Wilkinson, People Dancing, 202.

129 Benjamin Simpson, Reports on Indian Affairs, Oregon Superintendency, 1864, 103 in Barth, Quiet on the Yamhill, 126.

130 Wilkinson, People Dancing, 202-203.

131 Corvallis Gazette, December 2, 1865 in David D. Fagan, History of Benton County, Oregon (Portland, Oregon, A. G. Walling, 1885), 337.

132 Benjamin Simpson, Third Annual Report, October 3, 1865.

133 Alfred L. Lomax, "Ellendale Woolen Mill", Oregon Historical Society Quarterly (September 1930), 232-236.

134 Bancroft, Oregon, Vol. I, 651-652

135 Benjamin Simpson letter of April 29, 1865, Oregon Central Military Road Company records, Ms 993, Oregon Historical Society Research Library, Box 3. (hereafter: OHS Mss 993).

136 Benjamin Simpson to Judge R. E. Stratton, February 28, 1865, OHS Mss. 993.

137 Benjamin Simpson to Board of Directors, May 19, 1866, OHS Mss. 993.

138 Benjamin Simpson to Hon. J. B. Underwood, April 27, 1868, OHS Mss. 993.

139 Benjamin Simpson to W. S. Ladd. William Ladd was a prominent Oregon banker and director of numerous Oregon companies.

140 Bancroft, Oregon, re military road/what page? C

141 New York Times, March 21, 1888.

142 Lomax, Ellendale Mill, 233.

143 Faye Marie Brown Lightburn, Revolutionary Soldier Samuel Brown and Some of his Family, Supplement (Baltimore, Maryland, Gateway Press, 1993), 20. The Coopers are not listed on the passenger list for the Brother Jonathan.

144 Sam Simpson, "The Brother Jonathan" in Mike Helms, ed., A Bit of Verse from the Lockley Files (Eugene, Oregon, Rainy Day Press, 1983), 93-95.

145 San Francisco Chronicle, May 28, 1999.

146 United States Senators were elected by state legislatures until 1913 when the 17* amendment to the United States Constitution authorized direct election of Senators.

147 George H. Himes, "History of the Press of Oregon", Quarterly of the Oregon Historical Society, Vol. III, 360.

148 Kincaid, Biennial Report, 61-62, 67-68.

149 Transactions of the Oregon Pioneer Association, 1902, 360.

150 "Salutatoria", The Oregon Statesman, August 20, 1866, SPL.

151 Ibid.

152 Ibid., December 24, 1866.

153 David Newsome letter, August 1, 1866 to the Oregon Statesman in Newsome, Western Observer, 153- 154 Chang and Eng Bunker (1811-1874) were conjoined twin brothers born in what is now Thailand and the source of the term "Siamese Twins"

154 The Morning Oregonian, "New Candidate and his Qualifications", September 27, 1866. The Republican candidate for US Senate in 1870 was Joel Palmer whose primary public service was in Indian Affairs.

156 William D. Felton, "Political History of Oregon from 1865 to 1876", The Quarterly of the Oregon Historical Society, December 1901, 347-348.

157 Journal of the Proceedings of the House of the Legislative Assembly, Fourth Regular Session, 1866 (Salem, Oregon, State Printer, 1866), 115-116. Journal of the Senate, 1866 (Salem, Oregon, State Printer 1866), 70.

158 Geer, Fifty Years in Oregon, 490

159 The Elinora sailed the Pacific Coast under other owners until 1897 when it sank off Cape

Mendocino, California. Don Marshall, Oregon Shipwrecks, (Portland, Oregon, Binfords and Mort, 1984) 65-66. 160 Medorem Crawford letter to Benjamin Simpson, March 17, 1870. OHS Collection. 16l "Indian Census", Portland Oregonian, April 16, 1867.

162 Fagan, Benton County, 484.

163 Indian Affairs Report, September 21, 1870, Letters to Meacham, Vol. II-III, Box 4. 164 Portland Oregonian, July 17, 1871.

165 Ibid.

166 The Yaquina Bay Lighthouse is in Newport, Oregon at the North end of the Yaquina Bay Bridge (Highway 101). The lighthouse is in an Oregon State Park and is open daily (except for holidays) with volunteer docents from the Lincoln County Historical Society.

167 George M. Collins, To Guide, Guard and Rescue: Building the Yaquina Lighthouses, Jetties and Life Saving Station (Newport, Oregon, George Collins, 2010), 1-10. Jim Gibbs, West Coast Lighthouses Seattle, Superior Publishing Company, 1974), page

168 Benjamin Simpson to Maj. Nathaniel Michler, undated, in Collins, Yaquina Lighthouses, 12

169 Pioneers Suggest Memorial Edifice Near Otter Crest, Shirlie Simpson, Oregon Pioneer, 46.

170 Fagan, Benton County, 414. Meacham was not a member of the third company.

171 The town of Oneatta was about five miles southwest of present-day Newport, Oregon near Yaquina Bay Road and SE Davis Road. The site is not marked.

172 Joel Palmer to Alfred B. Meacham, September 20, 1871 and February 10, 1872. Meacham to Palmer, November 6, 1871 and to Solomon Hirsch, December 21, 1871. Letters of Alfred B. Meacham, Coe Collection of Western Americana, Yale University. Meacham (1826-1884) was Superintendent of Indian Affairs in Oregon from 1869 to 1872.

173 Fagan, Benton County, 482.

174 Benjamin Simpson, Report of the Surveyor-General for Oregon to the U.S. Commissioner of the Federal Land Office, 1877, OHS Mss. 2346.

175 Fagan, Benton County, 490; Lewis Mc Arthur, Oregon Geographic Place Names (Portland, Oregon, Oregon Historical Society, 1952), 458. Collins, Yaquina Lighthouses, 34.

176 William H. Rector to W.P. Dole, June 2, 1862. Rector was Superintendent of Indian Affairs in Oregon from 1861 to1863. W.P Dole was the United States Commissioner of Indian Affairs 1861-1865.

177 Newsome, Western Observer, 277n.

178 Barth, Quiet on the Yamhill, 184.

179 Ibid., 138.

180 Ibid., July 14, 1864, 167.

181 Geer, Fifty Years in Oregon, 490. Geer interviewed Simpson "a few months before his death" in 1910.

182 Kincaid, Biennial Report, 74.

183 Portland **Daily Oregonian**, October 4, 1872, October 7, 1872, October 8, 1872. The Oregonian reprinted an editorial from the State Journal supporting the Simpson legislation

185 Benjamin Simpson to Matthew Deady, November 17, 1852 in OHS Mss Collection.

186 Deady, Diary, Vol. 1, March 20, 1872, 72. Wilson was elected but died before he took office.

187 Oregon Statesman, March 23, 1858 in Newsome, Western Observer, 69.

188 Bancroft, Oregon, Vol. II, 701.

189 Winther, Great Northwest, 261

190 Deady, Diary, Vol. 1, November 30, 1872, 102.

191 Ibid., October 21, 1872, 98.

192 Ibid., August 27, 1873, 134.

193 Clark, "Alias John H. Mitchell" and "The Election Frauds", in Deady, Diary. 151-152, 154-155. George Williams served in the U.S. Senate (1865-1871) and as Attorney General of the United States (1871-1874). President Grant nominated Williams to be Chief Justice of the U.S. Supreme Court. Williams was not confirmed when rumors of misuse of federal funds surfaced. He was elected Mayor of Portland in 1902.

194 Lang, Willamette Valley, 491-512.

195 Wilkinson, People Dancing, 208.

196 Simpson to Mitchell, June 1874, Ibid., 213.

197 U.S. Senate, Congressional Record, February 20, 1875, 1528-1529.

198 Smith to Simpson, July 17, 1875 in Wilkinson, People Dancing, 215-216.

199 Simpson to Smith, August 27, 1875, Ibid., 216.

200 Fairchild to Smith, September 2, 1875, Ibid., 216.

201 Simpson to Smith, October 28, 1875, Ibid., 217. 202 Lee Lau, "Oregon's First State-Mandated School Readers", OHQ, Winter 2004, 618.

203 S.J. McCormick, compiler, Portland City Directory for 1878 (Portland, Oregon, McCormick Printing, 1878) 34. The US Courthouse in Portland as built in 1869 and is listed on the National Register of Historic Places.

204 W. W. Robinson, Land in California (Berkeley, University of California Press, 1948, reprinted 1979), 168-172.

205 Ben Simpson, Report of the Surveyor-General, 1877.

206 The New Northwest, March 31, 1881.

207 Portland Oregonian, January 31, 1882. Harvey Scott, the editor of The Oregonian, was the brother of Abigail Scott Duniway and a major opponent of women's suffrage in Oregon.

208 Ibid.

209 The New Northwest, March 31, 1881.

210 Portland Oregonian, January 14, 1882.

211 Christopher "Kit" Carson's (1809-1868) sister was married to Nancy Cooper's father's cousin Robert Cooper.

212 Shirlie Simpson, Oregon Pioneer, 1.

213 Odell, Semi-Centennial Offering, 40-43. John Simpson attended Willamette but did not graduate. The graduates were Sylvester, Sam, Louisa, Nora, and Dora

214 Oregon Statesman, September 6, 1859

215 Sam Simpson, "Alie" in Burney, GGW, 272-273.

216 The spelling is inconsistent. The schooner was The Elinora. Willamette records show Eleanora and family records use Elnora.

217 Simpson, Oregon Pioneer, 60-89.

218 Burney, Gold Gated West, 7. The "alphabet in the ashes" story is repeated by several authors including John B. Horner, Oregon: Her History, Her Great Men, Her Literature (Corvallis, Oregon, Gazette-Times, 1919), 342 and Ralph, Friedman, Tracking Down Oregon (Caldwell, Idaho, Caxton Printers, 1984), 59.

219 Friedman, Tracking Down Oregon, 59.

220 Fred Lockley, "Impressions and Observations of the Journal Man", Oregon Daily Journal, January 13,1923 in Sam L. Simpson, Five Couples, 29.

221 W.W. Fidler, Personal Reminiscences of Samuel L. Simpson, OHQ, Vol. 15, December 1914, 273.

222 Sam Simpson, "An Oregon Pioneer", in Burney,, Gold-Gated West, 267-268.

223 TOPA, 5th Annual Reunion, 1877, 60-63, 94. The "register of members" erroneously lists Benjamin and Nancy Simpson with the emigrants of 1849.

224 Lone Fir Cemetery is in East Portland. The Simpson family plot is in the southwest corner of the cemetery. The year of Nancy Simpson's death on her gravestone is inaccurate.

225 Benjamin Simpson to Sylvester C. Simpson, April 12, 1897.

226 T. T. Geer, "Ben Simpson and his part in the Story of Old Oregon", Portland Oregonian, March 31,

227 Shirlie Simpson, Oregon Pioneer, 12.

228 Laura Woodworth-Ney, Mapping Identity: The Creation of the Coeur D'Alene Indian Reservation, 1805-1902 (Boulder, Colorado, University Press of Colorado, 2004), 82-83, 96-99.

229 Ibid., 156.

230 Ibid., 151-158.

231 Sam Simpson, "An Oregon Pioneer"

232 Sam Simpson, "The Campfires of the Pioneers" in Burney, ed., Gold-Gated West, 91-108. The poem is 518 lines long.

233 **Oregon Pioneer Association**, 31st Annual Reunion, 1903, 136, 170.

234 Ibid., 33rd Annual Reunion, 1905, 364.

235 "General Ben Simpson Dies....", Oregonian, May 18, 1910.

236 "92D Year Reached..", Ibid., March 29, 1910.

237 Howard McKinley Corning, Dictionary of Oregon History (Portland, Oregon, Binfords and Mort, 1956), 224. The Wikipedia entry for Sylvester Simpson, as of January 2011, contains several factual errors. He died March 3, 1913 in Berkeley, not May 3 in San Francisco. He studied law with a private attorney while teaching at Willamette University. Willamette did not have a law school in 1864. Eight of the nine children of the nine children of Sylvester and Frances Simpson were not born in Salem. Five were born in Salem, one in Portland and three in San Francisco.

238 Joseph D. Lee, Oregon Pioneer Association, 41" Annual Reunion, 1913, 66

239 Handwritten, undated note, signed "G.H.H." on letter from Sylvester Simpson to Matthew Deady, April 4, 1874. George H. Himes (1844-1940) was an Oregon printer, publisher, historian and archivist. He was one of the founders of the Oregon Pioneer Association in 1873 where he served as Secretary. In 1898, he became Curator of the Oregon Historical Society where he served until his death at the age of 96.

240 Ibid.

241 John T. Simpson in Shirlie Simpson, Oregon Pioneer.

242 Peter H. Burnett, Recollections and Opinions of an Old Pioneer (New York, D. Appleton and Company, 1880; republished New York, Da Capo Press, 1969), 20-21.

243 Winther, Great Northwest, 209-211.

244 The first public high school in the United States opened in Boston in 1821. By 1827, Massachusetts required all towns with 2500 families or more to offer high school instruction.

245 Bancroft, Oregon, Vol. I, 31-35; Horner, Oregon, 240.

246 State Constitution of Oregon, 1857, Article VIII, Education and School Lands.

247 The strict distinction between public and private institutions is modern. During the Colonial period, Harvard, William and Mary, Yale, Princeton and others received some sort of government subsidy but remained private in their governance.

248 Robert M. Gatke, Chronicles of Willamette: The Pioneer University of the West (Portland, Oregon, Binfords & Mort, 1943), 52, 87. John B. Horner, Oregon: Her History, Her Great Men, Her literature (Corvallis, Oregon, Gazette-Times Company, 1919); J. F. Santee, "History of Christian College of Monmouth", Oregon Historical Society Quarterly, Vol. XLII (1941), 133-138. Geer, Fifty Years, 59-71.

249 Dodds, Oregon, 145.

250 In 1838, Oberlin College in Ohio was the first coeducational institution of higher education in the United States.

251 Biennial Message of Gov. L.F. Grover to the Legislative Assembly of the Sate of Oregon, Ninth Regular Session, 1876 (Salem, Oregon, State Printer, 1876), 157

252 Gatke, Chronicles of Willamette, 225-228.

253 "Willamette University", The Oregon Statesman, October 29, 1866.

254 Ibid., Gatke, 230-231.

255 Sylvester Simpson, Protean, undated (most likely 1863 or 1864), Simpson Collection.

256 Gatke, Chronicles of Willamette, 266.

257 Odell, A Semi-Centennial Offering, 40-43.

258 Sylvester Simpson Papers, possession of the author.

259 Sylvester Simpson, "Annals", Willamette Alumni Reunion, 1866.

260 Ibid., 1866.

261 Sylvester Simpson, "Annals", 1876.

262 Ibid., 1877.

263 The 1860 presidential vote in Oregon was 5344 for Lincoln, 5074 for Breckenridge, the pro-slavery Democrat and 4136 for Douglas, the pro-union Democrat. 264 Sylvester Simpson to Matthew Deady, January 24, 1871.

265 Sylvester Simpson, "Debate at the Hesperian Society", October 18, 1867.

266 Sylvester Simpson,"The Death Penalty", no date.

267 Sylvester Simpson, "Against the Pardoning Power", undated.

268 Sylvester Simpson, "George Peabody", no date, 47 pages.

269 The Peabody Fund, as it came to be called, had a distinguished board of trustees and a professional staff person who reviewed proposals and administered grants to other organizations. Grant-making foundations use the Peabody model to this day. The Peabody Fund of 1868 is now part of the Southern Education Fund.

270 Sylvester Simpson to Matthew Deady, February 6, 1872 (S-119)

271 Sylvester Simpson to Matthew Deady, March 25, 1872 (S-120))

272 Sylvester Simpson, "The Geneva Conference", undated. The success of the Geneva Conference contributed to the development of similar multilateral international bodies like the World Court..

273 Deady, Diary, Vol. I, April 16, 1872, 75.

274 Sylvester Simpson, "The True Nature of Charity", undated.

275 Sylvester Simpson, "Oration", undated, and "Fourth of July Oration", undated.

276 Sylvester Simpson,"Oration for Good Templars' Festival", undated.

277 Sylvester Simpson, "Temperance Address", Capital Lodge, June 1, 1867.

278 Sylvester Simpson, "Friends of Temperance", undated.

279 Sylvester Simpson, 'Missionary Address No. 3", undated

280 Sylvester Simpson, "Mr. President", undated.

281 Sylvester Simpson, "Hesperian Hall", November 15, 1867.

282 Sylvester Simpson, "Contentment", undated.

283 Sylvester Simpson, ""The Farmers' Movement", undated.

284 Sylvester Simpson, "Course of Studies for District Schools", December 26, 1865.

285 Sylvester Simpson, "A Plea for Free Education", no date. Most likely presented as a lecture and subsequently published in a newspaper

286 Sylvester Simpson, "Ladies and Gentlemen of the Graduating Class," no date, 34 pages

287 Oregon Statesman, December 24, 1866. The author of the editorial is not identified.

288 Sylvester Simpson, "Arnold of Rugby", no date.

289 Sylvester Simpson to Matthew Deady, May 1, 1877.

290 Ibid. [May 1]

291 Sylvester Simpson to Matthew Deady, October 24, 1872.

231 Deady, Diary, Vol. I, October 14, 1872, 97.

293 Sylvester Simpson to Matthew Deady, January 28, 1873.

294 Ibid.

295 Sylvester Simpson to Matthew Deady, April 19, 1873.

296 Ibid., 1875. 297 A.G.Walling, Portland City Directory for the Year 1876 (Portland, Oregon, A.G. Walling, 1876), 14-15, 158; Gatke, Chronicles of Willamette, 261.

298 Marion County Superintendent of Schools in Sylvester L. Simpson, First Biennial Report to the Legislative Assembly, Office of the Superintendent of Public Instruction, September 14, 1874, 27.

299 Sylvester Simpson, Biennial Report, 39.

300 Sylvester Simpson, Course of Study.

301 Sylvester Simpson, Biennial Report, 45.

302 Ibid., 4.

303 Ibid., 34.

304 Ibid., 33, 44.. 305 Benjamin Simpson to Matthew Deady, August 14, 1873. Deady appears not to have written the endorsement letter Simpson requested

306 Oregon Statesman, April 30, 1879 in Lau, "School Readers", 620.

307 Anonymous letter, Portland Oregonian, September 4, 1873 in Lau, Ibid., 610.

308 Sylvester Simpson, Biennial Report, 38-39.

309 Col. Edward Baker was representing Oregon in the United States Senate in 1861 when he

was killed leading Federal troops in battle at Ball's Bluff, Virginia. He was the only member of the U.S. Senate killed

310 The Pacific Coast Fourth Reader (San Francisco, A.L. Bancroft & Company, 1875); S. L. Simpson, The Pacific Coast Fifth Reader (San Francisco, S.L. Bancroft & Company, 1875).

311 Anonymous letter, Portland Oregonian, September 3, 1873 in Lau,"School Reader", 616.

312 Sylvester Simpson, Portland Oregonian, September 5, 1873 in Lau, Ibid., 617.

313 Anonymous letter, Portland Oregonian, September 3, 1873 in Lau, Ibid., 613.

314 Lau, Ibid., 618-619.

315 C.A. Reed, Portland Oregonian, October 14, 1874 in Lau, Ibid., 618.

316 H.M.Daugherty, Portland Oregonian, February 26, 1876, in Lau Ibid., 619-620.

317 Sylvester Simpson, The Daily Oregonian, June 3, 1876.

318 Sylvester Simpson, Biennial Report, 3-4.

319 Report of the Superintendent of Public Instruction in Biennial Message of Gov. L.F. Chadwick to the Legislative Assembly of the State of Oregon, Ninth Regular Session, 1876 (Salem, Oregon, State Printer, 1876), 73, 100.

320 Kate Brown, Secretary of State, Oregon Blue Book (Salem, Oregon, State Printer, 2013), 136.

321 L. Samuel, compiler, Samuel's Directory, Portland and East Portland (Portland, Oregon, H. Himes, 1875), 106; Walling, Portland Directory, 1876, 155,176.

322 Sylvester Simpson to Matthew Deady, January 24, 1871.

323 Sylvester Simpson to Matthew Deady, April 4, 1874.

324 Ibid.

325 Sylvester Simpson, "Ladies and Gentlemen of the Graduating Class", no date, 34 pages.

326 McCormick, Portland Directory, 1878, 52 [where first cite?]

327 Stephen F. Chadwick, Biennial Message to the Legislative Assembly of the State of Oregon, 1878.

328 Oregon Statesman, October 8, 1878 in Lau, "School Readers", 621.

329 Ibid., 621.

330 Ibid., 623.

331 Brown, Oregon Blue Book, 2013, 136-137; Onstine, Oregon Votes, 86-87, 247-249.

332 John Walton Caughey, Hubert Howe Bancroft (Berkeley, U.C. Press, 1946), 59.

333 John H. Littell, The Commerce and Industries of the Pacific Coast (San Francisco, A.L. Bancroft & Co. Publishers, 1882), 645-648.

334 Sylvester Simpson, "The Modem Sodom", undated.

335 San Francisco Municipal Reports, 1880-1881 (San Francisco, George Spaulding & Co. 1881), 549-561.

336 Report of the Board of Trustees, San Francisco Free Public Library, Ibid., 67-73.I

337 The new City Hall was completed in 1899. Construction required 27 years and $5.7 million. In 1899 the City Hall was destroyed in the 1906 earthquake and fire.

338 James Beach Alexander and James Lee Heig. San Francisco: Building the Dream City (San Francisco, Scottwall Asssociates, 2002), 78-79.

339 John H. Young, San Francisco: A History of the Pacific Coast Metropolis, 1871-1883, Vol. II (San Francisco, S. J. Clarke Publishing Company, n.d.), 694-695.

340 Irena Narell, Our City: The Jews of San Francisco (San Diego, Howell North Books, 1981), 78-81.

341 Report of the San Francisco Law Library, Municipal Reports, 1880-1881, 590-591.

342 Henry G. Langley, The San Francisco Directory, 1879-1895; Crocker-Langley, San Francisco Directory, 1896-1905.

343 Himes note on Sylvester Simpson letter to Deady, April 4, 1874, OHS Mss. Collection.

344 Dessie S. Rathbone, as told to Dorothy O. Wilson, "Burnbrae: A History of the Cottage", no date, rewritten, two pages.

345 Klyce built more than 35 homes and civic buildings in Mill Valley during his career.

346 Vera S. Dickerson, Burnbrae Guest Book, May 30-31, 1947.

347 San Francisco Call, July 2, 1906; New York Times, August 15, 1941, 17.

348 Although Sylvester Simpson had five sons, only Lynn Simpson had a son who married. His son, Ray Venti Simpson had a son William Ross Simpson (1934-1958) who was the last male descendant of Sylvester Simpson with the Simpson name. He was a naval aviator and was killed in a flying accident in the Pacific.

349 He enlisted April 27, 1898 and was discharged September 21, 1899.

350 Johnnie is located in Nyc County, Nevada north of Pahrump and west of Las Vegas. It is now a ghost town.

351 The Simpson family plot at Woodlawn is Lot Number 396, Section G. Twenty-two members of the Simpson family and in-laws were buried at Woodlawn including John J. and Desidera McFarland, the parents of Frances McFarland Simpson. The dates on the Simpson family monument include several inaccuracies.

352 San Francisco Chronicle, March 5, 1913.

353 Himes note on Sylvester Simpson letter to Deady, April 4, 1874. John Whiteaker was a prominent Oregon Democrat. He was elected the first governor of Oregon after statehood (1859-1862), Speaker of the House (1868), President of the Senate (1876 and 1878) and Representative to the U.S. Congress (1878). He would have worked closely with Sylvester Simpson during his two terms as president of the Oregon Senate.

354 Burney, Gold-Gated West, 7-10; Coming, Dictionary of Oregon History, 224; Richard H. Engeman, The Oregon Companion (Portland, Oregon, Timber Press, 2009), 345; Friedman, "High Tide for Sam Simpson", Tracking Down Oregon, 58-70; George H. Himes, "Note", Oregon Historical Quarterly, Vol. 15, December 1914, 264; Horner, Oregon, 342-343; Sam Simpson, Five Couples, 33-41; Shirlie Simpson, Oregon Pioneer, 90-142. The biographical sketches of Sam Simpson contain much of the same information. Some have perpetuated Bumey's error about the year of the poet's death. Sam Simpson died in 1899. Engeman has several errors in the entry for Sam Simpson including his year of birth, the year Beautiful Willamette was written and his middle name. Otherwise, the information is accurate.

355 Friedman, Tracking Down Oregon, 58.

356 Mary Elizabeth Munkers (1836-1926), interview March 21-22, 1923 in Mike Helm, ed., Fred Lockley, Conversations with Pioneer Women (Eugene, Oregon, Rainy Day Press, 1981), 110.

357 John Simpson, Lockley interview, in Shirlie Simpson, Oregon Pioneer, 23.

358 Unidentified classmate quoted in John B. Horner, "Great Oregon Poem is Allegory of Life".

359 John B. Horner, Oregon Literature (Portland, Oregon, J.K.Gill Co., Second edition, 1902), 62.

360 "Valedictory", Oregon Statesman, December 31, 1866 in Turnbull, Oregon Newspapers, 134. Simpson was premature in his prediction. The Statesman had a three year hiatus between 1866 and 1869 before resuming publication. The paper is currently published as the (Salem) Statesman Journal.

361 Sam Simpson, "Beautiful Willamette", in Burney, Gold-Gated West, 19-20.

362 Fidler, "Reminiscences", 268.

363 Sam Simpson, "Only a Feather", in Burney, Gold-Gated West, 209-210

364 Samuel Leonard Simpson operated fishing boats and canneries in the Queen Charlotte Islands. He was the son of Eugene H. Simpson and grandson of the poet.

365 "Salutatory", Corvallis Gazette, March 19, 1870.

366 Corvallis Gazette, March 19, 1870.

367 Ibid.

368 Ibid., April 2, 1870; April 16, 1870.

369 Ibid., August 2, 1870.

370 Deady, Diary, January 19, 1871, 2.

371 Sam Simpson to Mathew Deady, March 29, 1871.

372 Sam Simpson, "Quo Me, Bacche?, in Burney, Gold-Gated West, 245-248.

373 Sylvester Simpson to Mathew Deady, December 19, 1872.

374 Fidler, "Reminiscences", 268.

375 Harrison R. Kincaid, in Sam L. Simpson, Five Couples, 63. Kincaid was the founder and editor of the Oregon State Journal for 35 years beginning in 1864. From 1868 to 1879, he was also on the staff of the United States Senate in Washington. He served as Secretary of State of Oregon from 1895-1899.

376 Mrs. H. V. Stitzel, What Became of It (Portland, Oregon, George A Himes, 1878).

377 Sam Simpson, "Adjeu" in Burney, Gold-Gated West, 211.

378 "Lurlina", Ib id., 215-217.

379 Oysterville, Washington is located on the Long Beach Peninsula on Willapa Bay.

380 Sam Simpson, "Poem", June 23, 1873 in Burney, Gold-Gated West, 178-187.

381 Sam Simpson, "Ashes of Roses". Ibid., 187-196.

382 "The Late Sam Simpson", Salem Oregon Pioneer, June 18, 1899; "Planting of the Pine" in Burney, Gold-Gated West, 169-178.

383 Sam Simpson, "Campfires of the Pioneers", Ibid., 91-108.

384 Sylvester Simpson letter to Mathew Deady, April 26, 1877.

385 Fidler, "Reminiscences", 264-276.

386 Sam Simpson, "The Mother's Vigil", in Burney, Gold-Gated West, 132-136.

387 Sam Simpson, "The Campfires of the Pioneers", Ibid., 91-107.

388 Fidler, "Reminiscences", 269.

389 Sam Simpson, "The Launching of the Battleship Oregon" in Burney, Gold-Gated West, 123.

390 "Astoria's Thirsty Bard", The Daily Astorian, January 29, 1982 in Shirlie Simpson, Oregon Pioneer, 119-121.

391 Sam L. Simpson, Five Couples, 38. The younger Sam Simpson never met his grandfather of the same name.

392 Alfred Powers, History of Oregon Literature (Portland, Oregon, Metropolitan Press, 1935), 295.

393 Friedman, Tracking Down Oregon, 66.

394 Sam Simpson, "A Romance of Life", OHS Scrap Book #266, 7. The poem is not included in The Gold Gated West.

395 Undated article, published in the Journal after the June 1899 death of Sam Simpson. Oregon Historical Society, Scrap Book # SB 266, 16.

396 Sam Simpson, untitled poem,, Ibid., 63-67.

397 Unknown author, OHS Scrap Book #266, 14.

398 Fred A Dunham, Pacific Monthly, July 1899 quoted in Powers, Oregon Literature, 296.

399 Many more of Sam Simpson's poems are scattered among 19th century newspapers and magazines. OHS Scrap Book #266 has at least eighteen poems not included in Gold-Gated West.

400 Burney, ed. Gold-Gated West, 9- lO.

401 "To Honor Poet'', Oregon Statesman, April I, 1905

402 William A. Warren, "Pioneers Honor Poet'', The Sunday Oregonian, September 25, 1927.

403 James Stevens and H.L.Davis, Status Rerum (The Dalles, Oregon, 1927), l.Davis, an Oregon poet and novelist, won the Pulitzer Prize for Fiction in 1936 for his novel Honey in the Horn.

404 Leigh Marble, "Inebriate Waltz" in Where the Knives Meet Between the Rows, Leigh Marble Videos, April 2012. An earlier version of"Inebriate Waltz" was recorded in 2008 as part of a video project by the Friends of Lone Fir Cemetery..

405 Lee Lau, "Sam Simpson Sweet Singer of Oregon's Beauty", Oregon Cultural Heritage Commission, 1999.

406 David Newsome to the Illinois Journal, October 5, 1855, Western Observer, 61-65.

407 "92nd Year Reached", Portland Oregonian, March 29, 1910.

408 Sam Simpson, "Disillusion" in Burney, Gold-Gated West, 260-262.

Accounts by Others on the Same Oregon Trail Journey

Following are accounts by Barnett Simpson and Mrs. Mary Elizabeth Munkers Estes who were on the same wagon train that Ben Simpson led in 1846.

Another fascinating account was a journal that Mrs. Elizabeth Smith wrote. She came across the Oregon Trail the following year of 1847. Her account of their journey was much more arduous. Here is a link for an audio file for her account:
https://simpsonhistory.org/MrsSmith/Mrs.Smith_Oregon_Trail_Diary.mp3

Barnet Simpson

From "Conversations with Pioneer Men" by Fred Lockley, compiled by Mike Helm, Published by Rainy Day Press, 1996.

Barnett was the youngest brother of Benjamin Simpson. The following is a newspaper article by Fred Lockley from the Oregon Daily Journal, from Portland, Oregon, published on March 18, 1925, about his experiences crossing the plains in a covered wagon on their journey to Oregon in 1846.

A representative of the Simpson family tells Mr. Lockley the story of the migration to Oregon in the 1840s. The narrative will appear in three installments. A feature of the opening chapter is the episode that resulted in the narrator's adopting unanimously an 18th amendment of its own.

"I'm not figuring on getting married or running for office, so I might as well tell you the exact truth about my age and anything else you care to ask me about. I was born in Platte County, Missouri, December 29, 1836, and was the youngest child of a family of 11. So as not to give a one-sided picture, I am going to tell you the things that are not creditable about myself as well as the things that are.

"For example, I might tell you my most vivid recollection of our trip across the plains in 1846. I was going on ten when we crossed the plains to the Willamette Valley. We crossed the river at St. Joe and camped for a few days to let the emigrants gather and to organize the wagon train.

"My oldest sister, Eleanor, married a man named John Anderson. Her son John was a year and a half older than I, in spite of the fact that I was his uncle. My father told me to look up a bridle that had been mislaid, so John and I started to look for it. While looking under one of the wagons John saw a stone jug. He pulled out the cork and smelled it, and said, 'This is whiskey. Did you ever drink any corn liquor, Barnet?' "My father was a Primitive Baptist preacher and was very strict, so I had never tasted liquor. I confessed that I had never drunk any whiskey and was curious as to its taste. John tipped up the jug and took a swallow and handed it to me. I didn't like to be a quitter, so I took a swallow. It nearly strangled me, but I pronounced it mighty good.

"John thought it would be funny if he could get me drunk, so he suggested that we drink some more. We took a generous drink and then resumed our search for the bridle. We found the jug in the middle of the afternoon, and by

5 o'clock we had pretty finished what whiskey there had been in it. We went back every few minutes to take another drink. John would tip the jug up and pretend to take a big drink, and would pass it to me and urge me to drink heartily. By 5 o'clock I couldn't walk. I fell in a stupor.

"John had drunk enough to make him drowsy. He sat by the camp fire. He had a new hunting coat my sister had made for him. A spark jumped out on the tail of his new hunting coat and he was so fuddled he didn't notice it till someone saw the smoke, and by that time the whole back of the coat was burned off. "They saw he was drunk and they knew I had been with him, so they began to look for me. Presently they found me, lying where I had fallen. They carried me to our wagon and worked over me all night. I foamed at the mouth and had convulsions and they thought I was going to die. The first thing I remember was along about 9 o'clock the next morning. I heard my brother Thomas, who was not going to cross the plains with us, telling Mother goodbye and saying, 'Don't worry. Mother Barnet is going to pull through all right. Give him a tablespoon of whiskey every couple of hours till he sobers up.'

"I rolled over toward him and said, 'I have had plenty. I don't want any more. As long as I live, never another drop of whiskey will ever go down my throat.' That was nearly 80 years ago, and from that day to this I have never tasted liquor of any kind or description.

"My father, William Simpson, was born in North Carolina. My mother, whose maiden name was Mary Kimsey, was born in Tennessee. I don't remember what year my father and mother were married, but Ben was their first child, and he was born in Tennessee in 1818, when my mother was 21. Mother was born in 1797 and Father in 1793. Father was 53 when he started across the plains and Mother was 49. They were considered old people. They called Father 'Uncle Billy', and Mother, 'Aunt Polly'. My brother Ben, who was 28 when we started for Oregon, was elected captain of the wagon train. Ben married Elzirah Jane Wisdom in 1839, when he was 21. They had one son, John T. Simpson. She died not long after her baby was born. My brother married Nancy Cooper in 1843.

When we crossed the plains in 1846, to Ben and his second wife, two more boys had been born – Sylvester C. and Samuel L. Sam was a baby, having been born about six months before we started for Oregon. Sam, my nephew, was the author of the book of poems entitled ***The Gold-Gated West***. I guess his "***Beautiful Willamette***" is his best known.

"Our whole family came to Oregon in 1846 except my brother Thomas, who did not cross the plains till 1852. Tom married Rosena Buff back in

Missouri and decided to let us come out and see if we like it and if we did he would sell out and come.

"When we started across the plains all our neighbors told Mother what a dangerous trip it was and how we were sure to be killed by Indians or drowned or die of cholera or be run over by buffaloes. Mother, who had heard how they buried people who died while crossing the plains, in a blanket by the side of the road, decided she would be fore-handed, so the winter before we left she carded and spun and wove a lot of cloth, dyed it and cut it up and made a shroud apiece for everyone in the family. No, we didn't get to use a single one of them. I think she cut them up after we got to Oregon and made clothes out of them. I was more interested in the hunting shirt she made for me than I was in my shroud.

"It will be 80 years ago next spring that we started with our ox teams and covered wagons for Oregon. We didn't have any particular trouble on our six months' trip across the plains. My brother Ben was captain of the train and he was the right man in the right place.

"The only fatality we had was one man killed. Two men went in together to come to Oregon. They pooled their resources and bought a wagon, a couple of yoke of oxen and supplies for the trip. They didn't get along any too well. One night the driver of the outfit lagged behind. They camped about three miles from the rest of the train. The next day the driver caught up with us. When they asked him where his partner was he said, 'The Indians must have killed him during the night. I buried him this morning by the side of the road.'

"We had not had any trouble with the Indians, so most of the folks in the train thought he had killed his partner for his share in the outfit.

No, we didn't do anything about it. There was nothing we could do. We were in a hurry to press on to Oregon, and even if we had turned back and dug his partner up we couldn't have proved that some prowling Indian hadn't shot him, so we went on, but the man whose partner had been wiped out so mysteriously wasn't very popular with the rest of the folks in the wagon train.

"The last man to join our train before we pulled out for the long trip westward from the rendezvous across from St. Joe was Uncle Ben Munkers.

The train rarely had the same number of wagons in it two days together. It averaged about 100 wagons. Sometimes some of the party would straggle and drop back with another train, or hurry up and get ahead, later dropping back to join us.

Lots of folks crossing the plains imagined the train ahead or the train back of the one they were in must have more considerate and congenial people in it. They usually found out they were mistaken when they dropped back or forged ahead to join the other train. Some folks always have good neighbors. Others always complain about having bad neighbors.

I guess it is the people themselves more than the neighbors that are at fault. "One incident of the trip that I greatly enjoyed was having a band of several hundred Indians draw up across the road and refuse to let us come on unless we would pay for passing through their country. They were nearly naked and all-painted up. They danced and whooped and scared the women and the little children half to death. My brother Ben gave the word for every man able to bear arms to get his gun and march toward the Indians ready to shoot if they made any hostile move. They gave way and let us through, for they saw our men meant business.

The chief, who spoke some English, said, "You scare all our game away. Won't each man give us a present of a charge of powder apiece to prove you are our friends?" My brother told the men to pour out enough powder from their horns for a charge for each of the Indians.

"While they were doing this an antelope ran by. Half a dozen of the Indians leaped on their horses and took after it. They dropped it within 100 yards. They shot it with arrows. Most of the band were armed with bows, though some had guns.

"Did we have any fights on the plains? I saw only one. A woman claimed that another woman in the train was trying to vamp her husband. The lady who was doing the vamping had very abundant and beautiful hair, so the wife of the man who was more or less willing to be vamped sailed into her. It was a lively fight while it lasted. They pulled hair, scratched, yelled, and cried and fought like a couple of cats. The lady with the beautiful hair had a lot less of it when the fight was declared a draw.

"We had to stop one day to let a herd of buffaloes go by along the Platte. Two miles before they came to us we could hear a subdued roar like the sound of the surf at Newport. They fairly shook the ground. There were thousands of them. They ran along paying no attention to our wagon train, though our oxen were mighty restless at the smell, the sound, and the sight of them.

"All I need to do today, nearly 80 years later, is to shut my eyes and I can see the vast, empty plains with their rolling land waves. I can see the wagons come to a stop, see the children pile out of the wagons while the men folks unyoke the oxen and all the women scatter as soon as the train comes to a stop, to gather their aprons full of sun-dried buffalo chips to cook the coffee and bacon.

"What did we eat for supper? Bread cooked in a Dutch oven, or cornbread with coffee, bacon, beans, and dried peaches or apples. We had some cows along, so we usually had milk. Sometimes we had buffalo or antelope meat in place of bacon.

Sometimes the women folks rustled sagebrush or willow wood in place of buffalo chips, but the chips made a quick, hot fire, and proved very satisfactory.

"I told you I saw only one fight while crossing the plains. Well, I'll stick to that statement, but there were a lot of fights I was in, but I was too busy fighting to stop and be an eye-witness to them. The Burnett boy was a year older than I, but I was a mite larger. My father, being a Primitive Baptist preacher, had taught me to turn the other ' cheek. My mother had also impressed upon me that boys who expect to be gentlemen don't settle their differences with their fists. The Burnett boy found he could lick me, so hardly a day went by that he didn't make my life a burden. I could hardly call my soul my own. He generally caught me where my folks wouldn't see us fighting. I put up a half-hearted fight, usually trying to avoid punishment more than to try to hurt him.

"One day my mother saw him licking me. She pulled him off of me and said to me, 'The time has come for you to take your own part. I want you to thrash this boy, and do a thorough job.' I could hardly believe my ears. I hesitated, and she said, 'You can take your choice. Either you whip this bully within an inch of his life or I will give you a worse licking than he ever gave you.'

"I knew my mother was a woman of her word, so I waded in, and what I did to that boy was plenty. After that all I had to do was double up my fists and scowl at him and he would beat it.

"One of the things I remember very distinctly is our stopping at Independence Rock. The men and women gathered around the rock and read the names of the emigrants who had registered during the preceding two or three years. Then they scratched their own names on the rock. Some of the men painted their names on with tar from the tar buckets that hung from the back axles of the wagons.

I doubt if there are many left of those who wrote their names on Independence Rock 79 years ago. There are a few of us left, but when I call the roll of my former campmates who crossed the plains with me in 1846, not many are here to answer the roll call.

"You can't spend six months with a couple of yoke of oxen in a covered wagon crossing the plains without having lots of peculiar adventures and misadventures that stick in your mind. My father and Uncle Ben Munkers were the oldest men in the wagon train. My brother Ben, who was captain of the wagon train, let them take turns leading the train with their wagons, so they wouldn't have to swallow so much dust. If there was any wind the drivers of the wagons in the back swallowed their share of dust, for the oxen kicked up the fine alkali dust till the wagons were in a heavy fog.

"One day when my father's wagon was in the lead a couple of young Indians met us and one of them threw up his hand quickly as a signal for us to stop. This scared our oxen, and they bolted. They ran down the hill, turned into the river, and splashed through to the other side.

The Munkers oxen also became panic-stricken and followed our wagon. Mrs. Munkers, with her son Jimmy, six years old, was riding on the front seat when the oxen bolted. She was a cripple. Wherever she went she had to carry her chair and, also, hobble on crutches. She was so frightened that she grabbed Jimmy up under one arm, reached back and got her camp chair under the other, jumped out of the wagon, as it was going full tilt, ran as hard as she could to a hundred yards or so, and then, realizing that she was a cripple and couldn't walk, she put down the chair and sat down.

"The oxen tried to climb the bank on the other side of the river, but the wagon turned over, so they got over their scare and waited for the men to come and fix things.

"Coming across the plains I usually rode one horse and led another, or rode and herded the stock. One day I was riding a big American mare and leading her mate. I went on ahead of the train, but finally decided I had better backtrack and join it. I rode back 12 or 15 miles without seeing any sight of the train. I finally came to another train and asked what had become of the Simpson train. The captain told me Simpson's train was about 10 miles ahead of them and I had better hurry if I wanted to get there before night. It was growing cold, so he loaned me a big coat, for I was in shirtsleeves. I retraced my way till I saw where our wagon train had left the road to camp on a small stream some distance from the road. It was about dusk. My mother was spreading the table cloth on the ground ready to serve supper.

She said, 'Where have you been, Barnet? I haven't seen you since breakfast time.' My brother Ben had missed me and, being afraid something had happened to me, he and three other men had struck out to look for me. They didn't get back till long after midnight.

"When we came to the Sweetwater, Ben decided to have the train lay over Friday, Saturday and Sunday for washing clothes, repairing wagons and drying out supplies that had got wet. We had three preachers in our train. My father was a Primitive Baptist, Elder McBride was a Campbellite, and I have forgotten what the other preacher was, but each of them preached while we laid over on the Sweetwater.

"The ox drivers decided to get a little of the dust off, so they made up a crowd to go swimming. With my nephew John Anderson, who was about a year and a half my senior, I followed them and went into the shallow water. When the men had dressed and gone, John and I decided to learn to swim. John said, 'We can't learn to swim in shallow water, so we'll go where it's deep.'"

"I said. 'Go ahead. I'll follow you. I don't care if the water is a thousand feet deep.' "We had hardly got out into the current till John was washed into a deep hole. He called out, 'Give me your hand, quick, or I'll drown.'" I started toward him, but before I got there the current had caught both of us and we were washed downstream. I can remember yet seeing John's head, first under water and then coming into sight again as he whirled round and round in a whirlpool. The next thing I remember I was washed up on a sandbar and John was climbing up the bank to go back to the train and tell Mother I was drowned. We made a solemn compact not to tell our folks about our narrow escape till we got to the Willamette Valley.

"When we got to Fort Hall, some of the folks in the train took the road to Sutter's Fort in California. Among them was my brother-in-law, Alva Kimsey. He came north to Oregon the following year. When gold was discovered at Sutler's Fort he took the back trail and returned, but he didn't have much luck.

"At Fort Hall my father exchanged all of the bacon and flour and cornmeal he could spare for an order on Dr. McLoughlin for a similar amount at Oregon City. This saved hauling this surplus across the Cascades. We came by the Barlow Route, which had just been opened, and it was a terror.

I guess none of the emigrants who came down Laurel Hill with men pulling on the ropes to keep the wagons from running over the oxen will ever forget Laurel Hill.

"We wintered at North Yamhill. In the spring Father leased a place and put five acres in wheat. We had a big crop. My brother James and I tramped it out with oxen. In the fall of 1847 Father took up a donation land claim in the

Waldo Hills. We had 18 inches of snow that winter. Father had no hay, so he fed our cattle boiled wheat. We lost all of them but one cow and three steers.

"I went to school in the winter of 1846 to Herman Higgins, a cooper. He was a son-in-law of Reverend Vincent Shelling, a Baptist preacher. Higgins taught school, as he was a cripple, and this was about his only qualification as a teacher.

He used to make tubs and barrels during school hours. If we children laughed he would look up from his work and say, 'Larn your lessons. Tend to business there and larn your lessons.' I stayed overnight once at his home. They had no dishes and no furniture. We sat on the floor, and when it came time for supper his wife stirred up some dough and gave us each a sharp stick on which we put the dough and held it over the fire in the fireplace to bake.

"My first teacher in the Waldo Hills was Paul Darst. I was married June 12, 1853. I sold my 150-acre farm in the Waldo Hills for $600 and moved to Salem. I was Sexton of the I.O.O.F. Cemetery there for 25 years."

Oregon Journal
March 18-20, 1925

Munkers: Crossing the Plains in 1846

As told by Mrs. Mary Elizabeth Munkers Estes while sitting by her fireside Christmas Eve 1916

Mark Goddard from www.oregontrailgenealogy.com provided this account by his ancestor, Mary Elizabeth Munkers Estes. Mary and her family were part of the same wagon train that Ben Simpson led. This account includes how their bedridden mother reclined in a wagon over a bag of $10,000 in gold and silver. This would be worth about $375,000 in today's dollars.

From nearby Liberty, Missouri, in early April 1846, about fifty families prepared to make the journey to the far away Oregon Territory, which then included what is now the states of Oregon, Washington, Idaho and part of Nevada. My father, Benjamin Munkers, was among them. His family was composed of an invalid wife, three married sons and one married daughter, besides five younger children, the youngest a boy of five years. I was then ten years old and still have quite a clear memory of the journey and of conditions of the early days spent in Oregon.

All the way across, Mother was unable to do anything, even having to be lifted in and out of the wagon. She made the entire ridden on a bed. It was my work to help brother's wife, who managed the cooking for our camp.

Mary Elizabeth Munkers Estes and her nephew, Thomas Munkers

The Munkers family started out with five wagons drawn by oxen; three yoke to each wagon, thirty head of oxen, fifty head of roan Durham cows and five saddle horses. These made up our herd. Most all the company drove through some stock but I think no other family had so many as we.

When we left Missouri, there was a train of about one hundred wagons but that was found to be too large a party to travel together as the teams must be kept up by grazing by the way. So they scattered out under leaders or train captains, as we called them. When we started, a man by the name of Martin was our Captain. Later when our train was much smaller, Ben Simpson, father of Sam L. Simpson, was our head man. The future Poet of Oregon was then Baby Sam of the camp. Many a time I cared for him while his mother was doing the family wash.

After we left Missouri, all the buildings I remember seeing were Forts Laramie, Bridges and Hall. As this was but the second year of "Crossing the Plains", the way before us was much of it through a wilderness and over a trackless plain. There were no bridges, no ferries and a stream too large to be forded was crossed by means of rafts, if there could be found timber along its banks to make rafts. If not, our wagon beds were used for flat boats.

We had no trouble with the Indians but we did have one awful scare. It was when we were in Utah. All at once our train seemed to be surrounded on all sides by mounted Indians! It was a war party going out to fight another tribe. I do believe there were ten thousand of them and we thought it was the last of us, but when they had seen us all they wanted to, they gave a whoop and a yell and away they clattered!

Of those long weary months I cannot clearly tell. I know it was April when we started and October when we reached the place that was to be our home in Oregon. Sometimes we stopped several days in camp where we found plenty of water and good grazing and while the teams rested and fed up, the men fixed up the wagons and helped the women wash and prepare food for the next drive ahead. Then there were days we toiled over the arid plains till far into the night to reach the life-giving water that was a necessity to us and to our trains. The children of the company walked many many miles....sometimes I think I walked half of the way to Oregon! Some days it was very hard to find fuel enough for our camp fires. Many a time our simple meals were cooked over a fire of buffalo chips and sage brush. The weather did not cause as much trouble. I recall but one real storm. It was on the Platte River in Nebraska. We were in camp on the bank of the river when it came on. The wind blew a hurricane! Thunder roared and lightening flashed! It was a dark as Egypt. The rain poured like it was being emptied from buckets. I will never forget that night! Every tent was blown down. No one was seriously hurt, though a babe was narrowly missed by a falling tent pole. The men chained the wagons together to hold them from being blown into the river. Our camp belongings were blown helter skelter over the country around about and our stock was stampeded 'till it took all the next day to get them rounded up.

But after all, we had but few hardships compared with some of the emigrant trains. Some years, you know, there was Cholera that wiped out entire families and trains that were raided by Indians and too, there were times when the oxen were diseased and died leaving families stranded on the plains. Yes, we were very lucky!

In the early Autumn we reached the Columbia River and we drove down through the Barlow Pass and came into the Willamette Valley. We made camp there where the Swartz place is now. Father was anxious to secure a place where he could have shelter for the invalid mother and when he found a chance to buy out a homesteader (a man by the name of Anderson) he was glad to pay him his price ($1000) and take possession at once. The place was on Mill Creek, four miles East of Salem. There was a comfortable log house of two rooms, a log barn and ten of the 640 acres was farmed. Thus, before the winter rains came on we were snugly settled. Father brought in what supplies he could for the house and for our stock, but most of the cattle were turned on the range.

The first winter's work was making rails with which to fence the farm. Then followed sod breaking and seeding, thus adding some acres each year to our fields. Father set out an orchard of apple and peach trees in the spring of 1850, I think it was. I don't remember where he got the nursery stock.

He brought a half bushel of peach stones from Missouri. The orchard grew nicely and I think it was in the autumn of 1855 that father had 100 bushels of apples to sell. Fourteen dollars was the price he got per bushel. I do not often hear it spoken of now, but there was a time in the settlement where we lived when peas and wheat were currency. I cannot now say what the face value was, but I think one bushel either represented $1.00 in debit or credit. Peas were much used for coffee and often the only sweetening to be had was molasses.

Oh no, we were not poor! Father brought $10,000 to this country. How? In gold and silver. You know mother was brought on a bedstead set right into the wagon. Well, underneath her bed was a box of bedding and in that box, the money was cached. Yes, we soon had pretty good homes started but the stampede to the gold mines in California in 1849-50 was a bad thing for our families. Four of my brothers went (Thomas, 14 years old; Ben, 16 years old; Riley, 19 years old; and Marion) Marion later died there. They would all have gotten ahead faster had they stayed home.

Where did I go to school? I did not have much chance to go to school after we came here. One winter the neighbors got up a school. There was a vacant house and they hired a man to teach the children awhile. I went. That was about all the schooling I had after I came to Oregon. Yes, I've been here a long time. Seventy years! I've seen Oregon grow up!

What became of those who crossed the plains in our train? Well, the Crowleys settled in Polk County and the Fullerson's also as well as Glenn Burnett, our train preacher. The Browns, the Blakelys, the Finleys and the Kirks settled in Linn County. Ben Simpson and family lived in Salem. Yes, I know most all the old timers. L.F. Grover, afterward Governor of Oregon and US Senator, was a guest at my wedding. Reverend Roberts, one of the early pioneers of Methodism performed the ceremony.

Do I remember the hard winter and the great flood of 1861 & 1862? Yes! What was the worst winter and the greatest flood in all the years I've lived here. Much of Salem was under water. The Court House was full of people who had been driven from their homes. Near the old Bennett house, the water was swimming to a horse. The Willamette was a mighty river...miles in width, sweeping houses, barns, bridges and everything in its course. No, of course the river hadn't been bridged then, but then all the small streams were adding wreckage to the Willamette. The flood was in December 1861. In January came the deep snow which lasted for six weeks and pretty nearly finished what the flood had left.

www.ingramcontent.com/pod-product-compliance
Ingram Content Group UK Ltd.
Pitfield, Milton Keynes, MK11 3LW, UK
UKHW022024190726
13853UKWH00005B/2106

9 798234 061959